Teachers Who Teach Teachers:
Reflections on Teacher Education

for Scott and Monica, Paul and Nicoline

Teachers Who Teach Teachers:
Reflections on Teacher Education

Edited by

Tom Russell and Fred Korthagen

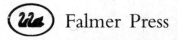 Falmer Press

(A member of the Taylor & Francis Group)
London • Washington, D.C.

UK	The Falmer Press, 4 John Street, London WC1N 2ET
USA	The Falmer Press, Taylor & Francis Inc., 1900 Frost Road, Suite 101, Bristol, PA 19007

First published in 1995

A catalogue record for this book is available from the British Library

ISBN 0 7507 0465 9 cased
ISBN 0 7507 0466 7 paper

Library of Congress Cataloging-in-Publication Data are available on request

Jacket design by Caroline Archer

Typeset in 10/12 pt Bembo
Graphicraft Typesetters Ltd., Hong Kong.

Printed in Great Britain by Burgess Science Press, Basingstoke on paper which has a specified pH value on final paper manufacture of not less than 7.5 and is therefore 'acid free'.

Contents

Contents

Acknowledgments

Our single greatest debt is to Jan Carrick, senior secretary in the Faculty of Education at Queen's University. Jan pored over revision after revision of each chapter, using her superb sense of language to make suggestions for improvement in the presentation of the material submitted by the contributors to this collection. We are also very grateful to Ria Gompelman, secretary in the IVLOS Institute of Education at Utrecht University, for her support throughout the editing process. We readily accept responsibility for any errors that may have escaped the eyes of these two individuals.

We also acknowledge the support of our own institutions, Queen's University and Utrecht University. The encouragement of colleagues within our own universities has made it possible to share more widely this collection of insights into the realities of teacher education.

Preface

On 7th July 1994, *The Independent* (London) used 'Teachers Who Teach Teachers' as the headline for a feature article about classroom teachers who take on major or complete responsibilities for initial teacher education. In the context of recent changes to teacher education in the UK, there may have been no doubt that the headline referred *only* to teachers in primary and secondary schools. Would any reader have thought for a moment that the headline might refer to university-based teachers who teach in programmes of 'initial teacher training' or 'pre-service teacher education'?

For the teacher educators contributing to this volume, it is crucial to think and speak of ourselves as teachers. We have lived too long in a world that pretends we are not teachers when contrasting us with those whom the term 'teacher' most readily suggests — those who pass through colleges and universities on their way to the important work of primary and secondary education. At the same time, to those enrolled in our teacher education courses at any given time, we *are* teachers and we are often expected to be 'super-teachers', because we have 'risen' into the academic world to a School or Faculty of Education. Even though teaching performance is probably distributed as evenly in schools of education as in the university generally, and in primary and secondary schools, there is an expectation that our location requires us to be far better than average.

Most of us try very hard to teach well, yet the realities of 'publish or perish', the 'ivory tower syndrome', and teaching loads that are often higher than elsewhere in the university work against many teacher educators. We have known for decades that teaching practice in schools means far more to those learning to teach than any other element of the preparatory program, and so teacher educators face an uphill battle from the start. There is an inevitable tension between 'theory' and 'practice' in teacher education, partly because the real world and first-hand experience speak so loudly, although not always clearly. The tension may also have its roots in the familiarity and apparent ease of teaching. No other profession prepares individuals who have more than 15,000 hours' experience (as students) within the professional setting (schools) where teachers do their work. Each teacher in a program preparing others to teach knows that there is so much to be covered, partly because most new teachers are not required to return for further study of teaching after they have acquired several years of experience. This too creates a tension, as we try to talk over and around 'the experience gap', hoping that our words will be remembered as experience accumulates. When experienced by teacher educators, these tensions are often discussed but are rarely analyzed and explored for significance. This book makes an important beginning.

This collection of reflections *on* teacher education *by* teacher educators opens with an introduction by Anna Richert, of Mills College in California, on the topic of 'learning to teach teachers' — a theme that permeates the entire volume. The ten chapters are organized in five pairs, beginning with reflections by two experienced teacher educators who recall their own development in the teacher educator role. Ken Zeichner, of the University of Wisconsin, looks back over several decades devoted to teacher education that made a significant contribution to social change in America. Ken speaks openly of the special efforts that this type of writing requires, noting that it also brings special rewards. Jean Clandinin, of the University of Alberta, sketches the development of her own role in teacher education as one in which learning to teach will always be a significant activity.

The second pair of chapters focuses on the special situation of individuals who are still beginning their careers in teacher education. Karen Guilfoyle of the University of Idaho, Mary Lynn Hamilton of the University of Kansas, Stefinee Pinnegar of Brigham Young University, and Peggy Placier of the University of Missouri-Columbia were doctoral candidates together at the University of Arizona until 1989. They have experienced the role of beginning teacher educator simultaneously, but in quite different settings. They interweave their voices in a rich account that tells a rarely-told story — assuming the role of teacher educator. Then Stefinee Pinnegar contributes a chapter that explores her experiences returning to the role of classroom teacher early in her career as a teacher educator.

The next pair of chapters describes two quite different ways in which teacher educators made deliberate moves to foster their own professional development. Gary Knowles of the University of Michigan and Ardra Cole of the Ontario Institute for Studies in Education share their correspondence over their initial years as teacher educators, making the tensions and pressures of the 'publish or perish' syndrome very clear indeed, but also revealing the power of writing as a way to make sense of personal experience and development. Tom Russell of Queen's University explored another route to personal development, by returning twice to the role of secondary school physics teacher with two objectives — better understanding what is expected of the new science teacher, and improving his teaching of a physics method course in a pre-service teacher education program.

The fourth pair of chapters describe two very different strategies for studying teacher education practices. Jack Whitehead of the University of Bath provides a brief 'world tour' of issues in action research before presenting a personal study of his own efforts to improve the quality of teacher education by showing one new teacher how to improve the quality of her own teaching. Then Ardra Cole and Gary Knowles present their second contribution to this volume — a personal account of the perils and rewards of a life history approach to self-study in teacher education.

The two concluding chapters take broader and more theoretical perspectives on the work of teacher education. Lya Kremer-Hayon of the University of Haifa and Ruth Zuzovski of the University of Tel-Aviv report on the professional development of teacher educators by comparing the views of beginning and experienced individuals. Then Hugh Munby and Tom Russell, who collaborate in teacher education research at Queen's University, apply the construct of the 'authority of experience' to data provided by student teachers in order to call attention to the importance of the basis on which teacher educators 'know what they know'.

The editors, Fred Korthagen of the University of Utrecht and Tom Russell of Queen's University, marvel that this volume has been prepared in a period as short as ten months since Falmer Press gave a 'green light' to proceed. Separated as we are by the Atlantic Ocean and a six-hour time difference, this has only been possible by the exchange of notes and chapter files by electronic means. This major exercise in international collaboration has been a very satisfying new phase in our sharing of perspectives on teacher education since meeting at a conference organized by James Calderhead in Lancaster, UK, in 1987. We have both been members of the Self-Study of Teacher Education Practices (S-STEP) Special Interest Group of the American Educational Research Association since its founding at the annual meeting of AERA in Atlanta in April, 1992, and many of the other contributors to this collection are also founding members. In fact, the idea for this book appeared as we participated in the very first meetings to establish the S-STEP group. We hope that *Teachers Who Teach Teachers: Reflections on Teacher Education* will help to sustain the growth and activities of that organization.

Fred Korthagen
Utrecht
Tom Russell
Kingston
February 1995

Introduction: Learning to Teach Teachers

Anna Richert

My students laugh when I claim that teaching is not boring; they already know that. For these student teachers who are in the thick of their process of learning to teach, the enormity of the challenge of teaching is as far from boring as despair is from passion and hope. The excitement these pre-service teachers feel for teaching is embedded in their view of themselves as learners. For beginners, learning is centrally aligned with teaching. In this introduction, I argue that learning, for all teachers, must be centrally aligned with teaching. Given the realities of change and uncertainty — which, ironically, may be the only two certainties there are in teaching — all teachers are in some ways beginners. It is the beginners' experience of learning and the power that this experience has for teaching that frames the understanding of learning to teach teachers developed in this chapter.

Let me begin by considering briefly what teachers do. From there we can consider what they need to know to be able to do those varied tasks. The learning requirements of teaching emerge quickly from such an exploration. To begin with, teachers plan lessons and deliver them. This merely opens the conversation. To accomplish these tasks they also choose texts, distribute them, and collect them. In between, they teach them. (My use of 'text' is broadly construed to include the various types of materials and activities teachers use in their work. Whereas a secondary English teacher may teach an actual text, for example, the text for elementary science might include those concepts and corresponding materials that represent the subject matter the teacher intends to teach.) Teachers talk with students, parents, school administrators, child welfare workers, police, book sellers. They read papers, observe student performances, evaluate student work. They console despondent teenagers, fearful children, weary parents. They foster hope, cajole commitment, celebrate joy. While this list of what teachers do goes on and on, it represents only one portion of the *doing* that is central to the work of good teaching. Equally important is the *thinking* that is associated with the task.

Teachers think about all the things they do, all the things they ought to do, and all the things they don't do. They think about what to teach tomorrow — how to teach Tolstoy, whether to join the curriculum committee, what kids know about velocity and force, why Johnny can't add, why Sonja can't read, why parents don't support school functions. They think about why algebra before geometry, why

Shakespeare instead of Morrison, who should sit near whom, and who should not. Of all the things teachers undertake, the most important, it seems to me, is *doing the thinking of teaching* or the reflecting about the complexities of their work. This 'doing and thinking' cycle is the cycle of reflection and action that Dewey (1933) spoke of generations ago. Dewey argued that these combined processes of reflection and action form the base for learning in teaching. Learning is continuous as reflective teachers engage in the work of thinking and doing in classrooms. In this way, *learning is central to teaching*.

What is true about learning for teachers is also true for the teachers who teach them. An early discovery of mine when I began to teach was just how complex an enterprise teaching is. The only thing harder, I figured back then, was learning to do it. These days I think learning to teach others to teach is more complex still. This book is about just that — learning to teach teachers. If we start with the assumption that teachers learn while teaching, then teachers of teachers learn while doing just that — teaching teachers. Drawing on examples of teacher educators learning from several of the chapters that follow in this book, I discuss the role of inquiry in teacher learning and the relationship between experience and reflection in learning to teach teachers. I conclude by positing a direct relationship between teacher learning and student learning. Without the former, I argue, the latter is less likely to occur. And without both, schools will not meet the needs of their clientele — the students and teachers they serve. The place to start this cycle of learning is with the first teachers involved in this process, the teacher educators.

Inquiry and teacher learning

Teachers learn by inquiring into their practice. They think about their classroom experiences in order to make sense of them. This process of 'making sense' begins when teachers confront the uncertainties of their work. Faced with a puzzling situation for which there is no easy or certain answer — how to teach negative numbers, for example, or how to reach a child who has difficulty learning or to explain motivation theory to novice professionals — teachers engage in the processes of reflective inquiry. Teachers gather as much data as they can about the situation that puzzles them. They then analyze those data to determine how they will act at future times. The nature of the teacher's reflective process necessarily depends both on the circumstances of their work (how much time they have, how free they are to determine their own action plans, and so forth) and the type and source of puzzle they need to solve (a point I return to shortly). Most often this process of inquiry is informal; teachers engage in it to some extent to answer some high percentage of the millions of questions they encounter about their work each day. Occasionally, the process is more formal and takes the form of research or action research (which we have come to hear much more about in the current conversations about school reform) and its consequences for improving teachers' work. Whether formal or informal, it is this constant and ongoing process of reflective inquiry that provides the basis for learning in teaching. Likewise, it is the centrality of learning in teaching that renders good teaching responsive to the uncertainties of the rapidly changing world of which it is a part.

As teachers of teachers, teacher educators strive to be learners of the sort I have just described. We can explore this idea of learning in teaching by drawing several examples from the teacher educators whose testimonies follow in this volume. It is learning about teaching teachers that provides the thread that connects the work of these authors, and offers greatest insight into the complexity of those processes that are discussed in this collection. I draw on this volume's chapters by Tom Russell and Ken Zeichner to illustrate the teacher-learning argument I posit. As other contributors do, Russell and Zeichner illustrate the important role of reflective inquiry in teaching, learning to teach, and learning to teach teachers. Their stories reveal the processes of learning embedded in the work of teacher education — processes, incidentally, that mirror those of reflective teaching in general. Their stories also provide good examples of the types of learning outcomes that can be generated from such inquiry, and the ensuing consequences of those insights for practice. Both stories begin with a puzzling situation such as that which Dewey suggested motivates reflection in teaching. However, the nature of the puzzle as well as the process used to examine it are different in each case. Together, the stories provide a continuum along which we can come to better understand inquiry and learning in teacher education.

Russell begins his chapter by introducing the puzzle he set out to examine. 'I took a leap of faith', he tells us, 'and returned to the classroom to find out if I was still a successful physics teacher'. In pursuing an action research project focused on this question of personal inquiry, Russell introduces a second question which this time has a direct teacher education focus. Together, the two questions (and Russell's process of framing and linking them) illustrate how questions in education are both multiple and connected; in teaching, one question typically leads to another that takes you back to the first and on to another, and so forth. Understanding his own work in order to do it better motivates Russell's process of inquiry and thus his continuous process of learning to teach teachers. He identifies his teacher education question as to whether or not (and how) 'the experiences of daily high school teaching would affect my ways of thinking about my regular work with people learning to teach physics'. In pursuing both questions Russell establishes himself as a learner. His chapter is rich with examples of how one question leads to another and how the pursuit of thoughtful answers leads to the generation of even more provocative questions. The process generates new knowledge that informs not only his teaching but that of his colleagues who have the privilege of examining the inquiry he presents.

Zeichner establishes himself as a teacher-learner as well. The learning tale he presents reveals the ubiquitous nature of teacher inquiry as he reflects on his process of making sense of his own work. Unlike Russell's inquiry, which was structured to examine several predetermined questions, Zeichner shows how the need to reflect on the uncertainty embedded within the work of teaching is necessarily an ongoing part of teaching practice. He contrasts the learning he does from this process of informal inquiry with his more frequently reported formal teacher education research, introducing his chapter with these words:

There is another aspect to my research, however, that I chose to focus on instead. This is the more informal research that I've conducted on my own teaching over the years, and how my teaching and the way in which I seek to organize a teacher education program have been influenced by my reflections on my practice.

The practical dilemma that motivated the reflection Zeichner reports in his chapter concerns a possible discrepancy between his beliefs and his teacher education practice. In reflecting (over time) on his teaching agenda for the student teaching seminar he directs, as well as student comments about that seminar, Zeichner began to question if his practice in that class matched his beliefs about teacher learning. He wondered if his abiding commitment to 'educational equity and to the building of a more decent and humane society' might, ironically, overshadow his ability to enact those very beliefs in his own classroom. His enthusiasm for imparting particular beliefs about equity and justice potentially left more latitude for his students to construct their own knowledge. Zeichner began his inquiry with the question of whether or not his classroom embodied a democratic and caring ideal. He wondered if students in his classroom were able to create and articulate their own deeply held beliefs about these issues, even if these beliefs were different from his own. By reflecting on his practice over time (which included both the generation of data and the examination of data already present), Zeichner gained clarity concerning the correspondence of his beliefs and his practice. This clarity led to new plans for future action. The inquiry process rendered him a teacher learner.

Just as in Russell's account, Zeichner's reporting of his process and its findings holds potential for influencing not only his own practice but also that of his teacher education colleagues who read his account and examine their own practice in light of his findings. Much the same can be said of other chapters in this collection. Ardra Cole and Gary Knowles provide two quite different chapters that show how writing and a life history approach to self-study can develop fundamental questions of practice. Stefinee Pinnegar, Karen Guilfoyle, Mary Lynn Hamilton and Peggy Placier show that the teacher-learner stance can be assumed productively in the very earliest years of a career in teacher education. Jack Whitehead inquires into his own practice from the base of an overview of action research on several continents. Jean Clandinin lives in her work and in her writing is the very process of continuous learning that I have taken as a theme in this chapter. Finally, the chapters by Lya Kremer-Hayon and Ruth Zuzovsky and by Hugh Munby and Tom Russell show how broader topics — professional development and the theory-practice tension — can be developed with unique reference to the contexts of teacher education.

Creating a culture of inquiry in teaching

Dewey explains that reflection begins in teaching when a teacher confronts a puzzling or uncertain situation. Interestingly, learning necessarily begins by venturing into the unknown. Given the wildly changing world in which teachers do their work, there is considerable 'unknown territory' in teaching; the puzzles of practice abound. The process of inquiry begins when the teacher enters that territory, ready to explore questions of practice in search of answers that will guide future undertakings. Teachers become learners as they inquire about their work. The very processes of asking questions, generating hypotheses, gathering and analysing data, and drawing conclusions are the processes that characterize learning in all fields. The puzzles teachers confront generate questions — why this? why not that? under what circumstances this? — that the teacher then sets out to answer. For example, Russell began with the coupled questions, 'Can I still teach physics well?' and 'What difference will that make for how I teach my physics student teachers?' For Zeichner, the puzzle was framed more generally: 'Am I doing what I want to be doing in my teaching?' In both instances, a question that emerged from practice motivated the reflective inquiry.

Posing the initial problem (or asking the question) is critical to the inquiry process in that it sets the stage for learning. However important, establishing the question at the outset of any inquiry is difficult to accomplish well. This is especially so in teaching — a profession that prizes answers rather than questions — regardless of the enormously uncertain and changing context in which the work of teaching occurs. The attempt to strive for certainty is evidenced in many ways in teaching: standardized measures for both teacher and student success; routinized procedures for classroom instruction, regardless of context; curriculum mandates that appear from local, state or provincial, and national sources; bells that ring at set times; classrooms comprised of set numbers of students; assessment procedures that typically privilege mastery over ingenuity, and so on. *In striving for certainty, the profession has established a culture that does little to promote inquiry*. It seems that, consciously or not, we have come to accept a definition of teachers as knowers rather than learners. In so doing, we have conceptually separated learning and knowing in teaching. Beyond that, the profession has structured teacher learning as linear and fixed; once a teacher moves from the learner to knower — a process that is seen traditionally to occur as a result of a pre-service training experience — she or he has little opportunity or support to circle back to the learner status again.

Given these cultural definitions, it is difficult for teachers to confront squarely the uncertainty of their work and to recognize that questions are as important as answers in the development of successful practice. The cultural milieu of teaching, therefore, renders it exceedingly important for teacher educators to reveal the learning requirements of their work and to model these learning processes in their practice. They must foster in their students an active acceptance of teaching's inherent uncertainty, as well as the skills of reflective inquiry. This process of inquiry is essential in teacher education for its consequences, both in teacher education knowledge and in the modelling that results for teacher education students. In this sense, the audience for the stories in this volume ought to include not just teacher educators but also the students of teaching in the classes where teacher educators teach. Those teachers who emerge from the classes these authors teach ought, in turn, to reveal their reflective processes to their students, who may then begin to embrace the centrality of learning in all of life.

The learning-to-teach-teachers examples that these stories provide suggest a range of starting points for the process. Russell, for example, began by stepping back from his teaching to examine questions he had about his work. In this way his learning process more closely approximates a traditional research model in which the teacher researcher defines or frames a question about which he or she wants to become more informed. The learning enterprise proceeds from there. Zeichner, on the other hand, began his inquiry when he noticed various forms of student resistance to some of the content of his course. Rather than stepping back from his teaching as Russell did to think through what he might want to understand more fully, Zeichner was taken aback by his students' lack of engagement with what he considered centrally important course material. It is interesting to note that Zeichner's reflective process happened over a period of several years. While some puzzles in teaching — a student does not come to class, for example, and thus repeatedly fails examinations, or an activity renders a class period totally chaotic — reveal themselves in obvious ways, other puzzles appear more slowly. Only after one engages in considerable reflection about one's work do some puzzles reveal themselves. For either type of learning — that in which a teacher learner steps back from practice to examine some aspect of it, or that in which one is taken aback by the puzzles being confronted — the culture of teaching needs to expect and promote in a deep and relentless way the vital place of learning in all teaching.

Why is learning so important to teaching?

In closing, let me review briefly why I believe learning is so important to teaching, and why the teacher education learning, such as that revealed in the chapters in this volume, is so important to the profession as well. The significance of teacher educator learning lies primarily in its potential for establishing norms in teaching that prize learning as a central value in teachers' work. If teacher educators see themselves as learners, and reveal to their students a reflective-learning stance towards their practice, they will engender more broadly a positive disposition towards teacher learning in the teaching profession.

Teacher educators need to be learners so that they can respond to the changing circumstances of their work and constantly learn to do it more effectively. Teachers need to be learners for the same reason that the students of those teachers need, in turn, to be learners. Never before has the importance of learning been so vital to humanity as it is in these times of upheaval, uncertainty, and change. Growing beyond our imaginations in almost every dimension of human existence, we are called upon to solve questions today that will be outdated tomorrow and obsolete the day after that. And so far we have not done as well as we must, in order to preserve the well-being of all life forms on this planet.

I began this chapter by invoking the image of the beginner's mind on the work of teaching. My argument for teacher learning rests on the belief that change and the uncertainties that accompany it render all of us beginners in some important ways. The area in which we may consider ourselves not beginners lies in our ability to frame important questions that can be studied in powerful ways to find significant answers that will in turn suggest the next round of important questions. Guided toward creating a more humane world, it is our commitment towards this collective journey of inquiry that holds the greatest promise for making the world a better place. As teachers we have no choice but to embrace the globe as learners so that our students will do the same. Ultimately, I believe our survival depends on it.

Reference

DEWEY, J. (1933) *How We Think*, New York, Heath and Co.

Part 1

Experienced Teacher Educators Reflect on their Development

1   Reflections of a Teacher Educator Working for Social Change

Kenneth M. Zeichner

Autobiographical introduction

I have been involved in teacher education since 1970 when, as a cooperating teacher, I first began working with student teachers in my grade 4–6 classroom in Syracuse, New York. Following that, I worked with the National Teacher Corps as a team leader and director of an Urban Teaching Center involving four elementary schools and Syracuse University. Since 1976, I have been a member of the faculty at the University of Wisconsin-Madison, involved in an elementary teacher education program as one of the directors of student teaching.

Throughout my career, I have been focused on the issue of preparing teachers to teach everybody's children, not just children like themselves, and particularly on the preparation of teachers for urban schools. I have been concerned with helping teachers examine the moral and ethical aspects of their practice and make teaching decisions with an awareness of their social and political consequences. I am also engaged in helping teachers see the relations between what happens in an elementary school or middle school classroom on a daily basis and the broader issues of equity and social justice (e.g., how students' life chances are potentially affected by classroom decisions). My work in teacher education has also been linked in my mind to other aspects of my life in which I have attempted to connect the way I live to the struggle for greater social justice (e.g., in what I eat, where I shop, how I try to raise my three sons, and so on). Thus teacher education has always been for me part of a larger political project and not just an intellectual or academic endeavour. This does not mean that I have only been concerned with equity issues and the struggle for social justice in my personal and professional life. It does mean however, that this political project is an important part of my being.

Educators who work in societies that claim to be democratic have certain moral obligations to try to teach in a way that contributes to a situation where those with whom we work can potentially live more fully the values inherent in a democracy. For example, in a democratic society all children must be taught so they can participate intelligently as adults in the political processes that shape their society (Gutmann, 1987). This is clearly not the case in North America, or in many other parts of the world in the 1990s. Although schools do not cause our social and economic problems, there is much that we can do as educators to contribute to the making of better societies. Regardless of our political commitments, we must recognize the reality that neither teaching nor teacher education can be neutral. We need to act with greater clarity about whose interests we are furthering in our work because, acknowledged or not, the everyday choices we make as teachers and teacher educators reveal our moral commitments with regard to social continuity and change.

I did not first come to the position about the need to connect my work in teacher education to the struggle for social justice by being enlightened in graduate school about the ways in which schools often contribute to the injustices in our society, although graduate school and my continuing academic studies since have greatly helped me conceptualize and make sense of what was first experienced at an emotional level. I first became politicized by growing up in the city of Philadelphia, and by attending Philadelphia public schools. I had some difficulty in school as a student and was often discouraged by school counsellors from setting my sights too high with regard to my plans for higher education. During high school, in a school known more for its street gangs than its merit scholars, my mind was often more on the basketball courts and the streets than it was on my studies and selecting which university I would attend. Because of the encouragement of a few of my teachers who saw academic potential in me that I did not see myself, I finally decided to give college a try and began studying at Temple University in Philadelphia the following year. I was one of the few students in my high school graduating class who went on to a university education.

After a difficult struggle that included several remedial classes, tutoring to make up for some of what I had missed out on in high school, and almost flunking out, I finally became more serious about my academic studies and started to make some headway. I was aiming for a career as a public defender in Philadelphia until the strong possibility arose that I would be drafted and sent to Vietnam. As an alternative to going to Vietnam to kill and/or be killed, in a war I didn't believe in, I decided that I would try to make a positive contribution with my life by becoming a teacher in the kind of urban school that I experienced in high school. There I could try to make a difference in the lives of city kids like myself who are often denied, in their education, things that are taken for granted in schools of the more privileged.

Immediately following my graduation from Temple University and some substitute teaching in the Philadelphia Public Schools, I enrolled in the Urban Teacher Preparation Program at Syracuse University, one of several graduate teacher education programs in the US then emphasizing the preparation of teachers to work in schools in poverty areas. Following a year-long internship in a Syracuse elementary school accompanied by graduate seminars on urban teaching, and despite drawing number 362 in the selective service lottery (a number that would have enabled me to go to law school as I had originally planned), I continued teaching in the inner city elementary school in which I completed my teaching internship and gradually drifted into teacher education as a result of the local Teacher Corps Project selecting our school and its community as a site for interns to work.

At the time I entered teaching, there was a great deal of social unrest through-out the US. Most of my peers in my teacher education program, and later my colleagues in my school, saw their work in education as I did, as part of a larger political project in which the social injustices of racism, sexism, poverty, violence, war, greed, and so on would be combated. Many of us were working to help build a new society, not just to help a lucky few in urban ghettos make it in the stratified and unjust society of the moment. We were concerned with helping our mostly African-American students from economically poor backgrounds gain the academic skills that would help them succeed in an imperfect society while at the same time working to reconstruct that society.

Throughout my years in the Syracuse School District, it was not hard for my colleagues and me to make problematic our practice or to focus our attention on the larger social and economic problems that were then erupting in violent riots in cities all over the US. Many of my students were several years behind grade level in reading and mathematics and were angry at a school they saw as having little relevance to their daily struggles for survival. The community had been extremely alienated from the school prior to my arrival, and during my first year there as a teaching intern, the school began a new status as a community school governed by a council composed of school staff and parents. An African-American principal was appointed who quickly sought to create a sense of ownership of the school in the community. Parents participated in the development of the school's curriculum, in hiring and evaluating staff, and in public forums that raised difficult issues related to race, social class and education that they felt had been ignored under previous school regimes.

I was immersed for a number of years in this environment in which previously marginalized parents and community members felt empowered to speak out, exerting their power so that they might realize their dreams of seeing their children receive the decent education that had been denied to many of them. This was a school where an African liberation flag hung in many of our classrooms and where each day was begun with the singing of 'Lift Every Voice and Sing' instead of the Pledge of Allegiance. It was an environment where a critical perspective on schooling and society and a commitment to work hard for greater educational equity and a better society were the norm. This environment where I spent my entire public school teaching career and a part of my life explains a great deal about my current educational perspectives.

What I have learned through research on my practice

Throughout my career at the University of Wisconsin-Madison, I have conducted or advised others on numerous formal research projects about various aspects of our elementary teacher education program, including the student teaching experience that I help direct. I have always sought to incorporate what we have learned in these studies directly into program changes, such as the evolution of our student teaching program into its current inquiry-oriented status (Liston and Zeichner, 1991). When

I thought about writing this chapter, I considered describing the various research projects with which I have been involved and tracing how our teacher education program has evolved over time in response to the research of our faculty and graduate students. There is another aspect to my research, however, that I have chosen to focus on instead: the more informal research that I have conducted, over the years, on my own teaching and on how my teaching and the way I seek to organize a teacher education program have been influenced by my reflections on my practice. My public writing, with a few exceptions (Gore and Zeichner, 1991; Zeichner, 1994), has focused on my more formal research and its relationship to teacher education program development. In the last few years we have begun to hear more of the private voices of teacher educators as they have shared their reflections and their struggles related to their teaching of teachers (e.g., Hamilton, 1992; Peterman, 1992; Clandinin, Davies, Hogan and Kennard, 1993). We have also begun to hear more of the voices of classroom teachers (Schubert and Ayers, 1992). This chapter is a contribution to this literature about the stories of teacher educators. Because it is also about me and not only about others, and because it reveals aspects of my personal world that I have rarely shared with the educational research community, this has been a difficult chapter for me to write. Typically, when I approach the task of producing a scholarly paper, I write a lot and very easily. This is a different kind of writing than I am used to in academia, and although it has been difficult, it has been more rewarding than the more distanced academic perspective that I usually assume.

The setting

My action research on my own teaching has focused on several different dimensions of my work. One of my major responsibilities at the University of Wisconsin-Madison is to help co-ordinate an elementary student teaching program that enrols about 175 students a year. This program includes a 20-week full-time teaching experience in an elementary or middle school in which student teachers assume total responsibility for a classroom program, and a weekly student teaching seminar that carries two university credits. The focus of my comments about student teaching in this chapter will be on the student teaching seminar. Until this year I have been responsible for supervising cohorts of 6 to 12 graduate student supervisors who teach the student teaching seminars and supervise student teachers in their field placements. In 1992–93, for the first time, Bob Tabachnick and I also taught our own section of the seminar in addition to supervising the work of the graduate students, because of our involvement with a research project on action research and the teaching of biology funded by the National Science Foundation (Tabachnick and Zeichner, in press).

The second major dimension to my work involves the preparation of teacher educators, and includes the teaching of three graduate courses. These courses focus on supervision, pre-service teacher education, and staff development, and are taken by both cooperating teachers and full-time Ph.D. students who are involved with many different teacher education programs on our campus. What follows is a discussion of two of the major dilemmas and tensions that have surfaced in my teaching over the years and the ways I have attempted to alter my practice to manage them. The first story is about the tensions that I have experienced between my commitments to my students and the creation of a more democratic and supportive classroom environment for learning, and my commitment to educational equity and the building of a more decent and humane society. The second story is concerned with a specific contradiction that I became aware of between my espoused theory and my classroom practice in relation to the idea of teacher research.

Story one: The tension between my commitment to my students and my commitment to a better society

Because of the political lens through which I view the educational world, I have faced significant tensions over the years as I have sought to educate both student teachers and teacher educators in a way that will contribute to the struggle for greater social justice. One tension has revolved around the conflict that I have often experienced between my care and concern for my own students (student teachers and teacher educators) and my commitment to their students and to the idea of a more caring, democratic, and just society.

Once I entered the world of teacher education, I quickly discovered that not everyone shared my outrage at the state of our country and our world. Many teacher education students and their teacher educators would have liked to live their lives untouched by the poverty, pain, and suffering experienced daily by so many in our country. Many of our student teachers were white and monolingual with very little direct intercultural experience, and they wanted to teach students who were just like themselves. At that time, several years before the conservative restoration of the Reagan and Bush years, there was a very active effort by many students in our program to avoid student teaching and practicum placements in schools attended by poor students of colour. Admission to the teacher education program was done mainly on the basis of academic test scores and grade point averages and ignored the level of development of students' social consciousness and commitment to educate all children. Outside the National Teacher Corps and TTT programs of the 1960s and 1970s, which were temporary and marginal programs in colleges and universities, there was little apparent concern in the US for educating teachers to teach students from economically poor families, especially poor students of colour. The state of US teacher education at the time I entered teaching in the late 1960s led Bunny Smith (1969) to characterize it as racist and discriminatory.

When I began to educate teachers, cultural deficit theories were popular in academic circles, and many educators blamed the problems that poor kids experienced in schools on the kids, their parents, pathological communities, and just about everything except the schools themselves (Deutsch, 1963). Unlike the situation described by my colleague Liz Ellsworth (1989), in which her students were disposed toward social and political critique and change, the world of teacher education is generally a very conservative one in which many students do not question the social and political conditions in which schooling occurs.

On the one hand, I wanted to create caring and democratic classroom environments in which my students felt empowered to speak out about issues that really mattered to them and where the personal and practical knowledge that they brought to the class was used as the starting point for inquiry. This kind of environment needs to be both challenging and supportive, a place where students feel free to express minority views and where there is a basic respect and caring for the individuals in the group, even during times of intellectual challenge. This environment must be a place where students feel that they are working on things that matter to them, things that are connected to their experiences as teachers and teacher educators. These were the kinds of educational experiences that were most meaningful to me in my own education and the ones that I wanted to create for my students.

On the other hand, I recognized that reflection about teaching practice and schooling does not necessarily lead to good things. In a mostly white university environment where many of the participants are those who have succeeded in the system without too great a struggle, it is very easy to ignore the perspectives of people of colour and to ignore equity implications in everyday practices of schooling. (My calling attention to race is not meant as neglect of the sense of disempowerment reported by many women in university settings, as Belenky, Clinchy, Goldberger, and Tarule, 1986, and others have written recently.) As the notion of teacher as reflective practitioner has gained popularity throughout the teacher education community, the position adopted by many has been that more reflective teachers are necessarily better teachers, no matter what they reflect about and no matter how they go about it (Zeichner, 1993). There has been very little attention to the fact that under some conditions reflection may lend greater legitimacy to practices that intensify inequities (Ellwood, 1992). I needed to confront the fact that, without intervention of some kind by me and my teaching assistants, issues of equity and social justice in schooling would not likely receive much attention in the seminars.

When I began trying to influence the student teaching seminars for which I was responsible, my approach was one of inserting 'critical content' into the seminar syllabus. I encouraged the graduate student supervisors to include in their courses readings that made problematic the social conditions of schooling that were most often taken for granted at that time — the hidden curriculum, and various ways in which the reproduction of inequalities was accomplished through curricular, instructional, and organizational practices. Often there would be assignments carried out in student teachers' schools that went along with these readings (Zeichner and Teitelbaum, 1982). Typical readings in our seminars in these early days were excerpts from Bowles and Gintis' (1976) *Schooling in Capitalist America*, Jean Anyon's (1981) 'Elementary schooling and distinctions of social class', Herb Kohl's (1980) 'Can the schools build a new social order?' and Mike Apple and Nancy King's (1977) 'What do schools teach?'. At no point in time did we try to indoctrinate student teachers with the 'correct perspective' about any of these matters. The emphasis always was, and remains today, on exposing students to different perspectives on particular issues (including a critical perspective that makes problematic the social conditions of schooling) and then trying to facilitate a process of deliberation in which students begin to develop their own positions on issues after having thought through the implications of a variety of alternative courses of action (Liston and Zeichner, 1991).

It became clear to me from my research on the program, and from reading hundreds of student evaluations of the seminars, that our approach of inserting critical content into the seminar syllabus was not having the impact that I wanted. Even though this critical content was part of a negotiated syllabus in which student teachers had a great deal of input into the topics included in the seminar, and although most seminar assignments were always connected to student teachers' work in classrooms and schools (e.g., doing case studies of particular children), many students still saw the seminar activities as something separate from the process of learning to teach, as just another set of academic hoops to jump through for certification. Although some students responded to this inclusion of critical material by becoming more committed and able to work against racism, classism, sexism, and the like in their teaching, most did not connect their greater awareness of the reproduction of inequalities through schooling to their own school situations and to their lives as teachers.

As a result of numerous discussions with my graduate student supervisors and other colleagues about this problem, I came to the conclusion that the seminar had to be constructed in such a way that the inquiry of the seminar begins with student teachers' own experiences and with the issues that they want to work on. I wanted to end the practice of trying to impose critical content on to students' perspectives and to begin the practice of facilitating more critical awareness through analysis of students' experiences (i.e., to have the greater critical awareness 'grow out of' the students' experiences by drawing attention to certain elements of their practice). Since 1984, action research has been one of the main vehicles in our program for doing this; examples of this work include Noffke and Brennan (1991), Gore and Zeichner (1991), Trubek (1993) and Zeichner (1994).

Over the last decade, we have moved our program practices somewhat closer to the place where students' own issues and practices become the starting place for inquiry in the seminar and further from the position of trying to impose a critical perspective from the outside (Gore and Zeichner, 1991). For example, during the 1992–93 academic year, Bob Tabachnick and I taught two sections of the student teaching seminar so that we could work on particular issues related to science education and on developing greater critical sensitivity from the ground up. In this class, students' action research issues formed the basis for the seminar curriculum. There were no required readings set at the beginning of the semester and no assignments other than the fact that each student teacher had agreed to carry out an action research project over the course of a 20-week semester and to keep a journal to which we responded in writing on a regular basis. The questions that student teachers investigated in these inquiries were selected by the students. Our goals were to support student teachers in their inquiries and to draw attention to issues of teaching science for conceptual change and equity and social justice as they arose in student teachers' written and oral discussions of their inquiries.

17

I have felt for a long time that the separations often made in the literature between 'technical' and 'critical', between 'micro' and 'macro', are distortions, and that *the critical* (i.e., that which makes problematic the social conditions of schooling and addresses issues of social continuity and change) *is in fact embedded within the technical and micro world of the practitioner.* Every classroom has a 'critical' dimension and all teachers can potentially explore the social and political dimensions of their practice along with its other aspects.

An example of starting with a student teacher's experience that appears on the surface to be unconnected to issues of social continuity and change, and then facilitating an exploration of the social and political dimensions of teaching experience, occurred in our seminar when a student teacher was describing her interest in finding ways to engage more constructively several students who were regularly disrupting her classroom. This kind of definition of a classroom problem by a student teacher is often interpreted in terms of classroom management or discipline and is looked down upon as trivial in academic circles. After lengthy discussion, it became clear from the descriptions of the situation that all of the students in question were students of colour in classrooms where only one-third of the students were of colour. I took the opportunity to use this situation to develop a discussion of cross-racial issues in teaching and directed the students' attention to the work of Ladson-Billings (1990), Villegas (1991) and Reyes (1992), who have explored the idea of culturally relevant and culturally responsive teaching. I also directed the students to an examination of the cultures of their own classrooms and schools.

It is important to read and discuss the work of those outside the immediate context of the seminar, but my goal has been to introduce readings to students as they become appropriate to the inquiries in which they are engaged. My role in this particular case was to draw my students' attention to the role of race and social class in a teaching situation in which they had been overlooked, so that when students continued discussing their action research, these dimensions of the experience could become part of the conversation. I have argued frequently that the critical domain is right in front of student teachers in their classrooms, and that the place to help them enter into reflection about the social and political dimensions of their teaching is by starting with their own definitions of their experiences and facilitating an examination of all of the different aspects of those experiences, including how they are connected to issues of equity and social justice. The experience is an inside-out process that is grounded in personal experience.

I have used this same strategy of engaging students in an analysis of their own practices as the starting point for inquiry in two of my graduate courses, 'Supervision in Teacher Education', and 'Seminar in Staff Development'. The difference between these courses and my student teaching seminar is that the graduate classes include a syllabus that designates topics and readings, while in the undergraduate course the topics and readings emerge entirely out of the analysis of practice initiated by students. In the graduate courses, students develop a semester-long action research project in which they explore various aspects of their practice as teacher educators. For example, in my supervision class, Jeff Maas (1991) completed a project in which he examined his use of writing as a tool for reflection with his student teachers. In another project, Jennifer Gore (1991) explored the notion of democracy in the student teaching triad. In an example of what Elliott (1991) terms 'second order' action research, Jessica Trubek (1993) examined her use of action research with her group of student teachers. In all of these cases, students explored the various topics of the course (e.g., alternative approaches to student teacher supervision, explorations of the role of experience in learning to teach) with their own supervisory experience at the forefront. I spend a great deal of time in this course reading and responding to students' journals, helping them to analyze their experiences and to make connections between what they are doing in the role of supervisor and the issues raised in the course readings.

When I started teaching this course at Wisconsin in 1976, it was a very traditional academic course with a set syllabus, and a major paper or formal examination at the end. Students always had many options for deciding the topic for their papers, but their own experiences as supervisors were not as central to the course as I would have liked. From the outset, students have always had to establish a supervisory relationship with a student teacher or teacher if they weren't already employed as a supervisor or cooperating teacher, and all students were asked to engage in some analysis of this relationship. Over the years I have gradually increased the importance in this course of the analysis of one's own supervisory practice, to the point where now all students are required to engage in an action research project on an aspect of their own supervisory practice as the major requirement for the course. How the course readings and other external literature help students make sense of their experience and clarify their supervisory agendas has become more and more my concern, in contrast to my earlier emphasis on the literature itself as a body of knowledge.

Story two: Teachers as knowledge producers: Rhetoric vs. reality

The second example of a tension experienced in my teaching that has stimulated much soul-searching and action in relation to my teaching, concerns my efforts over the past decade to use action research as a vehicle for student teacher and teacher reflection. Until 1992–93, when I first organized my own student teaching seminars in which a syllabus was not presented to students at the beginning of the semester, supervisors put together a course syllabus of topics and readings, often after negotiating with their students. This same practice was employed in my graduate courses for teacher educators.

As a result of some comments made to me at an American Educational Research Association meeting several years ago about how seriously we were treating the knowledge produced by our student teachers in their action research (as opposed to only using student teacher research as examples of how to do action research), I began to ask a series of questions about the degree to which my other graduate courses (most of which praised the value of teacher research and even engaged students in such research) incorporated the voices and practical theories of teachers.

What I found was that, despite my use of readings that were for the most part positively oriented toward teacher research and that challenged the hegemony of those who have sought to impose change in schools from the outside, the voices in these papers and books were mainly academic voices. Despite my commitment to the role of teachers as knowledge producers and to the practice of teacher research, my actual practice undermined my intended message to students. Were my students really learning about the role of teachers as knowledge producers and reformers if they never were given the opportunity to read anything written by a teacher or another student teacher?

The task, as I began to see it, was to find a more central place for teacher-produced knowledge in my work with student teachers and teachers. Thus I have tried to attain more balance between practitioner- and academic-produced knowledge in our student teaching program and in my graduate courses. In the student teaching program, I have made available to supervisors journals such as *Rethinking Schools* and *Democracy and Education* that offer teacher writing that explores teaching in a way that includes discussion of its social and political dimensions. I have also tried to help involve, as seminar instructors, public school staff who think about their work in a way that includes attention to its social and political implications. There are many efforts in the Madison schools, both by the school district and by individual teachers, to combat inequities in school outcomes among students. I have found that one of the most important things that I can do as a university teacher educator is to help put my students in touch with people within the public schools who are already working for social change; Marilyn Cochran-Smith (1991) makes a similar argument. Our earlier efforts to insert discussion of critical issues into the student teaching seminar through readings and academic assignments alone were too divorced from the practices of progressive teachers working for social change.

In some of my courses, such as 'Supervision in Teacher Education', achieving greater balance between academic- and practitioner-produced knowledge has been a very difficult process because of the nature of the available literature in the field. Despite these limitations, I have been able to 'import' from other areas literature that represents perspectives other than academic ones; I include here the perspectives (such as Sheppard, 1992) of student teachers on their own learning experiences. I have also used filmed and written case studies that enable my students' own voices to emerge more clearly as they react to various situations. The cases that I use, like the examples of teacher writing that I select, are those that raise issues about teaching in ways that include questions of equity and social justice; Stoddart's (1990) three cases of guided practice are very helpful.

Conclusion

These two stories illustrate how my reflections about my practice as a teacher educator have influenced the way I conduct my work. In both instances, I can see important changes that have occurred in my practice as a result of confronting the gaps between my rhetoric and the reality of my teaching. In the first story, I have tried to make my students' own experiences as student teachers or teacher educators the starting point for inquiry and discussion. In the second story, I have tried to create more of a balance between academic and other voices in the readings for my courses. Neither in these two stories nor in the numerous other dilemmas I face in my work have I totally resolved the tensions that the stories reveal. The process of coming to terms with teaching dilemmas is, of course, neverending.

I believe it is important for those of us who say we want to prepare teachers who are reflective practitioners to make more visible to our students our deliberations about our own work. They can then see 'up front' how a teacher experiences the inevitable contradictions and tensions of the work and goes about trying to learn from his or her teaching experience. Too often, what we hear at professional meetings and read in academic journals and books are stories of success, of all of the wonderful things we have done with our work. We all know that both teaching and teacher education are much more complex than they are often made out to be. We ought to let our stories about our work as teacher educators appear to others to be as complex as they really are.

There is another issue related to the question of where expertise about teacher education resides. Just as in the case of teaching, where there has been an attempt to create a so-called knowledge base without including the personal and practical knowledge of teachers (Cochran-Smith and Lytle, 1993), there is a danger in teacher education that a knowledge base will be defined without the voices and perspectives of teacher educators. Although there is less of an institutional division between those who do the work of teacher education and those who do research about teacher education than there is with regard to research on teaching (i.e., teacher education researchers are almost always employed in institutions that have teacher education programs), the actual involvement of teacher education researchers in teacher education programs is sometimes minimal at best. Most of those in the 1,300 or so institutions across America who are closely involved in teacher education programs and who identify themselves as teacher educators have little visibility in recent compilations of the so-called knowledge base of teacher education (Reynolds, 1989; Houston, 1990), despite the fact that most teacher educators are continually engaged in some type of self-study of their practices, such as those stimulated by program reviews and evaluations. Knowledge production in teacher education that reaches national visibility in the published literature is generated from only a handful of research universities that prepare very few of the teachers certified each year (Clark and Guba, 1976).

One consequence of this separation of teacher educators from what is recognized as teacher education research is that the questions, concerns, and voices of teacher educators are often not part of the official debate over policies for teacher education. It is frequently those who have a minimal personal stake in teacher education, yet who have built their research reputations on the back of it, whose voices receive the most attention. I have discovered recently, in a research project that seeks to document 'best practices' with regard to preparing teachers for cultural diversity, that some of the best work in this area has been carried out for many years by teacher educators whose work has received little attention in the teacher education literature (Melnick and Zeichner, 1994). I strongly believe that this is also the case for other aspects of teacher education as well. There is much good work going on in teacher education programs that we do not know about from reading journals and books, because those teacher educators doing this work are either too busy to write about it or have not been encouraged to write about it. Studies of the work of teacher education show large discrepancies between teacher education faculty and other faculty, including those in other departments in schools of education, in terms of resources to support scholarship. This includes heavier teaching loads that make it almost impossible to find time to write extensively about their work (Schneider, 1987).

The 'remote control' of teacher education is just as dangerous as attempts to manage teaching from a distance. It is time that we paid more attention to the voices of those who do the work of teacher education as we seek to determine the future of the field and to document the wisdom of teacher education practice. However, just as it is dangerous to glorify uncritically the personal and practical knowledge of teachers, it is also dangerous to accept, as necessarily good, everything that teacher educators reveal in their stories about their practice. As we begin to give more attention and respect to the personal and practical knowledge of both teachers and teacher educators, we need to learn how to assess the contribution of this knowledge to the common good. The stories of teacher educators must go beyond an exclusive concern with individual empowerment and personal transformation. These stories must also include a concern for social reconstruction that will move us toward a society where what we want for our own children is available to everyone's children. This is the only kind of world with which we should be satisfied.

Acknowledgment

An earlier version of this chapter was presented at the annual meeting of the American Educational Research Association, Atlanta, Georgia, April, 1993.

References

ANYON, J. (1981) 'Elementary schooling and distinctions of social class', *Interchange*, **12**, 2–3, pp. 118–132.

APPLE, M. and KING, N. (1977) 'What do schools teach?', *Curriculum Inquiry*, **6**, 4, pp. 341–358.

BELENKY, M.F., CLINCHY, B.V., GOLDBERGER, N.R. and TARULE, J.M. (1986) *Women's Ways of Knowing: The Development of Self, Voice, and Mind*, New York, Basic Books.

BOWLES, S. and GINTIS, H. (1976) *Schooling in Capitalist America: Educational Reform and the Contradictions of Economic Life*, New York, Basic Books.

CLANDININ, D.J., DAVIES, A., HOGAN, P. and KENNARD, B. (Eds) (1993) *Learning to Teach: Teaching to Learn*, New York, Teachers College Press.

CLARK, D. and GUBA, E. (1976) *Institutional Self-Reports on Knowledge Production and Utilization*, (RITE Occasional Paper Series), Bloomington, Indiana University School of Education.

Cochran-Smith, M. and Lytle, S. (1993) *Inside-Out: Teacher Research and Knowledge*, New York, Teachers College Press.

Cochran-Smith, M. (1991) 'Learning to teach against the grain', *Harvard Educational Review*, **61**, pp. 279–310.

Deutsch, M. (1963) 'The disadvantaged child and the learning process', in Passow, A.H. (Ed) *Education in Depressed Areas*, New York, Teachers College Press, pp. 163–179.

Elliott, J. (1991) *Action Research for Educational Change*, Buckingham, Open University Press.

Ellsworth, E. (1989) 'Why doesn't this feel empowering? Working through repressive myths of critical pedagogy', *Harvard Educational Review*, **59**, 3, pp. 297–324.

Ellwood, C. (1992, April) 'Teacher Research: For Whom?', paper presented at the annual meeting of the American Educational Research Association, San Francisco.

Gore, J. (1991) 'Practicing what we preach: Action research and the supervision of student teachers', in Tabachnick, B.R. and Zeichner, K. (Eds) *Issues and Practices in Inquiry-Oriented Teacher Education*, London, Falmer Press.

Gore, J. and Zeichner, K. (1991) 'Action research and reflective teaching in preservice teacher education: A case study from the US', *Teaching and Teacher Education*, **7**, 2, pp. 119–136.

Gutmann, A. (1987) *Democratic Education*, Princeton, NJ, Princeton University Press.

Hamilton, M.L. (1992, April) 'Making Public the Private Voice of a Teacher Educator', paper presented at the annual meeting of the American Educational Research Association, San Francisco.

Houston, W.R. (Ed) (1990) *Handbook of Research on Teacher Education*, New York, Macmillan.

Kohl, H. (1980) 'Can the schools build a new social order?', *Journal of Education*, **162**, 3, pp. 57–66.

Ladson-Billings, G. (1990) 'Culturally relevant teaching', *The College Board Review*, **155**, pp. 20–25.

Liston, D. and Zeichner, K. (1991) *Teacher Education and the Social Conditions of Schooling*, New York, Routledge.

Maas, J. (1991) 'Writing and reflection in teacher education', in Tabachnick, B.R. and Zeichner, K. (Eds) *Issues and Practices in Inquiry-Oriented Teacher Education*, London, Falmer Press, pp. 211–225.

Melnick, S. and Zeichner, K. (1994) 'Teacher Education for Cultural Diversity: Enhancing the Capacity of Teacher Education Institutions to Address Diversity Issues', paper presented at the annual meeting of the American Association of Colleges for Teacher Education, Chicago.

Noffke, S. and Brennan, M. (1991) 'Action research and reflective student teaching at the University of Wisconsin-Madison', in Tabachnick, B.R. and Zeichner, K. (Eds) *Issues and Practices in Inquiry-Oriented Teacher Education*, London, Falmer Press, pp. 186–201.

Peterman, F. (1992, April) 'Confronting My Personal Beliefs About Constructivism and Teacher Education: An Autobiographical Narrative', paper presented at the annual meeting of the American Educational Research Association, San Francisco.

Reyes, M. (1992) 'Challenging venerable assumptions: Literacy instruction for linguistically different students', *Harvard Educational Review*, **62**, 4, pp. 427–446.

Reynolds, M. (Ed) (1989) *Knowledge Base for the Beginning Teacher*, New York, Pergamon Press.

Schneider, B. (1987) 'Tracing the provenance of teacher education', in Popkewitz, T. (Ed) *Critical Studies in Teacher Education*, London, Falmer Press.

Schubert, W.H. and Ayers, W.C. (1992) *Teacher Lore: Learning From Our Own Experience*, New York, Longman.

SHEPPARD, S. (1992) 'The Research Says . . . Moving Away from Theory-Based Teacher Education Toward a Constructivist Action Research Based Approach', paper presented at the annual meeting of the Western Canadian Association for Student Teaching, Edmonton, Alberta.

SMITH, B.O. (1969) *Teachers for the Real World*, Washington, DC, American Association of College for Teacher Education.

STODDART, T. (Ed) (1990) *Perspectives on Guided Practice*, East Lansing, MI, National Center for Research on Teacher Learning, Technical Report 90–1.

TABACHNICK, B.R. and ZEICHNER, K. (in press) 'Using action research to support conceptual change teaching in science', in WATT, M. and WATT, D. (Eds) *Action Research and the Reform of Mathematics and Science Instruction*, New York, Teachers College Press.

TRUBEK, J. (1993) 'Learning from Ourselves: Doing Teacher Research with Student Teachers', paper presented at the Madison Area Action Research Network Conference, Middleton, Wisconsin.

VILLEGAS, A.M. (1991) *Culturally Responsive Pedagogy for the 1990s and Beyond*, Princeton, NJ, Educational Testing Service.

ZEICHNER, K. (1993) 'Connecting genuine teacher development to the struggle for social justice', *Journal of Education for Teaching*, **19**, 1, pp. 5–20.

ZEICHNER, K. (1994, April) 'Action Research and Issues of Equity and Social Justice in Preservice Teacher Education Programs', paper presented at the annual meeting of the American Educational Research Association, New Orleans.

ZEICHNER, K. and TEITELBAUM, K. (1982) 'Personalized and inquiry oriented teacher education', *Journal of Education for Teaching*, **8**, 2, pp. 95–117.

2   Still Learning to Teach

D. Jean Clandinin

Beginning as a teacher educator

It has been ten years since I began to live and tell a story of myself as a teacher educator. In January, 1984, I walked back into the classroom where I had been a teacher education student almost twenty years earlier. This time I walked into the class telling a story of myself as a teacher educator. I entered, for that first class, a room where twenty-three women and two men were seated, the students in my first early childhood education pre-service curriculum methods course. This was a two-term course and someone else had been teaching them for the first term as they waited for me to take up my new position at the University of Calgary, a mid-size university in a fairly wealthy city in western Canada. The students all lived in or near Calgary and, for the most part, they were in their early twenties. They were the first class in a new early childhood education program.

I had already spent some months trying to 'image' myself into a story of a teacher educator. The teacher education classes I experienced as a student some twenty years earlier had seemed to me uninteresting, and I spent my time either skipping classes or being present but *not* present in the same classrooms where I would soon be teaching. Whether I was there or not did not seem to matter much to me or to my teachers, at least not in the versions of the stories that I constructed for myself. As a student I had lived out, and now told the culturally expected story for a teacher education student. I had made up my mind that those stories were to be part of the landscape I reflected upon as I began my story as a teacher educator. I wanted to live a story as a teacher educator in which my classes would be *so* interesting, *so* relevant and *so* compelling (in terms of my relationships with each and every student) that no one could bear to miss them.

In preparation for beginning my story as a teacher educator, I talked with other early childhood teacher educators whom I considered quite progressive. I sought their advice on using films, discussion formats, problem-solving, case studies, guest speakers, visiting classroom teachers and so on. Assignments and examinations were to be practice-related and relevant to the students' real concerns about teaching. As a result, I felt confident with my prepared course outline, although I felt anything but confident that first morning as I walked toward the classroom I had known as a student. My course outline contained the list of topics to be covered, the textbook chapters and articles to be read for particular dates and a description of the assignments with the date when each was due. The students listened quietly and asked questions about the course requirements, about the readings and about the topics.

We spent those four months working through the list of activities on the course outline. Winter became spring and the course drew to a close. Standard course evaluations, prepared by the university and turned in by the students, noted that I was well-prepared and competent; I knew my subject matter; I was fair; I gave good and timely feedback. Some of the students from that first class still stay in touch; with some I have ongoing friendships. There was little to make me think I had much to learn about living my story as a teacher educator. That first term course set the plot outline for the story I was to live for the next few years. Even though I learned to give more thoughtful responses to journals, to allow the students to form their own groups, to allow class members to choose topics negotiated with me rather than to assign the seminar topics myself, and to vary the class activities to include individual tasks and small- and large-group discussions, *I lived the same story*. Although I learned to involve classroom teachers and children in more meaningful ways, moving from having 'real' classroom teachers come to class to lecture and from observing 'real' classrooms at the school board demonstration school to working closely with two teachers and the children in their classes through engaging my students in responding to the children's reading and writing, *I still lived the same story*. I still graded the assignments I designed, each year trying to design them in more classroom-connected approaches and endeavouring to imagine more thoughtful ways for the students to use research and theory to reflect upon what they were doing with the children and with the teachers with whom they interacted. My university-prepared course evaluations got better and better. It seemed I was good at what I did. There was little to make me question the character I lived out as a university teacher educator, nor anything to interrupt the basic plot outline of my story.

Within the basic plot outline scripted for me by the university, I was a 'good teacher': I prepared course outlines, evaluation processes were in place prior to the beginning of the course, examination requirements for undergraduate classes were met, and I lived a 'university teacher as expert' story. From my student evaluations, I learned that the students enjoyed our classes, felt challenged by the readings and discussions and felt 'heard' within the class times and within their journals.

In 1988–1990, I became dissatisfied with my story. I was uncomfortable about the separation between the university and the schools and with what I saw as a split in my relationships with my teacher colleagues. I was developing a concern about how we could infuse teacher education with an ethic of care, and with a desire to make more explicit a story of collaboration in teacher education. A group of six university teachers, twenty-eight teachers and twenty-eight student teachers came together to plan and live out an alternative program of teacher education. In the program we moved away from hierarchical arrangements toward collaborative conversations in which each participant contributed to the telling and living out of his or her own teacher education experience.

It was in trying to live and tell a new story, an alternative story of teacher education, that the plot line of the university story of teacher education became particularly apparent and constraining. As I became more aware of the part I was expected to live as a university teacher educator, I became increasingly uncomfortable developing my story within those scripted horizons. I began to wonder if my story as a teacher educator could change if the horizons did not change as well. For me, one of the most compelling stories from the alternative program involved assignments. This account of negotiating assignments is told more fully in a book written by some of the participants in the program (Clandinin, Davies, Hogan and Kennard, 1993). I retell it here in order to show both how I became more aware of the plot outlines of the traditional story of teacher education and how a new plot outline began to emerge for me as a teacher educator.

Finding a new story line

As the university teachers and co-operating teachers worked together to plan the alternative program, the co-operating teachers agreed to leave the matter of assignments and the evaluation of the curriculum courses to the university teachers. Because the descriptions of these assignments needed to be included as part of the course outlines distributed in the first week of university classes, we all agreed that this was reasonable. Neither co-operating teachers nor university teachers questioned the absence of student voices from this process. We conceded, mostly without discussion, that it was impossible to include the students' voices. We concurred that the assignments should be as open-ended as possible and that they should be connected to classroom practice. No one questioned the overall plot outline of the university-school relationship in the story.

Everyone told the story of the fall term as very exciting, full of what we would call 'awakenings' — retelling our stories — and 'transformations' — reliving our stories (Clandinin and Connelly, in preparation) — as students, teachers and university teachers. We read, talked, wrote and tried to hear each other's voices, and we tried to find ways to hear children's voices. For the university teachers, however, one of the main problems that autumn term was that few students were turning in the required assignments. 'Why?' we asked each other. The only writing that seemed to be occurring was in their journals. Where were all the assigned papers and projects about particular children, about particular attempts to teach subject matter, about particular teaching and learning strategies?

We heard the usual excuses (at least usual to me) of being busy, overworked, overtired, and uncertain how to proceed, none of which seemed to be adequate for those of us paying close attention to this teacher education inquiry. We talked with each other and reminded ourselves that only the voices of the university teachers had been heard in the design of the assignments. We agreed to meet as a whole group of students, teachers and university teachers to negotiate a new set of assignments — assignments that had the student teachers' voices at their centre. Those finally completed were, for the most part, pieces of work that illustrated a much more thoughtful consideration of learning and teaching than would have been likely from the original assignments.

As I reflected on this experience, I began to realize that much more was at stake, but at the time, it just seemed a more authentic way to allow students to work. There were more possibilities for collaboration with teachers and students. It was a different response to the taken-for-granted way of working with students and teachers, a way that seemed to value the voices of others. Perhaps it was also more democratic.

Retelling the story of learning to teach

Michael Connelly and I are now engaged in making more explicit the knowledge context in which we live — what we call teachers' professional knowledge landscapes (Clandinin and Connelly, 1995). In this work, we develop a set of terms and a way of understanding that help me retell my story of learning to teach. Thinking about living within a professional knowledge landscape allows me to reexamine and reinterpret my stories as a teacher education student and as a teacher of teacher education students.

In the current work we describe the professional knowledge landscape of teachers as composed of at least two different kinds of places: the in-classroom place where teachers work with students and the out-of-classroom communal, professional place. We describe the out-of-classroom place on the landscape as a place defined by the plot outlines of what we call a sacred story of theory-practice, a story in which theory is above practice; university teachers, policy makers and researchers hold knowledge to be given to teachers and student teachers; practice is applied theory; university teachers, researchers and others are the ones authorized to judge the stories of teachers and student teachers. We wrote that the sacred story assumes a metaphor of the conduit (Clandinin and Connelly, 1992) through which theoretical knowledge constructed in the university is handed down to the professional knowledge landscape of teachers and student teachers as a kind of rhetoric of conclusions. It is a powerful story, one that shapes the professional lives of teachers, student teachers and university teacher educators.

Describing a professional knowledge landscape as having separate places with different features allows us to look at the kind of dilemmas teachers experience, not only when they live in each place but also as they cross the boundary that separates the two places. Thinking about living within such a landscape has powerful consequences for telling how our narratives of experience have been shaped in the past and continue to be shaped in the present and future. What is particularly important for this chapter is to look at the story I lived and told as a teacher education student, at the story as I first attempted a retelling and reliving as a university teacher educator, and at the story as it was transformed again through the alternative program. While my first telling is in terms of storying and re-storying my own narrative of experience, I began to understand through the experience of the alternative program that a re-storying of the landscape was also involved.

As a student in my teacher education classes, I was a student character in what we call the sacred theory-practice story. I was there to be filled with theory that I could then apply to my teaching practice, first as a student teacher and, soon after, as a newly qualified teacher. Like many students, I had a sense that this was not a story to live by. My unnamed dilemma, however, was that I knew I needed to be judged as adequate by the ones authorized to judge my performance, that is, by the university teachers. So even as I recognized the inauthentic nature of the sacred story, I needed to learn to live and tell a 'cover story' that would convince my university teachers that I both knew enough theory and could apply it well enough in practice. Olson (1993) has now named this dilemma in the lives of student teachers but I moved silently through the experience. The two teacher education students in Olson's study spoke of trying to figure out the ways the sacred story is masked in a new language of teacher education.

As a student, I had no place to voice my dilemma. An experience in a music education class is illustrative. The requirements for the course were to learn enough music theory and to develop enough practical skills to play short pieces on the recorder — a musical instrument. I remember my resistance to undergoing this experience. I was clearly uncertain about the meaning I was to make of this set of expectations and I demonstrated my resistance by just pretending to play my recorder in group sessions where the grading occurred. My silent resistance through lack of participation earned me a passing grade and I used that as a kind of unnamed evidence to support my resistance to the plot outlines of the sacred story within my story of teacher education. At the time, I had no words to name my silent resistance, but I can see now how little I understood about the character I played as student in the story of teacher education. In silence I, like many of my student colleagues, hurried to escape what seemed to be a largely irrelevant set of activities. I wonder now about the many meanings of silence and about how my silence may have been read by my university teacher educators.

Retelling the story of learning to teach teachers

As I began my work as a university teacher educator I could see that, even though I was searching for ways to retell the story I would live, the plot outline of the sacred theory–practice story still constrained my living and telling. It had shaped my narrative as a teacher education student and as a teacher. My search for alternative methods that would allow better relationships, more relevant assignments and readings, and more integration of practice did not acknowledge the way the plot line of the sacred story shaped my lived and told stories. As I began work as a university teacher educator, the same plot outline continued to shape the way I lived that story. Without being able to step outside to try to imagine competing plot lines, I could vary the story only in small ways. Dissatisfied and uncertain about the constraints of what I can now name as the sacred story, the alternative program offered new possibilities.

In our negotiation of the assignments in the alternative program, we attempted to live out a new plot line, one that would be a competing story to the plot line of the sacred story. In our actions, we questioned who had the authority to give assignments, what meaning assignments had in the teaching–learning relationship, and what purposes they served in learning to teach. As we tried to live this competing story, multiple voices were authorized within the new story and the place of the university teachers (positioned above the professional knowledge landscape of teachers and student teachers) began to shift. We saw this as our awakening to the possibility of retelling the story and then to the possibility of transformation as we relived the story. Now, in yet another retelling, I present the story in new ways and see how, in our retold and relived story of assignments, we were still positioned as university teachers above the student teachers. We assumed authority for assigning grades and, in that way, maintained a partial telling of the sacred story.

It is tempting to retell the alternative program as a failure to completely transform the stories of all participants — university teachers, co-operating teachers and student teachers. It is tempting to say that we were merely unable, in that first attempt, to live the competing story we were telling because we were caught within our own autobiographical narratives, prisoners of our own familiar stories. Were that to be the version of the story I told, it would situate the story only within each of us as individuals. That would deny the place of the context (the landscape) in the story. The landscape shaped my living and telling, both as a student teacher and later as a university teacher educator. The professional knowledge landscape on which we storied the alternative program was still powerfully shaped by the sacred story. In the current work I can now articulate how difficult it is to imagine how to tell and to live a competing story as we re-storied ourselves *and* the landscape.

Elsewhere we wrote that university teachers who break from the sacred theory-practice story by relocating themselves outside the story of expert, knowledge production, certainty, and hierarchy are taking professional risks (Connelly and Clandinin, 1994). They give up a familiar and privileged story for the uncertainties of a new one of equality constructed through engaging in collaborative conversations with students, children and teachers. As university teachers begin to live and tell competing stories, founded on different epistemologies, these accounts become threatening to other university teachers, teachers and student teachers. To illustrate this threat, I return to a story of one of the student teachers from the alternative program. Sonia went on, at the completion of the alternative program, to finish the fourth year of her university program. One of the most striking things, for me, was Sonia's sense of herself as a 'threat' to her fourth year university instructors. Having begun to tell a story of herself as someone who had something to say and as someone who wanted to continue to explore her own lived and told stories, she was seen as threatening by those who still lived within the plot line of the sacred story. Her fourth year was a difficult year as she went back to living a story of 'playing the game' of the sacred story (Clandinin and Hogan, 1995).

Re-storying the professional knowledge landscape

Recognizing the threats that emerge from living and telling a competing story seems particularly important. In our recent work, we understand that telling and living stories that compete with the sacred story result in tensions that lead to questioning, to awakenings, to transformations. When these tensions appear, we often tell the stories only as accounts of our attempts at re-storying ourselves. Yet these tensions also call us to consider how our re-storying can change our professional knowledge landscape, as competing stories that challenge the dominant plot line are told as viable stories that can survive in a new landscape. Too often, 'competing' stories are restoried as 'conflicting' ones that require too much time and too many resources, have insufficient rigor, or require too much from students. When competing stories become too threatening to the sacred story, they tend to be re-storied as conflicting and are shut down.

As I return to my own story of learning to teach, I am left with a sense of unease. I continue to attempt to re-story myself in ways that illuminate how the professional knowledge landscape has shaped my story of learning to teach. I do that re-storying in conversations with myself and with others, some in face-to-face conversations and others in written conversations. But even as I live the tension between the sacred story, competing stories and the possibility of conflicting stories, I know that more is needed, and more than re-storying myself and those who live in community with me is necessary.

The enormity of naming the task in this way could maintain my sense of unease, perhaps even lead to despair. And yet I am hopeful. I have colleagues with whom I share in community. I continue to wake up to see possibility for transformation in my stories. And as Mary Catherine Bateson (1994) writes, 'Because we live in a world of change and diversity, we are privileged to enter, if only peripherally, into a diversity of visions, and beyond that to include them in the range of responsible caring' (p. 12). Without imagining, living and telling new competing stories that question the plot line of the sacred story, little in my lived story as a teacher educator and little in the professional knowledge landscape can change. Without opening up to the many possible visions that serve as possible storylines, I may find myself no longer still learning to teach.

References

BATESON, M.C. (1994) *Peripheral Visions*, New York, Harper Collins.

CLANDININ, D.J. and CONNELLY, F.M. (1992) 'The teacher as curriculum maker,' in JACKSON, P.W. (Ed) *Handbook of Research on Curriculum*, New York, Macmillan, pp. 363–401.

CLANDININ, D.J. and CONNELLY, F.M. (in preparation) *Narrative and Education*.

CLANDININ, D.J., DAVIES, A., HOGAN, P. and KENNARD, B. (1993) *Learning to Teach: Teaching to Learn, Stories of Collaboration in Teacher Education*, New York, Teachers College Press.

CLANDININ, D.J. and HOGAN, P. (1995) 'Shifting moral landscapes: A story of Sonia's teacher education', in CLANDININ, D.J. and CONNELLY, F.M. (Eds) *Teachers' Professional Knowledge Landscapes*, New York, Teachers College Press.

CONNELLY, F.M. and CLANDININ, D.J. (1994) 'The promise of collaborative research in the political context', in HOLLINGSWORTH, S. and SOCKETT, H. (Eds) *Teacher Research and Educational Reform*, Chicago, University of Chicago Press, pp. 86–102.

OLSON, M. (1993) 'The Authority of Stories in Teacher Education', unpublished doctoral dissertation, Edmonton, University of Alberta.

Part 2

Beginning Teacher Educators Reflect on their Development

3   Becoming Teachers of Teachers: The Paths of Four Beginners

Karen Guilfoyle, Mary Lynn Hamilton, Stefinee Pinnegar, and Margaret Placier

Introduction

> This is the most stressful job I have ever had . . . I don't know how I ever made it through [first semester] . . . I came close to not going back in January. (1/8/91-4) What I realize is what a nightmare last fall was [in my initial year] . . . I feel just as off-balanced and harried as I did last year. (9/8/90-1) When I think about my first year, several issues come to mind . . . In the staying sane area, . . . I think I flopped. Except that I called friends for support through the experience. They would bolster me, sometimes simply because they were having similar experiences. (11/8/90-3) I am becoming a professor, after continuing to behave like a graduate student for another year and a half, I guess. (12/14/90-2) (Guilfoyle, 1995)

These quotations illustrate how we wrote to each other about our initial experience in becoming teachers of teachers. In this chapter, we present and analyze accounts of how we learned about teaching teachers. Our purpose is not to examine the meaning of being a teacher of teachers, nor to provide strategies for training teachers of teachers. We are not trying to create a recipe for socialization, nor to illuminate the underlying pattern of learning to teach teachers. Instead, we present a multivocal account of the individual process we each went through in becoming a teacher of teachers.

It might be felt that what we are offering here has been presented elsewhere, in research on new professors, women academics, personal accounts of the professor's life, or in the teacher socialization literature. We believe that this analysis of our experience in becoming teachers of teachers offers a unique perspective. Current research on the new professor (e.g., Boice, 1991, 1992) focuses on how outstanding, effective, fast-start new professors shape their work and organize their time. Our study differs from this work because we are documenting and interpreting our own experience as new professors. The demands of academic life discussed by Boice — to publish or perish, to be a 'good' teacher, and to be a 'good' citizen of the university — result in personal pressures and have immediate consequences in our lives. Our accounts avoid the clinical and distanced voice of most discussions of this topic.

Our experiences in academe are different from the experiences of many of the new professors Boice interviewed and surveyed. When we began as assistant professors, we already had extensive experience as teachers, both in public schools and at the university level. From the beginning, we knew how to construct curriculum, carry out evaluation, use a variety of teaching strategies, and counsel students. Unfortunately, having and using this knowledge did not give us the edge we hoped it would. Because we teach teachers, concerns with and about teaching could not be easily or systematically resolved so that we could focus on the 'more important' concerns of getting ahead with our research — the tack taken by Boice's most effective beginners. In our case, our teaching and the teaching of our students was and is representative of all aspects of our responsibilities as university professors — research, teaching, and service. Guilfoyle (1995) articulated the complexity of doing this in documenting her attempts to bring together scholarship, teaching, and service with her responsibilities as a teacher educator. She explains how she reconciles the theory-practice divide in her own work by helping her students understand and resolve this conflict in their own education.

A strand of research begun in the 1970s and updated recently examines the role of the female academic (Aisenberg, 1988; Chamberlain, 1988). While this research informs us and provides echoes of themes we have lived, and also accounts remarkably well for our experience within the university community, it does not account for all of our experience. More importantly, it does not represent how female academics negotiate the troubled waters illuminated in the studies. The conclusions of the study give comfort to fellow travellers, but not direction. Martin's (1994) edited collection provides a clearer account. Hamilton's (1995) use of the metaphor of Dorothy from the *Wizard of Oz*, documents the impact of the 'tornado' of the institutional experience. It provides a provocative analytic synthesis of the lived experience of an untenured female academic in an account that goes beyond earlier work by embodying the analysis of this lived experience within an interpretive narrative framework. The accounts we provide here are informative not as models or maps but as possibilities.

Powerful restatements and assessments of academic lives, like those of Eble (1988), Booth (1988) and Getman (1992) were written by experienced, respected professors, not in the moment, but in retrospect. From the front porch swing in the later, tenured, revered years of successful academic lives, they relive sagas of old academic wars. They offer accounts from the perspective of the tenured male full professor in arts and letters and law, where academic life, while complex, has both higher status and less complexity than life in colleges of education, particularly in the often overlooked departments where undergraduate and even graduate teachers are educated. In contrast, our accounts are written from the perspective of female, untenured, beginning professors in teacher education. We offer the immediacy of accounts created in makeshift tents on the battlefield on the eve of battle, when the outcome is still in doubt. Placier's (1995) work accounts for her present difficulty of living her values of democracy while grading her students. Russell (in press) creates another such account about the tensions of being a teacher at both the university and a secondary school.

At times we have wondered how much our perspectives as beginning teacher educators could add to the literature because our experiences are similar, in some respects, to those of beginning teachers (Cole and Knowles, 1993). While the teacher socialization literature (e.g., Zeichner and Gore, 1990) has helped us think about our experiences, it has always been ironic for us because we are asked to lead students at a time when we feel just as vulnerable as they do to pressures of socialization, status and context. We would be the first to admit that becoming a teacher educator shares some features with becoming a teacher (Pinnegar, 1995), but we now realize that it is also quite different from becoming a teacher, in several important ways.

One major difference is our responsibility to conduct and publish research. We are hired to teach; we will gain tenure and promotion only if we publish. This condition immediately separates us from beginning teachers. In addition, while we share with all teachers the responsibility for the education of our own students, in our responses (institutional, curricular, and personal) to our students we must always be an advocate for the unseen children whom they will teach over their careers. The task of educating teachers has implications for all of education. The student teaching experience represents our responsibility. We have a moral obligation to all participants: the student teacher, the co-operating teacher, and the student in the classroom.

At the same time, the often fragmented relationships between universities and public schools increase the difficulty of fulfilling this obligation. As teacher educators, we foster ideas of teaching and learning often not evident in the schools where our students learned or where they will observe and teach. Our students bring with them mature beliefs about teaching and learning that tend to be more congruent with their past experiences than with the ideas we are asking them to consider. Our ability to make progress in helping them develop as teachers is complicated further by the limited amount of time that we have direct responsibility over them. Even if we insist that they act differently, once they enter their own classrooms they can teach as they wish, or as they are expected to by others in the school. Finally, our responsibility for teacher education is not just certification, but the continued growth and development of teachers.

New professors of teacher education must negotiate multiple layers of institutional politics and policies, both in the teaching of teachers and in the participation and negotiation necessary to continue within the academy. Teaching is always a political activity. Politics can be even more difficult in teacher education because of its lower status within the university and the larger culture and the increased number of institutional connections that educating teachers demands. We negotiate with most colleges on our campuses, as well as with all local school districts, state certification agencies, and national teacher accreditation bodies. In almost every contact, colleges of education come to the bargaining arena with little respect from the other participants. We must do this to educate an undergraduate student as a teacher, not because it is fashionable, builds stronger programs, or has prestige. This increases the fragmentation of the life of teacher educators.

In learning to become teacher educators, we have been informed by the research strands discussed here. When we recognized, early on, the ways in which this research could not completely account for our experiences in learning to teach, we began to study that process (Arizona group, 1994; Russell and Pinnegar, 1995). This chapter is part of our continuing effort to make sense of the process and to invite others to understand our experiences.

Outline of the analysis

We present both individual and group analyses of the process by which we learned about being teacher educators. The four individual narratives provide our personal interpretations of this process. However, we also wanted to provide a collective interpretation, one that accounted for our mutual experiences. The ideas that emerged in this group analysis were used to segment the narratives and to guide our arrangement of them under the subheadings in the section entitled, 'Becoming a Teacher of Teachers'. Our individual accounts do not appear in the same sequence each time; rather, we arranged them in ways that best defined and revealed our interpretation of a section. Thus the order of appearance varies, and an individual may appear more than once in each segment. During the past five years, as we have studied our experiences, we have collected, analyzed, and interpreted data and written about our experiences through the lenses of our own learning, teaching, and researching (Applebee, 1987; Bissex, 1986, 1988; Cochran-Smith and Lytle, 1993; Goswami and Stillman, 1987; Patterson, Stansell and Lee, 1990). These were our questions:

- What were our experiences?
- What were our questions?
- Where did we look for answers?
- What did we learn?

Re-examining these questions guided our individual analyses and led to the construction of the narratives. Analysis of data and reflection on our actions and interactions has been ongoing, informing and shaping each layer of data collection and analysis. Although not always clearly visible as such, we have been involved in cycles of action research (McNiff, 1988). As Woods (1986, p. 121) suggests, our analysis went through several stages: '1) speculative analysis; 2) classifying and categorizing; and 3) concept formation'. Our task in these stages was to interpret and make sense of the data, analyzing so that our findings would be trustworthy (Ely *et al.*, 1991). In constructing these narratives, we returned to a re-examination and analysis of earlier experiences in light of our current experience. We re-read our earlier papers, journals, letters, and other accounts of our experience. Then we identified the salient features of this process in terms of our current experience. The fact that each of us is under some type of institutional review (yearly, third year, or tenure) supported our analysis. Each of us constructed a narrative accounting for our process in becoming a teacher educator. If the reader is most interested in these narratives, a single one can be recovered by reading sequentially each segment of a particular person. These individual narratives provide one person's account of the process.

Rather than using the bulk of the paper to discuss the themes revealed in these accounts, with illustrative quotes from the narratives, we have provided the narratives in their entirety, thus inviting the reader into the analytic process. We have organized segments of the narratives using three issues that appear in all four individual accounts to provide the reader with additional analysis of our experiences. The three sub-headings — Questions and Biography; Memories, Images and Metaphors; and Process in our Learning — represent critical features of our experience. The categories are not always mutually exclusive; this results in part from our decision to present our complete, individual accounts. Sometimes issues that are discussed in the first section may emerge in the individual account in a later section in the document.

In presenting the individual segments, we begin with an introductory description of the sub-heading. This is followed by segments from our individual accounts, ending with a commentary. The individual accounts are not always presented in the same order. Instead, they have been presented relationally to help readers understand the definition we present initially and the commentary with which we conclude. This format invites the reader into a joint construction of the interpretation of the document.

Becoming a teacher of teachers

What follows are textually interwoven, individual analyses of the experience of becoming a teacher educator. Our separate accounts have been divided into thematic segments that are juxtaposed against each other to reveal the similarities and differences in our ideas about the experience of becoming a teacher of teachers. Questions and biography; images, metaphors and memories; and 'process' in our learning were the three critical features in our narratives and these provide the organizing frame for our collective story.

Questions and biography

'Questions' refers to those questions we asked ourselves about being and becoming teacher educators. While new questions surfaced during our experience, they emerged as we sought answers to the questions we began with. This heading also refers to the impact of our questions on our experience. 'Biography' refers to the personal histories we bring to our experiences as teacher educators and to their influence on our experiences.

Mary Lynn: When I ask myself how I became a teacher educator, I am left puzzling about the first time I thought about doing that or left wondering if I ever really initiated a learning-to-be-a-teacher-educator process. I suppose, though, that I first began the process long before I became conscious of it. In the unconscious moments, I worked hard to train teachers to integrate their curricula with multicultural perspectives or gender concerns. I spent long hours designing materials to be presented to teachers for use in their classrooms. But who taught me how to do that? Really, no one taught me. I learned by watching those people around me, by reminding myself about what happened in my own classrooms with high school students, by trying to remember the stages of development and how these might fit with what I needed to do. I also learned by making errors, major errors in front of the classroom. No class at the university discussed the process of becoming a teacher educator. Yet, somewhere, I decided that I wanted to work with teachers and support them in their desires to improve their practice. Somewhere, somehow, I decided that I could best support students if I supported their teachers.

So, how did I do that? What did happen along the way? Did I have mentors? Did I learn from my university instructors? How did I develop my knowledge about teaching teachers? What elements influenced my choices and decisions? As I ponder both the process and the procedure, I am struck by how single-minded and empowering the process has been. Although I have experienced moments of ambiguity and concern, now I feel quite empowered by the direction I have taken.

I notice that I have made decisions without much direct influence of others. This external influence has come in response to my reflections upon their ideas and actions. I have observed good teaching and I have spoken with good teachers, but rather than duplicate their ideas, I have reflected and responded. Even when I decided to attain my Ph.D., I made that decision based on wanting to make a difference in the lives of young students (K-12), not on how or why I might work with undergraduates. I never thought about teaching teachers, and I never wondered about how I might do that. I always assumed that I could.

Stefinee: My method of becoming anything is to get a glimmer of what that thing is and then begin walking in that direction. This particular walk began on the playground of the East Elementary School in St. George, Utah. One day when I was ten years old, in fifth grade, we learned what the abbreviation 'Ph.D.' meant. I remember standing on the playground and looking up at the sky and promising myself that if it took all my life, if I had to wait until children were grown and I was a grey-haired grandmother, one day I would get a Ph.D. When I entered a doctoral program at the University of Arizona, I was fulfilling the vow of that ten-year-old child. I was in some ways being a dilettante. I had left the vocation of teacher, unsure whether I would ever return. I did not plan on 'using' the Ph.D. in any way. I came to my doctoral program to learn about what had troubled me most as a teacher — how to teach all students, how to help students reach their potential regardless of their skill or mental ability. I never expressed these views. Like any well socialized graduate student, I quickly developed other language to express my goals.

At the University of Arizona a group of professors joined the faculty while I was a student; they changed my ideas. They (and others) taught me about qualitative research methods and research on teacher thinking and practical inquiry. I realized that if I wanted to re-experience the processes I wished to study, I would need to work in teacher education. Even then I did not label what I was choosing to do as becoming a teacher educator.

When I began my first academic appointment, I was preoccupied with two very basic questions: What did it mean to be a teacher educator? What did teacher educators do that made them teacher educators? I wondered what the developmental status of beginning teachers was and what would facilitate it. My own recently completed dissertation work suggested that the space between being a student teacher and an experienced teacher was so great it was difficult to see the roots of one in the other.

As I began, I felt silenced. I came to teacher education with good credentials. Yet it quickly became apparent that my expertise would be irrelevant. Though I was an experienced adult who had been a successful teacher both in public schools and at the university, I was treated as if I were a blank slate — someone who knew absolutely nothing. My senior colleagues catered to the public school's endorsement of EEI [essential elements of instruction]. While it was difficult for me to articulate clearly my own ideas of helping students learn to be teachers, these did not include teaching and enforcing this model of instruction exclusively. I wondered about Reynolds' (1992) list of knowledge needed for beginning teachers. I had studied the work of Schön (1983) and interpretations of how his views of professional knowledge related to development as a teacher. I wondered about 'technical rationality' and reflection on practice in teacher development. There was great interest in 'the knowledge base for teaching and teacher education', but I struggled to fit this perspective with my beliefs about learning to teach.

I had come into an arena where there appeared to be no way for me to contribute from the basis of my strengths. While there was an adolescent development course in the planning stage [the area of my education], I was asked to teach a general methods course and told to do lots of research. I knew little about general methods other than those I had used as a teacher. The faculty had agreed to teach courses in uniform ways, and I began by team teaching with another faculty member. While we had a good relationship, I felt that little I had or knew was of value here. I struggled with teaching the course for the three years I was there, because the conception of teaching that was embedded in the design of the course was quite antithetical to my own beliefs about teacher development. My expertise as a teacher of English and as a student of English language, human development, learning and qualitative research was for the most part ignored.

Karen, Mary Lynn, and Peggy's accounts of their course design experiments and their courage in living their beliefs in their classrooms were a support and a goad to me. I wondered how it would be to feel so confident about what students needed to become teachers. I was unsure. During this time, I struggled to create an unfragmented existence — teaching, research, service, family life, friends. Several of my colleagues were also beginners. We had rich conversations about theory, philosophy and teaching, and we laboured together to get our research interests going and to create an academic environment which would allow us to develop. I tried to reconnect with teachers so that I could continue to learn from them.

When possible, which was not often, I read. As I read I thought about the process of my own becoming a teacher. I also began written conversations about my practice with Tom Russell, Mary Lynn Hamilton, Karen Guilfoyle, Peggy Placier, Barbara Morgan, Luz Gonzales, Jack Whitehead and Glenda Wilkes. During this time, I taught English at an alternative high school for two six-week stints with students who had been removed from the public schools. This experience helped me remember what I did not know about teaching and learning to teach. It called into question most of what I did in my classroom and what we did in teacher education programs, including student teaching. My own beliefs about what I could do as a teacher educator emerged in the design of a new course on adolescent development and learning. I began to act on my belief about the need to understand the development of teachers' practical knowledge.

About this time, I took a new academic appointment. At this new university, the program seemed as fragmented and self-directed as the other had been managed and proscribed. Again, I felt my expertise denied. I could not see how to use anything I had learned. (A very ironic experience to be in a situation with little restriction and yet not know how to do what I thought would be best for students.) I spent the first two years working hard to determine how we were educating teachers and how theory and practice fit together in the program. Departments in the arts and sciences had power. They felt strong ownership over much of what I considered the content of teacher education. Public schools began to assert ownership over practice. In negotiations of ownership over the theory-practice divide, I often felt like shark bait between these two groups.

During this move, I came to think of myself as a teacher educator. This meant that I was committed to the education of teachers. I began to see more clearly ways I could move forward in enacting teacher education as I understood it.

Peggy: My process of becoming a teacher educator actually began about 24 years ago when I became the 'head teacher' of a Head Start centre in a very small northern Ohio town. The title of 'head teacher' was entirely inappropriate. As a beginning teacher, I was incapable of heading anything, but I was the only person at the centre with a degree and, therefore, senior to others with less education but more practical experience.

My own pre-service teacher education had been miserably inadequate. The model of in-service staff development in our regional Head Start program, in contrast, was stimulating and productive. Every Friday, the staffs of all four centres in the region met in the morning for a session with our staff development coordinator. We created activities and materials, shared experiences, solved problems, and occasionally listened to experts. In the afternoon we met as centres to plan the following week's program. This was my teacher education. Headteachers, teachers, and teacher aides alike, whatever our educational backgrounds or titles, we were all teachers educating ourselves and creating our own practice. My most important mentor was a teacher of about my age who had dropped out of school to marry at age 14, had four children by age 20, and was attending college classes with the help of a grant from the program.

Despite the strengths of the program, however, I had a terrible first year. When left alone with my class, I could not manage Bernie, a big, strong 4-year-old who pulled hair, kicked, and smeared faeces on the bathroom walls (today, special educators would no doubt label him 'behaviour disordered'). On the last day after the busload of children had pulled out, I sobbed uncontrollably for a solid hour. The board met to consider whether I should be fired, but for some reason they were merciful. The next year things smoothed out. Even the program nurse, who from her passing observations of my performance had thought I was hopeless, told me I was a good teacher.

As a beginning teacher my major concerns were day-to-day planning and survival in a new environment. While I was politically aware, concerned about the war in Vietnam and civil rights, I was not aware of the deep political meanings of my work for the Head Start program. I was not aware, for example, that the program was based on a 'cultural deficit model' of 'compensatory education'. I was not fully aware that it was part of a grand liberal strategy, a War on Poverty. I was not aware of myself as an agent of the federal government intervening, for better or worse, in the lives of children and families. I was just a teacher of children, worried about what to do the next week, day or (in the case of Bernie) minute.

It is important for me to remember this personal history, because it takes me back to the place where many of my students are today. Most are not aware, for example, of the effects of the report, *A Nation at Risk*, on American schools (including the ones they attended) in the 1980s. Most cannot evaluate the potential consequences of recent federal 'Goals 2000' legislation, or the decision by a judge in our state to equalize per-pupil spending in all districts. As a teacher educator in the foundations of education field, it is my job to persuade them that such knowledge is indispensable to them as future teachers. It is not easy. One day a student remarked, 'Why do we need to know all this stuff? We aren't going to be administrators'. At other times, students have accused me of being 'too negative', because I often focus on the political failings of schools rather than the positive, practical aspects of teaching. Most, quite naturally, would like to go on thinking of teachers as good and innocent people and schools as benign institutions.

For me, one aspect of becoming a teacher educator has been to recover my memory of my beginning-teacher self in order to understand my students' point of view. My graduate education distanced me from that long-ago self. As a foundations scholar, I developed a social reconstructionist position based on a critical analysis of American schools and educational policies. It was this position that I wanted to transmit to my teacher education students. Many of my mistakes and surprises as a beginning teacher educator have derived from my assumption that this position would be as self-evident to my students as it now is to me, that on exposure to it, they would shout 'Eureka!' Instead, most are on paths of their own that collide or diverge rather than converge with mine.

Karen: I came to teacher education with limited understanding of the context of academe. The struggle started when I began to comprehend the complexity and multiplicity of the roles, and the tensions and dilemmas a teacher educator faces. Even though I had twenty years of experience in schools, teaching emerged as one of the primary challenges in my struggle and continues to be after five years. Using self study as a methodology embedded in teacher research, I am exploring my journey as a teacher of teachers. For me, teacher research is an empowering way to understand teaching and offers a 'radical alternative to traditional epistemologies of research on teaching and teacher education' (Cochran-Smith and Lytle, 1993, p. xiii). Since my purpose for entering teacher education is change by promoting justice and equity for *all* learners, the methodologies of teacher research act as a form of social change and support my inquiry.

In my inquiry, I am exploring my interactions in the context of academe and the classroom. I had not anticipated that teaching would be one of the major mountains for me to ascend. To my surprise, it became an issue on several levels — in the classroom, with my colleagues, within the structure of academe, and eventually in the community. My philosophy and theories, grounded in whole language, a social constructivist view of learning, and critical pedagogy, represent a minority view in academe and create problems to address. With the tensions and dilemmas I face, I recognize I can travel this road because 'I get a lot of help from my friends' (Guilfoyle, 1992, p. 1). Reading, reflecting, and researching also facilitate my journey. In a journal entry during my third year, I wrote:

> It would not have been possible to come where I am in my journey without the interaction I have had with others — students, colleagues, mentors, teachers in public schools, and my family. Researching my journey has clearly helped me . . . and it did not come as a major shift. It was a process.

These segments of our accounts reveal that questions and biography were important precursors and contributors to the process of our development as teacher educators.

Personal biography is fundamental in this development, just as Bullough *et al.* (1991) and Knowles and Cole (in this volume) would suggest. What is particularly interesting is *how* biography played a role. Each of us speaks of very significant experiences: the remembered vow of a ten-year old — marking the beginning of the journey; the specific incident — sobbing on the last day of school; the pattern of the learning to teach process being similar to the process of learning to teach teachers; and the background of twenty years as a public school teacher. As we recount our experiences, biography did not play a straightforward or obvious role in our development. In fact, our personal biographies led to commitment and insight. Our past experiences gave us insight into our current experiences, and this brought new understanding, an enrichment of the meaning of being a teacher educator and greater commitment to the development of teachers. Part of our biography now is the realization that our movement from teacher to teacher educator, while based on experience, emerged gradually, or at least more gradually than we had realized.

Memories, images and metaphors

This section refers to our figurative, imagistic, mental conceptions of ourselves, both in our roles as teacher educators and in our understandings of our experiences. Here we explore the memories, images and metaphors that guide life decisions. Our narratives show we differ significantly from this perspective, yet personal images have had an important impact on the work of each of us. For Mary Lynn and Karen, imagistic thinking is represented as metaphors, like the quilt or the journey. For Stefinee, imagistic thinking is literally an image of herself as tap dancer or as member of a community. For Peggy, imagistic thinking is evident in the replaying of a specific memory of herself on the last day of her first year as a teacher. While 'biography' refers to ways in which our past experiences have merged to leave us the person we are at a particular moment in time, 'memories, images, metaphors' refer to deeper, more holistic, more elusive, interpretations of the experience.

> **Karen:** When I reflect on my experience, I think about how often I am reminded of a 'journey'. In constructing the meaning of my journey as teacher educator, I see it as 'The Struggle'. For me, it is a struggle to navigate the terrain of academe. I continually encounter sharp curves, steep hills, and detours that are difficult to understand in a system that outwardly speaks of creating knowledge, change, restructuring education, and rethinking curriculum at all levels. Through action research, I endure the struggle and change it as I travel along learning about it. In the process, I am learning how to address *some* of the issues I encounter, and realizing there are others that will continue to be problematic because of my experience, beliefs, theories, and commitment to demonstrate practice that promotes justice and equality for all. Sometimes the intensity of the struggle moves me to contemplating the other roads I could take and wondering if this journey is the one I want to be on.

Stefinee: In my development as a teacher educator, I have had three domin-ant images. One image articulated in our letters to each other (Arizona Group, 1994) was a dream vision of community where colleagues and administrators and public school teachers unite together to foster the development of the students who are going to be teachers in the ethos of the African proverb: 'It takes a village to educate a child'. In such a dream, I see all co-operating and sacrificing so that beginning teachers will develop into their best and not worst teaching selves.

Peggy: As I replay the last day of my first year as a teacher, I gain empathy for what lies ahead for my students and how they feel in my classroom. Recon-necting with my beginning-teacher self reminded me that 18–22 year old col-lege students have their own vocational and developmental tasks to accomplish. Growing up in the 1980s, they also have different world views and political ideologies from my 1960s self. I cannot assume that the knowledge I find essential for understanding and re-evaluating my own teaching experience has intrinsic interest or value to them. Becoming a teacher educator means learning how to link the curriculum to their interests, values, and identities, without com-promising mine. I have found myself thinking as much about who my students are and what they know, think and believe, as what I want them to be and know, think and believe. This has created further dilemmas, as I find out that what some of my students believe (e.g., racism, sexism, extremely judgmental attitudes toward certain children and families) seems to me to be incompatible with the ethical obligations of teachers in a democratic, pluralistic society. Academic freedom means that they have a right to express their opinions. But what is my ethical obligation to my students' future students? Are we even justified at times in closing the gate to teaching based on attitudes or ideology?

Stefinee: When I began teaching future teachers, my image of myself was the image of a beginning tap dancer. First you get the beat, then you add fancier steps, then you add hand motions, then you pick up the cane. But I kept dropping the cane or losing the beat and ending up arms akimbo, tangled in a heap. I never saw myself getting the beat. It is ironic that I would ever think of myself in the image of a dancer because I am completely uncoordinated. I think this initial image represented the denial I felt of my own voice and talents, an incredible self focus, and my struggle to balance it all.

Mary Lynn: If asked to imagine a metaphor that might best explain my learning-to-be-a-teacher-educator-process, I would have to select the meta-phor of quilter. Women used to quilt for families to produce the necessary blankets to survive the winter. These were often artful and creative — visually lovely, yet functional. For social as well as practical reasons, women of the surrounding community would assemble to help with the final stitching of the quilt. As the women came together, they shared ideas and suggestions for the next quilt as well as other life experiences.

In this image, I can see myself sitting in a small desk chair with my quilt surrounding my feet and the chair. And as I look at the quilt, I know that each square of fabric represents an idea shared or a strategy suggested by a student or colleague. I am the person creating the quilt — selecting the pattern and placing the squares — yet my colleagues and friends offer direction and advice. Slowly, with every stitch on my soft, bright fabric, I am creating a quilt that represents the story of my teaching life.

Just as the quilter chooses her material and her thread, I have selected my direction and designed my lessons. Sometimes I have matched my desired directions with the wrong strategies, but I adjust for those errors as soon as I see how they do not work. Sometimes I am simply forced to rip out the stitches and start again. Fortunately, both materials and students are resilient. So, how did I learn to become a teacher educator? I have to say simply that I learned to teach teachers by doing it. Just as quilters learn to quilt by quilting, I learned to teach teachers by teaching. I became familiar with my own comfort levels as well as those of students. I discovered what worked for me as a person responsible for the learning as well as the interest level of the students involved. In turn, as I learned, I shared ideas with my colleagues who responded and provided further opportunities for reflection and thoughtfulness. Reflecting upon my teaching is, for me, the most critical element of the learning-to-teach-teachers process.

Upon what do I reflect? Just as the quilter draws upon her knowledge and experience as a stitcher to make decisions about patterns and colours, I draw upon my knowledge and experience of learning and teaching. I reflect upon articles and ideas I have read about in the past, upon strategies and methods I have used in other settings, and upon the activities and ideas of my students. All of my experiences come together in the moment to affect what I do next in the classroom. I am infinitely involved in a development process. As I progress, responding to student responses or ways of learning, I adapt my thinking and actions. My quilt could not be made without input from other people and experiences, but I am the essential element in its creation.

Culture and beliefs are important in the learning-to-teach-teachers process. As a quilter selects her colours, patterns, and stitching strategies, her personal history, her background, and the beliefs based upon that history and background, influence her choices. She could not make the choices she makes without those influences. And that is how it is for teacher educators — or at least for me. My history, my thinking, my learning, all influence each choice I make. For example, I believe in the importance of identifying students' prior knowledge before introducing new concepts. Consequently, before I begin a lesson, I always engage in a discussion about the concepts to be presented so that we can construct the current parameters of my students' knowledge.

In my teaching, I am also driven by my desire to save the world. I want to wake my students up to the injustices in the world and that aim is manifested in my reading choices and discussion directions. I do not hesitate to raise controversial issues in my classrooms or challenge my students in their thinking.

47

I also welcome their challenges of my ideas. This, of course, underscores my belief that change can not occur in peoples' thinking until they are conscious of what they believe. Once conscious of their beliefs, people, myself included, can decide whether or not to shift their beliefs.

Stefinee: My current image of myself as teacher educator builds more directly on the underlying image I discussed initially and removes me as awkward tap dancer from centre stage. This is the image of teacher education as a solution to the three person problem: the teacher educator, the future teacher, and the student of the future teacher. In this representation, the teacher educator is responsible for teaching a student who will become a teacher of students and has simultaneously a moral obligation to both. With the emergence of this image, I saw myself most clearly as a teacher educator. I also found my voice and ways to respond to this image in my academic life.

Our images of ourselves as teacher educators are a two-edged sword. They can provide a glimmer, a holistic yet fleeting idea of what it means to be a teacher educator at a particular moment in time. They sometimes seem nebulous, but because they capture succinctly and insightfully for us how we think and are, they may blind us to how we might be. For example, the image of the awkward tap dancer was so powerful that it was difficult to refocus on the larger image that included self in relation to other where the other took centre stage.

Memories of ourselves as teachers, often replayed over and over again, remind us of specific instances of our past and make the experiences even stronger in our minds than they were initially. Such memories are invisible to those watching us and are a stark reminder that neither we nor our students come to any learning situation 'blank' or as 'empty vessels'. We bring with us recollections that limit, direct, and support our current learning.

Sometimes the literature of teacher thinking reads as though images, metaphor, memory, and reflection can be separate, capturable, categorizable characteristics that teacher educators can manipulate. Our experiences and these accounts indicate that, like personal biography, they are intertwined with each other. Moreover, it is these images, memories, and metaphors that generate and regenerate the passion we feel for teaching and teacher education.

Process in our learning

For us, learning is a process. It emerges across time. While 'questions and biography' guide our learning and 'memories, images, metaphors' guide our interpretations of our learning, our current knowledge reflects the interactions of these against our ongoing experiences. As we live and learn our biography, our questions change and new memories, images, and metaphors emerge or old ones are reinterpreted and renewed. This section is our attempt to account for this process.

Mary Lynn: Thus far, I have stated that reflection is an essential tool for becoming a strong teacher educator and that beliefs and culture are essential influences on reflection. I have not, however, really answered the questions, how did I learn about being a teacher educator? how did I learn? how did I learn to be a teacher? Would I answer the questions the same way? I think I would. I learned to be a teacher educator by developing my desire to learn more about learning. I wanted to be able to convey ideas and watch people discover what they know, so I became a teacher/teacher educator. And I learned how best to do that through honing my skills as a questioner and thinker. Actually, as I write this, I realize that I have always observed myself and, in observing myself and the world around me, found out what works and does not. I do not mean to imply that everyone is like me, but understanding myself provides the necessary insight for me to look beyond myself. As I look beyond myself, I can formulate my own theories and ideas about the workings of the world and share them with my students.

Did I have mentors in my learning-to-teach-teachers process? No, not really. I did have people that I admired and people I sought out. But, with regard to teaching, to some degree, I can truthfully say that I learned about teaching teachers on my own. Now I want to address that. Often, when students say to me, 'I never learned anything until I started student teaching', I become irritated. However, now I understand. Over the course of their education, they have reviewed information, observed teachers, and thought about teaching, but only when they are in front of the room, personally bringing together their knowledge and their experiences to convey information to their students, do they really *teach*. I understand. I feel the same way.

I wager there might be people who would claim influence on me — that there are people who think they taught me about teaching. This is not, however, true. They did not teach me how to teach. They might have provided me with suggestions; they might have made me conscious of my beliefs; but I was the one who brought those ideas together in just that way. Of course, I do not mean to demean their influence, but they did not teach me how to teach. Their influence is deep upon my thinking about my understanding, but the teaching part is mine.

Stefinee: Recently, I have considered how my becoming a teacher educator was like my becoming a teacher. My university experience was not always pertinent yet, retrospectively, I see its relevance more clearly than I did while I was learning. Confronted with real people and responsibility for them, I did not know how to use what I had been taught. Education, I see now, is about learning to learn not about technical rationality. I forgot that being educated meant I had the knowledge and skills to teach myself. But the gap between university course work and experience teaching, either as a public school teacher or a teacher of teachers, is one which fascinates me. In my view of myself as teacher educator of beginning teachers, I am convinced that we need to capture aspects of the slippery arena of practice and let our students try out those elusive, ambiguous spots while they are still with us. We need to be available to show them how the things we are teaching might be useful in the real world of practice. But teacher education extends beyond my students at the university to teachers in schools. Thus, I constantly seek ways to participate in teachers' examinations of their own thinking about their practice and the change in their practice that begins to emerge. I have committed myself to look clearly at my own practice and regularly ask my students how they perceive the work we do together. In this difficult arena, I feel I refine myself as a teacher educator and gain insights into the processes of becoming a teacher and becoming a teacher educator. I am constantly learning about how to teach from my memories, my experience, my reading, and the interconnections I make among them. Learning from experience in this way, I am teaching myself to be a teacher educator as I teach my students to teach themselves to be teachers.

Peggy: My beginning-teacher experience, as painful as it was, was exciting because I was constructing it for myself, along with my colleagues. If I listen to that old self, I know that I must provide opportunities for students to construct their own understandings of the politics of education, even if we disagree. My battered but still unbroken belief in participatory democracy reinforces this stance. Indoctrinating students into my point of view, or coercing them to express that point of view even if they privately retain their own, is inconsistent with democracy. Becoming a teacher educator, therefore, has increasingly meant sharing the floor with students and downplaying my role in order to draw out students' opinions for discussion and debate. Peer education at times seems more effective than professorial pontificating in complicating and challenging students visions of teaching and schooling.

In attempting to be a democratic teacher educator, a major contradiction I have encountered is between the ideal of sharing power with students and the professors' monopoly on the power to evaluate and grade students' work. While I have had some success at resolving this dilemma with individual classes in which I am the sole instructor (Placier, 1994; 1995), I have not been able to convince my colleagues in multiple section classes or the college in general of the necessity to challenge the grading system. This is where I crash up against the norms and authority of the 'system' I am always urging my students to change. I may be no more willing than a beginning public school teacher to become engaged in systemic politics until my own teaching dilemmas are resolved and my job security is established (Placier, 1991).

Becoming a teacher educator means looking back not in disdain at my beginning-teacher self, but with more loving eyes. No one is exempt from political and ethical responsibility in this enterprise of schooling. I make that very clear. I have not relinquished my critical position. While I would like them to reconstruct rather than reproduce the way schools work, that is a heavy burden to place on beginners. I am learning to allow the beginners their excitement about becoming teachers and their hopes about beginning.

Karen: In whole language, approximations are celebrated by recognizing learning is a process. My experience learning the roles of a teacher educator is also a process of approximations, as is teaching. One does not *become* a teacher, rather, it is a process that evolves over time. Connections are made between experiences, and new knowledge is constructed which later shifts as other experiences are encountered. Each semester, I build on what I am learning and extend the meaning of teacher educator. I do not do this by myself. The process is social.

For me, social relationships with others, inside and outside academe and the classroom, serve as a major support in my development. I attribute much of my current understanding to these voices. Students' voices in the classroom and in their journals and self assessments have been especially valuable to my teaching. For example, this student's journal entry made a major impact on my thinking and practice:

> I am having a very difficult time with this new paradigm of teaching and learning. My time in this class is spent being frustrated and often angry no matter how hard I try to remain calm. I think the biggest reason for this is the huge change in my whole way of thinking that this paradigm is asking me to make (2/7/1992-JM).

As interactions support and/or push my thinking, reading and writing extend my meaning. Connecting my thinking with others as they explore learning and teaching provides the support to move forward. An example is how, at one point in my journey, Peterson's (1992) text helped me through a bog and to understand further the role of experience in learning. He wrote:

> I see teaching responsibility as one of helping students uncover words that interpret what it is that they are experiencing. Often this is difficult because it is so easy for teachers to push their own ideas off on students, thereby distancing them from their experience. (p. 99)

Since I continually deal with resistance in my teaching, it is often the focus of my inquiry. Peterson's words, and reading Lather (1991) and other feminist writers (e.g., Guilfoyle, 1994), were instrumental in my moving to review the resistance.

Reflecting on the actions and interactions of myself and others provides a frame for both my teaching and researching. Reflecting empowered me as a learner and facilitated many of the transitions I have made. My experience using reflection contributes to my developing understanding and aids me in supporting other learners coming to value its potential.

I am learning about teaching teachers and making transitions because as a learner I am actively involved in the process, committed to teaching, and feeling passionate about transforming schooling to support *all* learners. In attempting to understand my struggle as a teacher, I hope to extend my knowledge about learning and teaching to support other travellers. This experience is helping me rethink teacher education and leads me to challenge the simplistic view of teaching presented to pre-service teachers. It also challenges theories about the development of teachers. Through teacher research, I am aware that my development has been a learning process influenced by multiple factors. Inquiry supported through dialogue and critique pushes experience to the edge and opens new roads to travel. It doesn't remove the struggle, but it does help the teacher understand the journey.

Mary Lynn: If I can return to the quilter metaphor once again, consider a room filled with materials, threads, colours, and ideas. As a quilter, I select how I will use those items and where I will use them. Importantly though, my quilting teachers, my friends, my comrades, have affected my understanding of my art and my skill. They have influenced me at a very deep level — I could not be creating my quilt without them! If they had not been there to help me develop, I would not be working on this particular quilt. I would not be teaching how and what and why I am teaching without the influence and the effect of those teachers, and colleagues and comrades.

Again, how have I learned about becoming a teacher educator? I have learned about the learning-to-teach-teachers process by engaging in conversation, listening to my teachers, observing the world around me. In so doing, I have learned the world, reflected upon it, and brought it to my classrooms.

Although we see ourselves as self-taught teachers of teachers, we have learned new things about how that happened. Our understanding of our process of learning makes us think differently about the education of our students. Across all our studies of this process, each of us sounds a particular theme. These themes are evident here and reveal our individual commitments: Mary Lynn's theme of the vital role of culture and context; Peggy's focus on living democratic values; Stefinee's insistence on wholeness and community; and Karen's commitment to process and to empowering all learners. These themes capture what we try to do in our lives as teacher educators. Like our biographies, they underlie the story of our experience just as they mark our clear commitment to it. We see ourselves as less and less centre stage. Our own past memories make us view even recalcitrant students with more loving eyes. We understand that, in the moment of teaching, what we taught will be there in the action but perhaps not the reflection of our students. Studying our own process of learning has been central to our ability to progress.

Conclusions

Critical to our understanding of our development as teachers of teachers is the way that experience played such a critical role in the process of our learning. Memory shaped our experience. Experience shaped our experience. Memory of our experience shaped our experience. Our biographies brought us to the arena of teacher education. These, coupled with our current experiences and interpretation of them, led us to commit ourselves to a different kind of teacher education. We study our own practices. We examine both our successes and our failures, and we ask our students to join us in this examination. Because we expect our students to create classrooms that will support the learning of their students, we try to create classrooms that will provide them with similarly supportive experiences. We recognize the power of our students' beliefs, images, and biographies, and we try to enlist them in expanding their own understanding of teaching and learning. Whatever we want our students to do in their own practice — study and reflect, use innovative pedagogy, be a change agent — we ask of ourselves.

Like the other contributors to this collection, we proudly name ourselves as 'teacher educators'. That name represents the professional and personal essence of our perceptions of ourselves. Yet it is a problematic title. We know its traditions and reputation, and we sometimes feel marginalized, unnamed, and distanced from others' use and definition of the title, 'teacher educator'. Thus we see ourselves as different from, yet connected to, the representations of this title in the work and lives of our colleagues in teacher education and its institutions. Personally, our practices as teacher educators re-create and redefine teacher education. We find the title essential to accounting for ourselves and our work.

Our commitment to a different view of teacher education and our support from each other led us to risk taking to our students the kinds of educational experiences we thought they needed. Our attempts to watch, analyze, and report what we saw happening in our development and theirs is a hallmark of our process and the reason that this account exists. As Munby and Russell (1994) suggest, the authority of our own experience has a powerful voice and influence, one almost ignored in development processes generally and in the development of teachers specifically. Movement in understanding what we were doing as teachers of teachers was connected to interactions with other people and demonstrated that learning is social. Reading, reflecting, researching and analyzing guided, supported, and facilitated the process. We have become and are becoming teacher educators. Individually and collectively, the paths we have chosen are alternative ones, but we believe they have the most potential to help us understand what it means to teach, to teach teachers, and to gradually re-create education practices. We encourage others to begin walking their own alternative paths, documenting them as they go.

References

AISENBERG, N. (1988) *Women of Academe: Outsiders in the Sacred Grove*, Amherst, University of Massachusetts Press.

APPLEBEE, A. (1987) 'Teachers and the process of research', *Language Arts*, **64**, 7, pp. 700–714.

ARIZONA GROUP (1994) 'Letters from beginners: Negotiating the transition from graduate student to assistant professor', *The Journal*, **8**, pp. 71–82.

BISSEX, G. (1986) 'On becoming teacher experts: What's a teacher-researcher?', *Language Arts*, **63**, pp. 482–484.

BISSEX, G. (1988) 'On learning and not learning from teaching', *Language Arts*, **65**, pp. 771–775.

BOICE, R. (1991) 'New faculty as teachers', *Journal of Higher Education*, **62**, 2, pp. 150–173.

BOICE, R. (1992) *The New Faculty Member: Supporting and Fostering Professional Development*, San Francisco, Jossey-Bass.

BOOTH, W. (1988) *The Vocation of a Teacher: Rhetorical Occasions, 1967–1988*, Chicago, University of Chicago Press.

BULLOUGH, R.V., JR., KNOWLES, G. and CROW, N.A. (1991) *Emerging as a Teacher*, London, Routledge.

CHAMBERLAIN, M.K. (1988) *Women in Academe: Progress and Prospects*, New York, Russell Sage Foundation.

COCHRAN-SMITH, M. and LYTLE, S. (1993) *Inside Outside: Teacher Research and Knowledge*, New York, Teachers College Press.

COLE, A. and KNOWLES, J.G. (1993) 'Shattered images: Understanding expectations and realities of field experience', *Teaching and Teacher Education*, **9**, 5/6, pp. 457–471.

EBLE, K. (1988) *College Teaching and Learning: Preparing for New Commitments*, San Francisco, Jossey-Bass.

ELY, M. with ANZUL, M., FRIEDMAN, T., GARNER, D. and STEINMETZ, D. (1991) *Doing Qualitative Research: Circles within Circles*, London, Falmer Press.

GETMAN, J.G. (1992) *In the Company of Scholars, The Struggle for the Soul of Higher Education*, Austin, University of Texas Press.

GOSWAMI, D. and STILLMAN, P. (1987) *Reclaiming the Classroom: Teacher Research as an Agency for Change*, Portsmouth, NH, Heinemann.

GUILFOYLE, K. (1992) 'Learning about Teaching/Learning as a Teacher Educator: "I Get a Lot of Help from My Friends"', paper presented at the annual meeting of the American Educational Research Association, San Francisco.

GUILFOYLE, K. (1994) 'Finding Out More Than I Want To Know: Teacher Research and Critical Pedagogy in Teacher Education', paper presented at the annual meeting of the American Educational Research Association, New Orleans.

GUILFOYLE, K. (1995) 'Constructing the meaning of teacher educator: Learning the roles', *Teacher Education Quarterly*, **20**, 3, pp. 11–29.

HAMILTON, M.L. (1995) 'Confronting self: Passion and promise in the act of teaching or my Oz-dacious journey to Kansas', *Teacher Education Quarterly*, **20**, 3, pp. 29–43.

LATHER, P. (1991) *Getting Smart: Feminist Research and Pedagogy With/In the Postmodern*, New York, Routledge.

MARTIN, R. (1994) *Transforming the Academy: Struggles and Strategies for the Advancement of Women in Higher Education*, Earlene, Iowa, Graymill Corporation.

McNIFF, J. (1988) *Action Research: Principles and Practice*, London, Routledge.

MUNBY, H. and RUSSELL, T. (1994) 'The authority of experience in learning to teach: Messages from a physics method class', *Journal of Teacher Education*, **45**, 2, pp. 86–95.

PATTERSON, L., STANSELL, J. and LEE, S. (1990) *From Promise to Power*, Katonah, NY, Richard C. Owen Publishers.

PETERSON, R. (1992) *Life in a Crowded Place: Making a Learning Community*, Portsmouth, NH, Heinemann.

PINNEGAR, S. (1995) '(Re)experiencing beginning', *Teacher Education Quarterly*, **20**, 3, pp. 65–83.

PLACIER, M. (1991) 'Being Political: The Ambivalence of Beginning Teacher Educators', paper presented at the annual meeting of the American Educational Research Association, Chicago.

PLACIER, M. (1995) '"But I have to have an A": Probing the cultural meanings and ethical dilemmas of grades in teacher education', *Teacher Education Quarterly*, **20**, 3, pp. 45–63.

REYNOLDS, A. (1992) 'What is competent beginning teaching?: A review of the literature', *Review of Educational Research*, **62**, 1, pp. 1–35.

RUSSELL, T. (1995) 'A teacher educator and his students reflect on teaching high school physics', *Teacher Education Quarterly*, **20**, 3, pp. 85–98.

RUSSELL, T. and PINNEGAR, S. (Eds) (1995) 'Becoming a professor of teacher education' [special issue], *Teacher Education Quarterly*, **20**, 3, pp. 5–9.

SCHÖN, D.A. (1983) *The Reflective Practitioner: How Professionals Think in Action*, New York, Basic Books.

WOODS, P. (1986) *Inside Schools: Ethnography in Educational Research*, London, Routledge and Kegan Paul.

ZEICHNER, K. and GORE, J.M. (1990) 'Teacher socialization', in HOUSTON, W.R. (Ed) *The Handbook of Research on Teacher Education: A Project of the Association of Teacher Educators*, New York, Macmillan, pp. 329–348.

4   (Re) Experiencing Student Teaching

Stefinee Pinnegar

Introduction

As teacher educators, we recognize student teaching as the most salient experience in the education of teachers. We are often frustrated that material taught in university courses does not appear to survive student teaching and seldom seems to become part of the practice of the teachers we educate. Public school teachers often criticize the teacher education coursework that was offered them as 'too theoretical' — not merely unhelpful, but unrelated to issues in classrooms. Teacher education programs constantly attempt to overcome the barrier of practice; the debate about the relationship of practice to theory and theory to practice continues. This study is based on my reflections from teaching in an eighth grade English classroom under the direction of a third-year teacher, where I struggled to negotiate the theory-practice divide. During this experience I wrote daily reflections so that I could examine my own thinking about teaching.

Of many purposes for this study, the essential question was one of personal competence. Could I teach in the ways I was telling future teachers they should? I wondered whether what I learned in university coursework and what I had been teaching my students would survive in reflections on teaching practice. I returned to school to explore anew the dilemmas of practice that I still carried in my head from my first years of teaching. Now, 20 years later, working as a teacher educator, I wondered whether I had learned anything that would enable me to teach the kinds of students with whom I began my teaching career.

I experienced a nightmare image during those years on the Navajo Indian Reservation: I was pushing my hand into a box of sand up to my elbow, then pulling my hand out, watching the sand fill up the imprint of my hand, and thrusting my hand in again. During the two years I taught on the reservation, three of my students died. One was found hanging with his hands tied behind him; another was discovered bruised and naked inside a culvert where he had crawled to get warm in the subzero weather; the third was stabbed to death by two of my other students. School lunch was the only meal some of my students could count on eating. Many of my students had children. One of the girls in my ninth grade class had a two year-old child. One student quit school in her senior year because she was pregnant with her fourth child, and her mother told her that her five-year-old could not take care of a new infant as well as the two-year-old she already had.

Several of my students were alcoholics and had been since elementary school. One student had watched both parents and one sibling burn to death in two different car crashes; he was left helpless outside the car, unable to reach them. The complications of their young lives were heartbreaking.

In the spring of 1992, I returned to teach in an eighth grade public school classroom in a situation not unlike those in which we place student teachers. The lead teacher, a former student of mine, had invited me to come, but because I did not hold a teaching certificate in that state, I needed to be 'supervised'. The third-year teacher who had been somewhat coerced into accepting me in his classroom was not just wary but truly sceptical of my ability to teach his students. Because I was a teacher educator, he questioned both whether I would be able to manage the kinds of students he taught and whether I would indeed stay to work with them until the end of the year. His doubts about my competence and endurance were similar to those held about any student teacher. As a result of his scepticism, he limited the demands of the context. I was not allowed control of the system of accountability; I could not participate in negotiations with central administration, nor with parents. The economic constraints of the setting were not imposed on me. While I was allowed to put things on the walls, I did not feel comfortable rearranging or reorganizing things. It was clear to me that the aquarium, book cases, and file cabinets were his property. I used only the surface of the desk. In most ways, I felt like a guest in the classroom. The regular teacher, whom I will call Jay, described the setting and his feelings about it and me as follows:

> This is a three-year alternative high school. The student body consists of kids with a variety of problems. These may include poor attendance, drug use, lack of academic progress, poor reading skills, [all] resulting in a variety of behavioural problems. Within the majority of the kids is an overriding lack of interest and poor motivation for learning. All of the kids entered into the program because they had not been able to function in the 'regular' school setting. Many of these kids are simply 'buying time' until they turn 16 and drop out.
>
> I was one of three staff members for the program . . . I was in my third year at [the school] and had already begun to see signs of 'teacher burnout' in myself. This was a particularly difficult group of kids to deal with, and I left school many days feeling frustrated, beaten, and lacking a sense of professional accomplishment. I had become very cynical in my view of the learning potential of these kids. Because of this I was very reluctant when our lead teacher talked of the possibility of my team teaching a poetry unit with Dr. Pinnegar. I was convinced that the kids would do all they could to make this a miserable experience.

This description could apply equally to any novice — any student teacher — entering this setting. Because my experiences in this setting had many of the constraints of student teaching, when I first began to analyze my daily entries, I wondered whether I would fall into a survival mode as student teachers reportedly did.

I wondered if I would come away from this experience unable to see how any of the things I had learned or taught students actually applied in teaching in public schools. In the analysis that follows, I focus on the ways in which theory did emerge in my reflections on my practice and on the ways in which theory could be used to frame and interpret those reflections.

The data source for this study is a set of daily reflections that I wrote following each session and before the next. I added clarifications and expansions as I transcribed these reflections, marking them with brackets ([x]) and dating them to distinguish these additions from the original reflections. As I analyzed, I designated additional reflections or explanations with double brackets ([[x]]). I organized the reflections chronologically. I first read them through completely without making any marks on them, and then I read and coded them for themes. Next I examined them for patterns across the themes and over time. Finally, I re-examined them for evidence of theories that I, as a teacher educator, had taught to my students — evidence of specific mention, reference to or descriptions of particular theories. I discuss my findings within the following categories: problem representation, reflection, planning and management. I close with discussion of a major theme — trust — that was apparent throughout my reflections on my teaching.

Problem representation in teaching

As a teacher educator, I frequently remind my students that problems of practice do not come to us labelled, either theoretically or practically. A student does not wear a sign on the head that says, 'Think about Attachment Theory here' or 'Alcoholic' or 'Sexually abused by mom's boyfriend at 2 a.m.'. Situations are not labelled as 'problems with the token economy system' or 'students attributing success to external locus of control sources'. Therefore, an important part of teaching is identifying a problem and setting the problem constraints. As I worked with Jay in the setting described, I became aware that, although we were together in the same classroom, observing the same behaviour, what we defined as problems that needed solutions were often very different. On Day 11, I wrote:

> If I do this again, I want to do this again next spring. I want him to write what he sees, because we are seeing this so differently. I can tell because of what he says bothers him about the kids and what bothers me. I'm much more bothered by anger directed at me and [by] passivity, which is just turned off-anger, than I am by disruption. With the two of us we can always bring back disruption, but passivity is ice.

Note that I realized that we saw the classroom responses of children very differently. My concern about student behaviour focused on lack of response from students or on personal anger from them. Both of these indicated to me that the students lacked trust either in me or in some other aspect of the educational system. In contrast, horseplay, talking amongst themselves, teasing and poking, which might erupt at any time, were less threatening for me because I thought that Jay and I had good management skills and could together meet such problems.

Nickles (1981) proposes that, once problems are represented, the solution path is articulated. In fact, when problem constraints are constructed in certain ways, what was originally defined as a problem may no longer be perceived as one. Langer (1989), in her book on *Mindfulness*, indicates that an important cause of mindlessness is premature cognitive commitment. In practical settings, where, as Doyle (1986) suggests, action must be taken rapidly because of the simultaneity, multidimensionality, history, and publicness, teachers identify problems and respond quickly. The way in which the teacher identifies the elements in the event leads to what is identified, not seen, or ignored. The constraints that define the problem in the teacher's original conceptualization create the solution path. Yet Langer's (1989) work would suggest that part of being able to resolve problems is being able to act out one solution without being blinded by that construction of the problem and being able, on future occasions, to entertain other constructions of the problem.

Nickles' (1981) idea about constraints is important here, because I realize now that the differences in what we *saw* in the classroom reflected a difference in what we perceived as our major responsibility in the classroom. Part of my desire to return to teaching in this kind of classroom was an interest in applying some of the things I felt I had learned about teaching English. Jay was concerned with maintaining standards of behaviour in the classroom. Doyle (1986) suggests that teachers have the twin responsibility of presenting content and maintaining order. I was struggling to teach students poetry, to get them to learn to read poetry in ways often used only in teaching advanced students. Both Jay and I saw content as my major responsibility. For the work I wanted to do, I was more concerned about negotiating the kind of power fissions, chasms, and fusions discussed by Foucault (1978) than I was with many of the management concerns that seemed to preoccupy Jay. I was more concerned about whether students would risk discussing the issues that might be raised by poetry such as 'Dream Deferred' or 'My Life Closed Twice'. As the regular teacher, Jay saw maintaining order as his major responsibility. As a result, he identified as problematic and urgent those events that posed threats to the system of order in the classroom.

This division was also apparent in the aspects of the team-teaching situation that he was willing to let me assume. I was not given access to the accountability system. He informed the students on the first day that as long as they all 'produced, were co-operative, and at least attempted the work in class', they would receive a grade of A and he would keep track of their participation. This policy freed me from the kinds of anger engendered by discussions about grades, particularly when the tasks were highly ambiguous. Because Jay had reduced the academic task dimension of risk, I could work even harder to insure that the ambiguity dimension remained high (Doyle, 1983). In addition, Jay indicated that I would only need to teach four days a week, one hour each day, though I was willing to come five days a week and teach for more than one hour. As already noted, his limits on my responsibility in many ways cast me in the role of student teacher. He controlled access to the amount of time I was allowed to teach. He communicated clearly to the students that he, not I, would be assigning grades.

A second issue of problem representation, one that appeared as I examined my own reflections, concerns 'backtalk' created by a problem. This concept is discussed by Schön (1983) and expanded on by Russell (1986). Wanting to go back to the school became a clear signal to me that something had gone wrong that day. I wrote on Day 15: 'I felt O.K. but I wanted to go back. That's how I can sort of tell that things are weird. I want to go back and fix it.'

As I wrote this entry, I found myself rethinking the situation and trying out other solution paths for this day. Following Nickles' (1981) view of problems, I put different constraints in place that would have led to a different solution path. I wrote: 'I should have had Jay do the poem. He's good at that kind of stuff too. Then I could have worked with the students. They wanted my attention.'

In my reflections on this day, I first wrote a description of the original problem representation (how I decided to carry out the plan for the day). Then I created a re-representation of the problem just quoted. The sentence starts 'I should have'. In addition, I have other re-representations of the problem listed on this reflection. When I went back to type the notes, I added an aside about my perception of the problem between me and the regular teacher. I recorded additional asides each time through the paper. One important aside indicates a realization that on this day I had given both responsibilities of teaching — the content and the management — to the regular teacher, and yet he was not secure in the content. I wrote the following comment, on reflection: 'What does capturing events allow as you revisit both the event and your earlier interpretation of it?'

The reflection on Day 15 and the additional asides indicate that backtalk from a situation can lead the teacher to try to reteach the class, at least mentally. The teacher can then try out other solution paths developed by mentally changing the constraints used in defining the original problem.

Finally, I notice in my reflections another kind of problem representation, a form that focuses on understanding the individual students. One example, again from Day 15, is my observation of a parent's response to her child. I knew several things about the mother and her daughter. As I watched the mother's response to the daughter, I was forced to rethink the mother's motives. I posed an alternative explanation for why the mother made the daughter sit through a trial for the mother's boyfriend who murdered the girl's father. Nickles' theory of problem representation provides a very helpful frame for representing multiple facets of my reflections about teaching.

Reflection

The importance and power of reflection in the education of future teachers has generated considerable discussion. I found myself engaging in several kinds of reflection on my practice. First, I found the elements of backtalk discussed by Russell (1986) to be a possible spontaneous source of teachers' development from practice.

Backtalk represents the way in which an undesirable resolution of a situation leads the practitioner to revisit and rethink the event, mentally constructing and tracing a different solution path. I also found evidence in my notes of 'in-flight reflection'. During teaching, the teacher is thinking about what is happening and why, and making adjustments in the lesson while teaching it.

Another kind of reflection that I found among my notes consists of the teacher's thoughts immediately after teaching. Usually, my reflections were made immediately after I finished, but sometimes I did not write until the next day or over a weekend. I found differences in the focus and content of the reflections written later. Immediately after teaching, connections to all a teacher knows about practice may not be as readily available as when time has elapsed. In addition, integration time may result in a qualitative difference in thoughts about what happened. I began to wonder if there might be significant and instructive differences between immediate reflections, delayed reflections, and postponed reflections made long after teaching events.

I also found I had made non-linguistic reflections. We know very little about just what teachers can and do see in images when they think about their teaching. In one reflection, I indicated that I could clearly see the classroom, the faces, the students and the actions. Later, when I commented on this event, I indicated that I could no longer 'see' the event as I remembered being able to 'see' it when I first wrote that reflection.

I returned the next year to teach again at the alternative high school. I began to rethink what had happened the first year in light of seeing the students again. The second year I had a clearer memory of the teaching context and some of the students, and this memory had an impact on what I thought about them, both during and after teaching. I am convinced that reflection on teaching can help a teacher gain insights in many ways. But these various kinds of reflection are a constant reminder of the fluidity of memory and of its interactive and reconstructive qualities.

Planning

Planning has been a frequent theme in my reflections on teaching. Two aspects of planning for instruction reveal theoretical underpinnings. The first is pre-planning for instruction prior to seeing any students. The second is daily planning for instruction.

Pre-planning

In planning for teaching in this setting, I used several of the theories I taught in my undergraduate teaching and other ideas that came from my own past educational experience. I recognized that underlying any teaching I ever do in English are my own theory of the content of English and my beliefs about the intellectual capability of students to engage in the interpretation and reinterpretation process that I see as a foundation to reading and understanding language and literature. In addition, I believe that the more clearly students can articulate their ideas, the more control they can gain. As a result, my reflections consistently reflect a concern with students developing flexibility and fluency in language production and in process writing techniques; I want students to produce lots of writing that can then be shaped and reshaped. I include with techniques of process writing things I was taught during my studies for my M.A. degree in English concerning Kineavy's theory of discourse, Peter Elbow's work, and others' suggestions and theories; staff development I received during my teaching experience; and my own reading of Linda Flower's work.

Theoretically, I accept Vygotsky's (1978) view that an important aspect of linguistic development is the ability to make simultaneous experience sequential. As I worked with students in interpreting poetry, the poem represented an event, and the discussion was designed to help them articulate multiple paths through the meaning of the poem. Also evident in my plan for teaching these students is my acceptance of Vygotsky's (1978) concepts of the Zone of Proximal Development and the more capable other. In negotiating this zone, the more capable other does not do the work, but through questioning leads the students to do the work themselves. These two ideas were central to the way I planned and conducted discussion in this classroom.

In deciding how I would interact with these students, I realized that I would be confronted both with real inadequacy in reading and with motivational problems that might appear as inadequacy in reading. With this in mind, I decided to teach poetry because it would allow me to use Multiple Oral Rereading, a technique I had used with students with learning difficulties in another setting. The students and I could collectively read poems several times before the students had to work with poem content. In reading the poem I could model the pattern of reading and the mode of questioning that reading for meaning requires. This repeated reading is more difficult with a novel or even a short story. Shorter poems that could also be connected to their own life experience could be used to approach poetry, at least initially, from a concrete perspective. This concern reflected my understanding of Piaget as I realized that, even at 14, many of these students would not be formal operational thinkers (Flavell, 1984).

Finally, from an information processing approach, I realized that working and reworking a poem would cause students to integrate thinking about the poetry with reflecting on life experience, a form of interpretation that they had not done in the past. I was also concerned that students might on occasion reach cognitive overload. They would not be able to consider aspects of the poem because their working memory or short term memory might be at capacity, or they might not be able to hold all the pieces in their minds.

The purpose of this account of pre-planning is to demonstrate ways in which various theories of thinking, my own theory of the content of English, and the nature and needs of the students contributed to my planning of instruction. An additional important issue in pre-planning for me as a researcher was the idea I have always had that certain content never reaches the classroom because it is filtered out when teachers weigh activities against their understanding of the capability and typical behaviour patterns of the students. A teacher's interactive and reconstructive memory of a classroom of students may screen out certain kinds of content or activities during the initial planning process. For example, in planning for this course, I prepared a set of behavioural objectives that focused on teaching students to use alliteration, metaphor, simile, rhyme scheme and meter pattern as interpretive tools. The classroom teacher's response to the list of objectives led me to focus instead on a few more basic concerns. I abandoned content that I would have attempted because I felt implicit pressure from the classroom teacher. Student teachers and beginning teachers often feel a similar response to their ideas about what or how to teach when they discuss their teaching plans with experienced teachers.

Daily planning

Two issues in daily planning are relevant to this discussion: (1) my response to behavioural objectives, and (2) the constant multiple planning that I did for teaching the class. On Day 10 I wrote:

> I don't feel like a failure today. It just didn't go well, yet. The whole time I was there, I thought of the music teacher in Tucson that said, 'One day it's good and that is its own reward'. It isn't good yet. Maybe I need to help them know when it is good. I also realized how worthless behavioural objectives are to me in my teaching. They are such a good idea. They seem like they should work — why don't they work for me — what is it that I do to plan instruction? I think objectives focus more on the content than on the kids. Is that it?

This passage reveals the influence of several ideas from research. One from social learning theory concerns the way in which things can be self-reinforcing, not requiring external reinforcement or reward (Bandura, 1986). The comment on behavioural objectives links with work by Langer (1989), who indicates that an important root of mindlessness is education for outcome. She suggests that students confronted by an outcome make an immediate assessment of their own capability to reach that outcome. If they judge themselves as incapable, it is difficult to get them to begin the process of reaching that outcome. Similarly, if teachers judge students incapable of reaching that outcome, they may have a difficult time focusing on helping the students begin the process by which the outcome might be reached. This occurred with Jay's judgment of these students when I handed him my list of objectives. He judged his students as incapable, and he could not imagine a path which could lead them to competence.

The second issue, my multiple daily planning, is revealed by the following excerpts from my reflections. On Day 13 I wrote:

This morning something happened that has happened several times and so I am going to write about it because I think it is an important thing to remember. I had prepared two poems to read. As I was riding to school, I suddenly thought, 'I need to have them write. They need to have me keep working on fluency'. Maybe we'll begin with 'Dream Deferred' tomorrow and then have each person write about a dream-something they want.

We did not discuss the two poems I had brought, but instead worked on a variation on free writing that I call 'writing on the cube' and then worked on a choral reading of a ballad, 'Git up and Bar the Door'. Then on Day 14, I recorded:

I had a long struggle with myself on the way to class today about whether I ought to have the students take the stuff they had written about weekends and turn them into paragraphs or whether we ought to start on found poetry. In the end when I walked into class, I asked Jay how the students were today. He said he had had them write . . . I decided then and there that we would focus on reading, 'The Charge of the Light Brigade' and starting on found poetry.

While these reflections may seem to others to reveal a sort of improvisational approach to teaching, as Yinger has labelled it, they cause me to recognize the fluidity of the planning process in teaching. Every day I went to class with a plan. In my reflections on the day, I would often outline plans for a full week, but then when I would reflect on it the next day that is not what I did. Each night I spent time preparing to teach for this class. I remember often coming in with several plans, with the material to implement those plans, and then making a decision when I saw the students about what I would really do. My underlying goal in working with these students was to help them develop articulate voices in reading and interpreting poetry, voices that would carry into their own writing. What I could do with them in working toward this goal depended on where they were and how willing they were on a particular day to mentally engage in a task. In my reflections, I commented on a student who each day that he was in class would fall asleep in his chair, bolt upright, looking right at me. One comment I made on students is relevant to my discussion of planning. On Day 3, I wrote:

I thought this morning how hard it is to teach in settings where children come late or only occasionally because so much of having a wonderful classroom is creating a community. So you have the tone set and then a child walks in half-way through bringing usually some reluctance or reticence — depending on why they are late. The class begins to feel good as a group, to have bonds of trust and caring and then in plops someone who hasn't come for days and it's hard with this group to keep the web of caring in place.

Perhaps the continual flux in my planning was an appropriate response to the fluidity in the life of these students. They did not always come. They changed boyfriends often. Life was not always predictable for them. What we were doing was difficult mental work, and the constant fluidity of plans was evidence of the way in which I changed the classroom work to connect with them and yet keep the ambiguity intact. Constant over the fluidity of planning was my assertion to the students when I wanted them engaged in a discussion, that I would wait for them to respond, that I wasn't going away, that I would continue to ask. In my reflections I continually articulated a focus on my goals, juxtaposed against the multiplicity of plans that were changed, altered, or abandoned in response to my reading of the class.

Management

As I explained earlier, Jay and I initially at least divided the responsibilities for teaching: I assumed the responsibility for content, and he assumed the responsibility for management. Jay indicated to me by leaving me alone in the classroom occasionally and by making a few direct statements (though they are not recorded in my reflections) that he felt comfortable with my management skills. Yet he never really allowed me to take over the task of managing this classroom. Throughout the time we taught together, he signalled to the students in concrete yet subtle ways that he was still in charge.

For example, he told the students to show me respect. When I arrived on Day 9, Jay had assigned seats. In my reflection, I commented: 'The assigning of seats, though Jay didn't realize it, was the reassertion of his power in the classroom and sent a clear message to the students about who was in charge'. On day 11, he threatened the students. On Day 14, he offered them free cokes if they would do their best job in reading the passage. He hunted down the students who were a minute or two late. He sent home the sick students. He only occasionally left the classroom, and when he left the students would go silent, actually stop what they were saying mid-sentence. They did not act disruptive, but it was hard to bring them back to the discussion. In fact, one student actually commented that they were doing this because he had left the room.

As a result of comments I made on my own management style, I came to realize how Jay was able to continue to manage the class. On Day 11, I wrote:

> I find touching and body language so valuable to teaching because it allows
> you to signal what you want and what you will tolerate without making
> it public with everyone in the classroom.

As I reread this reflection, I realized that Jay had used his own body language and casual movement around the classroom to continually manage this class. He may have felt that the behaviour of the class was a reflection of his own competence as a teacher. At least initially, he was also concerned that the students would drive me out and he would have to resume complete control of the class. On the last day, he told the students that I had lasted five weeks longer than he had expected. Although Jay subtly managed the classroom, I felt he respected me as an educator. He began to try out techniques I used with the students in other areas in the curriculum. He commented at one point that he liked to watch me with the students because what they said did not anger me. He also noticed that they would say more in my discussions with them than they had said before when he was teaching them. My observation of Jay's ingenious forms of management helped me realize the subtle ways in which cooperating teachers can continue to manage the classroom for student teachers without the student teacher even being aware of it.

Trust

The theme of trust recurred throughout my reflections on my teaching in this alternative high school. On Day 4 I commented: 'So, it's getting [Jay's] trust as well as the students'. I realized that in attempting this task, I had to trust my ideas gleaned from a university education, gain the trust of the teacher, and build the trust of the students to ensure that the ideas would work. In reflecting on the students on that day, I wrote:

> My teacher questions:
>   How to get them to trust and risk getting involved?
> My personal question:
>   Why should they want to give up their safe apathy and care about anything?

The next day I continued:

> There has to be a safe place in classrooms not to trap students into caring but give them reason to care and trust.

In these reflections I focused on a theory of experienced teachers that teachers need to exhibit confidence so that students can trust and then risk doing their best (Pinnegar and Carter, 1990). In my reflections I focused on this dimension of trust in different ways throughout the weeks I spent teaching in this setting. I found that when I teach, I focus on trust in teaching future teachers, but I do not teach them about it.

In reviewing these reflections on my teaching, I note some changes in trust after about a week, then again at five weeks, and then again at the end. There is a qualitative difference in my engagement with the students that I commented on at Day 5. I simply said that things were different. There is another change in the way I commented on their engagement with me at about the third or fourth week. In fact, I seemed to run a check on each student to see how our relationship of connection and trust was operating. Finally, it seems at the end that the relationship began to dissipate as the year ended and teacher and students would separate for the summer.

Conclusion

Many of the things I reflected on led me to realize that student teaching may not be the most helpful and educational event we can provide for pre-service teachers, even though they always refer to it as the most important part of their teacher preparation experience. The constraints placed on them by experienced teachers may contribute to and exacerbate the kinds of reality shock that Veenman (1984) identifies as a given for beginning teachers. In my own reflections on teaching at an alternative high school, I was able to identify the ways in which theory guided, framed, and emerged in my thinking about my practice. As teacher educators, I feel that we should take the example of Virginia Richardson in her work on teacher beliefs. We should get beyond the question of whether theories, ideas, and research taught in teacher education programs are evident in the practice of teachers, to focus instead on *how such learning is evident*. Perhaps some of the problems of practice might be more clearly explained by examining *how* theories emerge rather than discussing *whether* they do or do not.

References

BANDURA, A. (1986) *Social Foundations of Thought and Action: A Social Cognitive Theory*, Englewood Cliffs, NJ, Prentice-Hall.

DOYLE, W. (1986) 'Classroom organization and management', in WITTROCK, M. (Ed) *Handbook of Research on Teaching*, 3rd ed, New York, Macmillan, pp. 392–431.

DOYLE, W. (1983) 'Academic work', *Review of Educational Research*, **53**, pp. 287–312.

FLAVELL, J.H. (1977) *Cognitive Development*, Englewood Cliffs, NJ, Prentice-Hall.

FOUCAULT, M. (1980) *The History of Sexuality* (translated by HURLEY, R.) New York, Vintage Books.

LANGER, E.J. (1989) *Mindfulness, Reading*, MA, Addison-Wesley.

NICKLES, T. (1981) 'What is a problem that we may solve it?', *Syntheses*, **47**, pp. 85–118.

PINNEGAR, S. and CARTER, K. (1990) 'Comparing theories from textbooks and practicing teacher', *Journal of Teacher Education*, **41**, pp. 20–27.

RUSSELL, T. (1986) 'Beginning Teachers' Development of Knowledge-in-Action', paper presented at the annual meeting of the American Educational Research Association, San Francisco, ERIC # ED 270 414.

SCHÖN, D.A. (1983) *The Reflective Practitioner: How Professionals Think in Action*, New York, Basic Books.

VEENMAN, S. (1984) 'Perceived problems of beginning teachers', *Review of Educational Research*, **54**, 2, pp. 143–178.

VYGOTSKY, L.S. (1978) *Mind in Society: The Development of Higher Mental Processes*, Cambridge, Harvard University Press.

Part 3

*Ways to Promote One's Development as a
Teacher Educator*

5 Teacher Educators Reflecting on Writing in Practice

J. Gary Knowles and Ardra L. Cole

As university professors and teacher educators, we devote a significant part of our professional and personal lives to writing. It is an integral part of our professional practice. It is part of our 'cultural capital'. Because both the process and product of writing play such an important role in our academic lives as teacher educators, we include it, along with researching and teaching, as an area of our work that requires systematic, introspective attention. In this chapter we use the reflective milieu of written dialogue to explore the writing element of our professional practice and its role in facilitating our professional development.

For many years, as classroom and school practitioners, we engaged in various reflective activities to help us think about and make sense of our developing practice. When we moved from the field to the academy, we naturally continued to think and write about and question what we were doing, and we encouraged pre-service and in-service teachers with whom we worked to do likewise. As part of our ongoing quest for professional self-development, and to keep up with the research and publishing demands of the academy, we began to write publicly about the importance of developing reflective and reflexive practice and the use of various strategies for encouraging that practice. Much of this writing focuses on our own professional development through self-study as we endeavour to 'practice what we preach'. Through systematic reflection through writing, we continue to extend the boundaries of our thinking about our individual practices and the contexts in which we work, and about teaching, research, and teacher education more generally. Through our writing we seek to understand the multiple roles, contexts, and relationships that comprise our practices. Thus we explore, reflect, and write about the many facets of our work. We have written about our roles as teachers (Knowles and Cole, 1995; Knowles, 1993a), researchers (Cole and Knowles, 1993, 1994; Cole, 1994a), thesis supervisors (Cole, 1994b), field experience supervisors (Knowles and Hoefler, 1989) and, more generally, as teacher educators and faculty members (Knowles and Cole, 1994). We have also written about elements of our pedagogies (Knowles, 1991, 1993b). In this chapter we explore our roles as writers working in the creative tension that is created by the demands of scholarship and the demands of practice.

A significant part of our self-study program takes place through dialogue, in different forms of conversation (our other chapter in this book provides a detailed account of our self-study methodology). This dialogue is central in our work and is based on our view that 'the other' plays a central role in constituting the self (Bakhtin, 1981; Mead, 1934; Sampson, 1993). Following Sampson, we believe that we, as persons, 'are fundamentally and irretrievably dialogic, conversational creatures, whose lives are created . . . and sustained or transformed through conversations' and, further, that, 'how we think, how we reason, how we know, how we solve problems, and so forth — are best grasped by examining the conversations in the social worlds we inhabit' (Sampson, 1993, p. 109). In this chapter we draw on our writings about writing — our surface and electronic mail correspondence. Implicit in the framework and focus of this chapter are our many conversations about writing, for it is they that have helped develop the form of this account and allowed us to draw on our writing-in-relation. In essence, the excerpts from our correspondence are, themselves, examples of self-study through writing.

Over the almost seven year span of our professional correspondence we have amassed considerable 'data' on our experiences and development as university faculty members. We have conversed extensively about general and particular aspects of the various roles and responsibilities we assume, and how we, as individuals, respond to expectations and demands associated with those roles and responsibilities: as teachers, researchers, supervisors, colleagues, and writers (the focus of this chapter). Reflected in our correspondence is the changing nature of the issues and concerns that have been salient for us throughout the course of our employment at our respective academic institutions. Also represented are topics or themes of a more permeating quality. For example, within the context of our roles and responsibilities as writers, much of our correspondence in the early years of our professorial appointments focused on becoming familiar with and gaining entry to the publishing community, and on understanding the role of writing in relationship to our other roles and responsibilities. As time passed, and workload demands seemed to exponentially increase, our conversations shifted to concerns about finding time to write and needing to be more holistically integrative in our teaching and researching, including our writing. In the more recent period of our correspondence, the tenure and promotion review process has provided the context for much of our dialogue as we tally, reflect upon, assess, and speculate about our writing efforts. Present throughout our correspondence are expressions of and commentaries on our individual values, goals, and aspirations with respect to the form and content of our writing. Also present is a kind of running commentary on our development as writers.

We come to writing about writing with no formal preparation or expertise in writing as form or process. Neither of us specifically aspired to being a writer per se; being a writer is a role that comes with the territory of researching and professing in high profile institutions, a role that constantly challenges each of us. Nevertheless, after several years of writing, we now see the role of 'writer' as being central to our professional and, to varying extents, personal identities. In the early years of our professional relationship, our correspondence took place mainly by letter exchange through international surface mail. We have always been professionally situated in different cities and countries. Recently, electronic mail has been our main vehicle of professional correspondence. Thus the writings that follow, presented chronologically, are excerpts from some of the surface mail exchanged from November, 1988 to February, 1992 and from electronic mail exchanges from April, 1993 to August, 1994.

We do not offer an extensive analysis of our writings. Rather, we offer our correspondence as windows into our thinking and responses to our roles as writers, and as examples of our ongoing dialogical reflection on our practices. In so doing we hope to both inform our understandings of ourselves as writers, and to publicly acknowledge and consider the role of writing in teacher educators' professorial practice. While not necessarily germane to all, we hope our experiences will resonate with others in roles similar to our own. Thus we hope that, in sharing some of our reflections, others will be encouraged to engage in similar kinds of conversations with colleagues in their own institutional contexts and about their own practices.

Writings

November 1988 — June 1990

It is clear in the first set of exchanges that, as neophyte university faculty members, we experienced significant discomfort with respect to our new-found roles as academic writers. With years of teaching experience behind us, we entered the professoriate with considerable confidence in our abilities to carry out our teaching responsibilities; however, we did not feel sufficiently prepared to adopt a writing persona easily. Although we saw the publishing of our research and writing as the primary means through which we could contribute beyond our own local practices to understandings of teaching and teacher development and to the ongoing improvement of teacher education, we struggled to find our voices and places as writers in the teacher education community. Whereas teaching was so embedded in our professional identities that it seemed to come naturally, writing for publication was something with which we had little experience. In our early years as teacher educators, to be a reputable published writer seemed such a far away goal.

Salt Lake City, November 6, 1988

Dear Ardra,

I've been thinking about my sometimes painful experiences of beginning to write. Unlike practices associated with beginning to teach — where my actions were transitory and ephemeral, and my mistakes could be blotted out in my mind (although, mind you, not necessarily in my students' minds) as I constantly reframed my work and actions — writing has a sense of permanency about it that sometimes renders me wordless. Yet, I also feel that, to be a successful scholar in the academy, I have to become comfortable with the notion that my perspectives, writing style, research epistemology, methodological approaches, and intellectual interests will each and together evolve as I grow personally and professionally.

Gary

London, December 3, 1988

Dear Gary,

I have another article from my thesis research ready to send off to be reviewed for publication. How are you going about finding appropriate journals for submissions of your work? I've just spent several hours in the periodicals section of the library — a disheartening experience. Of the hundreds of different educational journals on the shelves, only a handful seems to publish other than traditional (positivistic) research, and, of those, only a few focus directly on teacher education and development issues. I am beginning to understand why most of the research and literature I resonate with seems to be published in the same journals. That's all there is! And, of course, this is doubly problematic for me (and perhaps for you?) because I can't yet imagine seeing my name in the Table of Contents of many of those journals. I can't yet see myself as a *bona fide* member of the publishing community — especially as an author within that elite caste of refereed journals.

Even though I've already had one article accepted for publication in a refereed journal, and even though I think this one is also of sufficient quality for publication in a refereed journal, I'm still tentative about subjecting my work (and myself) to a review process and reviewers that I have heard can be piranha-like. (Why is it that I think the first acceptance was a stroke of luck?) I guess I've left the sheltered cove of graduate school, and am going to have to brave the open, rougher waters. All I can do is jump in and hope for the best.

Ardra

Salt Lake City, April 1, 1989

Dear Ardra,

I have been wondering about the wisdom of professors telling graduate students to proceed with publishing their work only *after* they have finished writing their dissertation. I also often heard suggested 'Writing up your research for publication is very difficult and distinct from the dissertation process — don't get the two confused. Get your dissertation completed!' This advice shaped the actions of some of my graduate student peers. . . . I largely rejected this advice. For others and myself, that advice seemed potentially dysfunctional because it separated the public presentation of one's research in journals or books from the private presentation of scholarship within the relative safety and support of a dissertation committee. . . . Don't get me wrong, I'm not suggesting that work associated with a dissertation is inferior to work published in journals. It's just that going public with one's work is such an important part of what we, as teacher educators, must do and yet doing so is much easier said than done!

Gary

London, May 5, 1989

Dear Gary,

I am one of those who was nurtured within what you call the safe environment of the dissertation committee and, you know, now that I have left the nest, so to speak, I wouldn't have wanted it any other way. I was advised to focus all my energies on completing my thesis before starting to worry about publishing my work. And I was encouraged in my writing by a supervisor who believed in me and my abilities as a writer. But I don't see that as being misled, as I think you do (if I understand correctly what you said in your most recent letter). To some extent I think I was being 'protected', from what I am beginning to see as the 'big bad world' of academic publishing, but I am thankful for that safety because within that protective context I was able to acquire a level of confidence in my development as a researcher and writer. . . . I also developed a strong belief in and respect for the kind of work that I and my graduate school colleagues were doing — work that in many ways challenged academic convention.

If I had focused attention on 'learning the publishing game' and then set about writing to conform to conventional rules and standards, I have a hunch that such an experience would have severely restrained my creativity and channelled my work in a particular direction or style. And I might have ended up with a traditional kind of formulaic thesis that lacked the passion and originality with which I think mine was imbued. Perhaps it is a naive view but I believe in what I did and how I did it, and, to me, that counts for a lot. Of course, the disadvantages are, as you imply, not having any publications at the outset of an academic career and starting out without having initiated a link between one's writing and the publishing community. But I'm not sure I was ready to publish then. Anyway, I'm sure we'll come back to this topic as we continue to 'test the waters' of the publishing community. Will we sink or swim?

Ardra

Salt Lake City, May 28, 1989

Dear Ardra,

Like I think I mentioned to you, I was told that I'd never get a job of my choice without publications. Perhaps I was really being told that I needed to improve my writing. Because I tend to be stubborn, that kind of response only fuelled my determination. Obviously you weren't disadvantaged by not having a publication at the time of obtaining your position. I know, however, that I got the job here because I had published. Whether or how that initial publishing experience has made it easier for me to assume the role of writer along with my other professional responsibilities remains to be seen.

Gary

London, June 25, 1989

Dear Gary,

This has been a terrific week — another article has been accepted for publication in a refereed journal, and I heard back from a publisher to whom I sent a book prospectus (I don't know where I got the nerve to do that) and she is interested! I was so excited, I literally ran down the hall to Margaret's office. Margaret is one of my colleagues; I had to share the news with her. Actually, what I really needed was someone to reassure me that I was not misreading the letter. Whenever I get a positive response to my work I tend to think that someone (either myself or those reviewing my work) has made a mistake. When I shared this idea with Margaret she gave me a lecture on the notion of the 'impostor syndrome'. Are you familiar with that notion? Hope all is well.

Ardra

Ann Arbor, November 2, 1989

Dear Ardra,

I, too, have to pinch myself every time I finally have my work accepted for publication, especially after several rejections from journal editors. When I was a budding, somewhat naive writer, at the beginning of graduate school, I thought that writing was a relatively simple process. Write. Revise, maybe once or twice. Polish and bring to convention. And, publish or present to others. My experience and perceptions of myself as an undergraduate led me to believe that I was a good writer. I wasn't — and this view of myself as writer eventually caused difficulties as I tried to make the transition from early graduate student scholarship to well polished dissertation work, and publishable, professorial scholarship. I am certainly much more aware now of the depth required of me as a scholar and writer. As well, journal reviewers generally seem less sympathetic to work that seeks to break new ground, especially in form, and I've found that my writing needs many revisions (sometimes upwards of 10 or 15) in order for it to get to an 'acceptable' form. Just for interest, at this point in my career I have two published articles, one on the way, and two in progress. Oh, and I submitted a proposal to a publisher for a book on field experiences. Oops, I've just started counting! Is this what tenure and promotion committees do? Does this bode well for the future?

Gary

Ann Arbor, December 13, 1989

Dear Ardra,

I have some thoughts on my development as a writer. . . . I think my readiness to write — the maturing of my writing — has been evident in the last year or so. The dissertation writing helped a great deal. Bob, my dissertation committee chairperson, was extremely helpful in the process. He pushed me to clarify, and clarify, and clarify. . . . And, having the opportunity to review his writing and work that we co-authored gave me an intimate window on the processes of writing and publishing. Also, the process of becoming a *bona fide* writer wasn't rushed, and that helped. Granted, I was in graduate school seven years! Somewhere in my fifth year, I began to feel as though I had something to say. I knew that my research was sailing into relatively uncharted waters, that I was taking a different tack on learning to teach and beginning teaching. I simply 'found the wind', as sailors would say. So it was then that I began to feel as though I were a writer. I knew that I had a very long way to go but I started acting like a writer. I took writing seriously, spending long hours composing and revising text — mainly stories of classroom practice — from which I derived great pleasure . . . and a sense of accomplishment.

Gary

The multifaceted need to integrate researching, writing, and teaching is expressed in the following two letters. Then, as now, we struggle to respond in authentic ways to our own professional development needs, the demands of the institutions within which we work, and the demands of the field.

Ann Arbor, May 14, 1990

Dear Ardra,

How do I merge my scholarship with my teaching? I find such a fusion to be a real need. I cannot live a bifurcated life in academe. Some of my colleagues seem to have such disparate researching and teaching agenda. I don't know how they do it! For me there needs to be an internal consistency and a kind of economy of scale in my teaching, researching, and service activities (the latter is less of an issue, though) within the university. I hope to achieve a high level of inter-relatedness and synergy among these various activities and roles. Is this too large an expectation? I hope not! I'm working on making it a reality. Actually, [the consistency and congruency] were present in my work when I began here but the pressures to get involved with various projects not of my conception — such as the work with a professional development school and other research and practice efforts — somewhat crowded out those qualities. Caution!

For me, the power of researching and writing rests in the potential for both of them to involve my whole being, and to be something that I care about immensely. . . . This year's been a real bust! . . . My goal for the next academic year is to become more integrated. Ho, ho, ho!

Gary

Kitchener, June 29, 1990

Dear Gary,

I couldn't agree more with your point about the need to integrate teaching and scholarship. Within the university context, with the pressures to publish and obtain research funds on top of the demands of a heavy teaching load (in your case), or of significant field work responsibilities (in my case), plus other responsibilities, integration of one's work is necessary for survival. This is especially true for people like us who invest so much time and energy in our teaching and who engage in systematic inquiry into our practice as part of our pedagogy. Since, as we both know, in the merit structure of the academy, research and publishing are 'worth' much more than teaching, all the more reason to closely link the two. Besides, from a professional standpoint, we have a responsibility to practice what we preach. I don't think we can continue to advocate that teachers engage in ongoing reflexive inquiry into *their* practice if we are not prepared to do the same.

Ardra

August 1990 — March 1991

Our letters in this period reflect some of the tensions we experienced with respect to our creative needs and interests, and both real and imagined institutional constraints.

The more comfortable we became in our roles as writers, the more possibilities we saw for creative representations of teacher education and development issues, and the more time we wanted to spend experimenting with non-traditional forms of academic writing. We became acutely aware of the 'tacked on' nature of professional writing in our lives as teacher educators, and how difficult it was to find the time and space for the creative demands of writing.

Ann Arbor, August 13, 1990

Dear Ardra,

A couple of things: I've just sent off paper presentation proposals for the [American Educational Research Association] Annual Meeting — hope they, or at least one of them, get accepted. I'm quickly coming to understand that the review process, whether for articles or conference papers, is primarily a political one, despite the claims for objectivity and anonymity in the review process and so on. It's about the politics of ideas and power rather than about support for the generation of ideas and innovation. I'm becoming a little blasé about my publishing effort. In a sense, I am trying very hard to not have too much invested in any one manuscript . . . and so, in order to survive I am trying to make sure that I am writing what *I* want to write, rather than wholly serving the agenda of another or the institution. Yet, as I say this, I know it's going to be easier said than done.

Gary

Kitchener, November 9, 1990

Dear Gary,

My bookshelves are reorganized once again. I've caught up on two months' worth of filing. I've created a new computer directory and renamed some existing files because their identification seemed confusing. My pencils are all sharpened and neatly arranged on my desk, left to right in descending order according to length. (This is serious stuff!) I have a brand new pad of paper positioned on my desktop at the precise angle for my handwriting. A fresh glass of water, and I'm all set [to write that article that is supposed to be completed soon] — well, almost. I just realized that I owe you a letter. Avoidance? Never! Well, maybe a bit. I said, 'Yes' to an invitation to write for a journal, uncertain at the time about how I would address the topic, but confident that something would come to me eventually. So far, nothing has come and the deadline looms near.

When I was writing my dissertation I had tacked on the wall above my desk a quote that frequently gave me inspiration. I copied it from a story set in sixteenth century England in which one of the characters, supposedly Shakespeare, responded to the narrator's comment about his writing, 'A page a day', said he, 'doth do a wonder in a year. And so he was always at it'. Well, time is quickly running out and right now even completing a page seems inconceivable. Maybe I'll go and read something. That sometimes helps. Perhaps I'm trying too hard — trying to prematurely squeeze out my creative juices when they need to be left to ripen a bit more until they're ready to flow freely.

I'll get the article done. Eventually, and when I least expect it, I'll have an idea and I'll be off and running. It always happens that way. What I'm experiencing here reminds me of a comparison Annie Dillard [1989] makes in *The Writing Life* between splitting wood and writing. She spent days and nights of agonizing cold in a cabin, to which she had retreated to finish a writing project. She did not know how to split wood sufficiently well to keep a heat-radiating fire going. After mornings of 'chipping flints' and 'attacking the wood', and nights of trying to figure out how it was done properly, the answer came to her one night in a dream. 'You aim at the chopping block, not at the wood', the dream told her. 'Treat the wood as a transparent means to an end, by aiming past it'. And so it is with writing she asserts. 'Aim for the chopping block. If you aim for the wood, you will have nothing. Aim past the wood, aim through the wood; aim for the chopping block'. [Dillard, 1989, p. 59]

I need to go and chop some wood. . . .

Ardra

Kitchener, March 13, 1991

Dear Gary,

I have been thinking a lot lately about the writing responsibilities associated with our positions, about your recent struggles to infuse your artistry with your academic life, and about my own desires to do other than conventional forms of scholarly writing. Is there not a touch of irony in the fact that you are having such a difficult time finding a place for other than traditional forms of representation of ideas in an institution that supposedly should support innovative ways of thinking and representing thought? And, isn't it also ironic that, despite the fact that we, as professors, are expected to produce volumes of written material, I don't think we are seen as writers — at least in the literary sense? We're expected to be [writers], in somewhat the same way that faculty members in most university departments and with no background in teaching are expected to be teachers.

I have noticed, however, that I am increasingly seeing myself as a writer. I have even begun to explore the possibility of writing non-academic prose. I like the way 'being a writer' feels although I'm not sure I'm 'there' yet. For example, I don't see myself as a writer like I see you as a visual artist. What can you tell me about when you finally decided that you *were* an artist and presented yourself in that way?

Ardra

Ann Arbor, March 25, 1991

Dear Ardra,

In one way I have always seen myself as an artist. Although I can't tell you the exact time I decided I was more than a closet or backyard artist, my experience goes something like this: As you know, I had worked in Fiji and Papua New Guinea, and other 'exotic' locations in the South and South West Pacific before coming to the United States, and for years had taken photographs of various subject matter in these settings. Somehow, though, snapping pictures wasn't very satisfying. The photographs never really represented *my* view and experience of the landscape and the elements within it, although they were 'good' photographs. So, on a return visit to Fiji, I figuratively threw away my camera and started to paint. I was interested in recording 'my journey', and it was an empowering experience. Often crowds of people clustered around me as I painted, and I got the sense that they *really* thought I was an artist. They expressed appreciation for my representations of the natural and cultural landscapes and *they* labelled me 'artist'. Later on that same trip, I had the opportunity to visit a New Zealand artist's exhibit in Suva, the capital city of Fiji. I showed him some of my work and he suggested that I display it. He gave me some names of galleries; I showed my work to gallery owners and I sold many of the pieces.

When I returned to the United States I focused on developing my talents as an artist. I enrolled in an informal, term-long water-colour course where I was encouraged by the art teacher. She introduced me to some very basic techniques and left me alone to my own inclinations, doing no more than saying, 'You do good work', and, 'You have an artist's eye'. Over the course of the term, while most students did one or two paintings, I did nearly 40. I painted a series representing the patterns of autumn colours in the foothills of the Wasatch Mountains in Utah. When I lined up my work side by side, I saw evidence of my artistic development — and was amazed. Soon after, I had my first exhibit in the United States (and sold many pieces). The formal public display of my art work was the signal that I had some validity in claiming to be an artist — analogous to publishing my first article?

Although I had always seen myself as an artist, I wore the label more easily at the encouragement of onlookers — other artists, fellow teachers and students, those who bought my paintings, and friends — who expressed appreciation of my work. The audience is very important. If I had no possibility of having anyone respond to my work, would I be an artist? Would I be a writer? I now think not. I want people to respond to my work. As an artist I paint for myself — my own creative, artistic, and emotional well-being — and I paint for others. And I write for similar reasons, although those reasons are tempered by my role as teacher education researcher. Artistic endeavour involves investment in and attention to both process and product, as well as consideration of the ways in which artistic work is presented and viewed by others. . . . We should talk more about the parallels between writing and painting — communicating, symbolizing, interpreting, and suggesting through words and sentences, or colours and shapes, on paper or on canvas — and between me being a visual artist (and a writer) and you a writer.

Gary

Toronto, March 30, 1991

Dear Gary,

Alongside the parallels of writing and painting I see a strong line associated with our professional development within educational contexts. It highlights the interrelated nature of personal and professional development. For what is professional development but development of the self? The development of my writing self has come about because of increased confidence in my various roles as teacher educator. Through teaching in the university classroom and working with teachers and school boards in the field I have gained new insights which inform my writing and help me portray practice more authentically. I think that your artistic work displays an authority which rests in the centrality of the subject matter — the landscape, topography — and artistic perspectives in your life, and it's that kind of centrality that we both need to claim and exhibit as teacher education scholars. I'm moving in that direction, I know.

Ardra

January 1992 — April 1993

The next set of letters highlights the ongoing struggle to find time and opportunities for professional writing amid other work demands and responsibilities. Our commitment to writing about our teaching seemed, at times, hard to uphold in spite of its intrinsic value.

Ann Arbor, January 17, 1992

Dear Ardra,

I seem to be in a phase in which I question the value and place of nearly everything I do. . . . I am especially concerned about the value of my writing for others. Have you felt like this? Many of the issues I often raise about writing (and the kinds of questions I ask) come from having a very full teaching and researching agenda. Sometimes the incredible imbalance in my professional life catches me off-guard. I find myself being very passionate about my teaching, or at least certain elements of it, but as I become encrusted with weariness that comes from working very long hours under pressure, teaching sometimes becomes less than fully engaging. These feelings also rest in the fact that, for me, teaching can become all-consuming, because much of it is highly collaborative and team-based, so that there is very little time left for other scholarly or professional development activities. Usually it is my writing time that is squeezed out. So, I wonder, given that much of my writing seems rushed, inserted into small temporal spaces, do I really have anything to say that will be helpful to readers? With over 1800 educational research and practice journals published, so I'm told, the chances of originality in perception, framing, and articulation of pressing teacher development and educational issues seems slight indeed. Somehow, the thought is very sobering!

Gary

Toronto, February 6, 1992

Dear Gary,

I know what you mean about the need to maintain some semblance of professional balance. All the more reason to define our classrooms as our 'field site', so to speak. Having said that, however, I must admit that I find it incredibly difficult to articulate a written analysis of my teaching. I can write about aspects of my professional life in general terms, and about elements of my personal life, but writing autobiographically about my teaching is very difficult. . . .

Recently, in going over transcripts of taped conversations and observation notes about my teaching, I was struck by the congruity between what I said I did (or wanted to have happen) and what was seen by an observer in my classroom. If I were a researcher exploring someone else's teaching, I would be excited by the validating quality of those congruencies. For example, in my doctoral research I explored how teachers' images, values, and beliefs played out in their classroom practice. When I saw connections between their verbally articulated beliefs and beliefs expressed in classroom practice, and then shared those observations with them, it was such an affirming experience for all of us. And, it was so easy to write about because the 'evidence' was vividly present.

. . . But with my own analysis it is different. When I look at the data, the evidence is just as vividly present. It is exciting to see the interconnectedness of instances of practice with their underlying values and beliefs, and to understand the personal history roots of those values and beliefs. There is a completeness about it, an authenticity. And yet, I still cannot very easily write about it.

If the connections were not so obvious, if the information pointed out major flaws and gave me opportunities to be self-critical, would it be easier for me to write about my teaching? . . . Why is it easier to be self-critical than self-affirming?

Ardra

Ann Arbor, April 22, 1993

Dear Ardra,

There is a delicate balance between spending time in teaching and investing time in researching and writing. Now, after a few years in the professoriate as an assistant professor, I am a very different writer. Back when I began [here at The University of Michigan] I had considerable freedom of time and space in which to write. I remember sitting in my office over the course of the first year and writing profusely at the computer during the day and revising hard copy at night. From time to time during that year I thought that I had a tide of students washing against my office door, but now, in retrospect, given my increased teaching load and other responsibilities, it seems as though they were only the small frontal waves of the surging swell, an indication of the rising tide. Now, it is rare that I get any time at all to write while at the office. Recollect how we wrote *Through Preservice Teachers' Eyes* [Knowles and Cole, with Presswood, 1994] together — on weekends, in every spare moment we had, 'between the cracks' as it were. Isn't that how most of our scholarship has been achieved? And others? How do they work? Perhaps I have fundamentally misunderstood notions about the life of a scholar. A scholar's mind never rests! A scholar, so it seems, is forever thinking, finding it difficult to rest the mind, to put aside the books, to put down the pen. But to do all of this on top of a 60 or 70 hour week? How do others maintain their enthusiasm, the quality of their work, and the freshness of their perspectives?

The culture of the university — especially as it embraces the notions associated with the publish-or-perish adage — places a very real and felt pressure on scholars, perhaps especially on untenured professors like us. Even recognizing that pressure, my greatest difficulty in my professional day is finding time and space to write, a time that is free of interruptions and distractions, and a space that is conducive to the articulation of both simple and complex thoughts. And, given my personal disposition — being easily distracted by visual images, colour, and movement, for example, and distressed from unwelcome noise or music — I need a secure, quiet place to reconstruct the internal workings of my mind.

Gary

Toronto, April 23, 1993

Dear Gary,

Your comment about the life of a scholar reminds me of something I read a while back when we began to explore the literature on the teacher education professoriate. Do you remember how Mager and Myers [1983, pp. 29–30] characterized the work of becoming a professor?

> The work of becoming a professor is . . . a matter of developing a life of the mind: sculpting a block of knowledge, making it one's own, identifying colleagues who respect and contribute to that work, and making that work available to the larger public. . . . [The number of hours beginning professors work, however,] calls into question their capacity for sustaining a career which spans a quarter of a century, or longer, and doing so with fervour.

Isn't that precisely the incongruity you were pointing out — expectations of high levels of energy, creativity, and productivity in institutional contexts that, in reality, militate against those very things? And, if that is not sufficiently discouraging, listen to this short excerpt from Annie Dillard's *The Writing Life*:

> Much has been written about the life of the mind. I find the phrase itself markedly dreamy. The mind of the writer does indeed do something before it dies, and so does its owner, but I would be hard put to call it living. [Dillard, 1989, p. 40]

Feeling better now? . . .

Ardra

Toronto, April 24, 1993

Dear Gary,

I know you haven't had time to respond to my last message but I had to share this with you. I thought you would appreciate what Dillard has to say about writing spaces, since I know how important context is to you. I started reading *The Writing Life* again after your last message when I looked up the quote about the life of the mind. She describes at great length how she goes about creating 'unappealing workplaces'. No matter where she is — in the mountains, by the ocean, in a busy urban setting, or in her home environment — she works to block any access to the outside world and minimize 'distractions' within her workspace. She says she doesn't care where she works because she doesn't notice things around her. 'One wants a room with no view', she argues, 'so that imagination can meet memory in the dark'. [Dillard, 1989, p. 26] What do you say about that?

Ardra

Ann Arbor, April 27, 1993

Dear Ardra,

I don't think Annie's criteria for a writing place quite meet my needs! Perhaps it's the kind of writing that we do that makes my needs very different — or that we're very different persons. I think my page would be perpetually blank if I were to try and write in the kind of place she described. . . .

My office at the university is a very comfortable space, small but bright with two very large windows looking out on two spruce trees. The room is reassuring because it contains many easily accessed resources, books and journals tightly stacked in tall, steel bookshelves. I've decorated the room with my photography and paintings, the handiwork and artwork of children (including my youngest son), a small round conference table, a white board, and 'Steelcase' office furniture (file cabinets, desks, and, upholstered chairs). . . . Together the compact arrangement and presence of these various items and pieces of furniture provide a window into my personal and professorial lives. My office presents a glimpse of my personal history — shelves of books about professional and personal experiences, water-colour paintings of silos and sand mines, mountains and machines, photographs of tropical places and people, artefacts of teaching and travel — which stimulates memories of my work in Michigan, Utah, and lands beyond North America. Within the room's purposely arranged and organized cosy clutter, I am able to write (provided I have uninterrupted time, which is usually in the early morning or early evening). It is as I imagine a writer's den to be — close, cosy, comfortable, convenient — and a place where I can be centred. . . .

I often prepare for writing by hanging a 'Do not disturb' sign on the outside door knob, locking the door, disengaging the phone, arranging source and other materials on my desk, and easing into the high backed office chair to begin actually composing, engaging the keys of my Macintosh computer keyboard one by one. . . . Without some of these rituals my writing process is likely to be interrupted and the writing itself staccato-like. Of course, all this suggests or implies that I have something to say, a point of regular self-questioning.

Even as I compose, I strive to know what to say and how to say it. But, more significantly, I strive to understand the greater meaning of my work and its fit. In a sense, this is a constant personal confrontation — to understand the potential value and place of my experience, and my theoretical and practical insights for readers, the wider audience of fellow teacher educators, including those residing locally, nationally, and internationally. As I write these words I'm very much aware of how sometimes I labour over the mechanical articulation of my thoughts as I place the words on the computerized page, hunting and pecking at the individual letter keys, never really knowing the development of smooth flowing composition — never really feeling it as the life-giving warmth of blood coursing through veins — until many revisions later. Writing is usually pretty enervating! Is my scholarship dead, I sometimes muse? It must be easier than this! . . . Yet at other times (and I can't quite tell you *when*, but perhaps it happens when I'm extremely passionate about something), I *know* that writing becomes something like a life-sustaining endeavour and is very invigorating.

Gary

November 1993

The next two letters represent a kind of self-assessment as we paused to look back over our past several years as university professors and teacher educators. We remind ourselves and each other of the importance we place on our personal-professional growth as educators, and of the sustaining power of following our professional passions and interests.

Ann Arbor, November 25, 1993

Dear Ardra,

I know we've talked a great deal about the tenure and promotion process, especially in relation to our researching, but I want to talk about it again — this time about the way the mythical standards and expectations have influenced our writing. Are you up for it? . . . After asking each other many questions about standards in our early years, do we have any more or better answers now, just a short time before we apply for tenure and promotion? Have we sold out to pressures connected with current moods and topics of the day, and institutional demands, and have these affected our writing? Perhaps! Maybe not! Have we followed our powerful personal interests and passions for particular issues and work? Have we made the kind of contribution to understanding teacher education practice and issues that we (implicitly) set out to do several years ago? Have we written from the heart *as well as* the mind? Research is never meant to be from the heart, right? . . . Oops! That's my Calvinistic background coming out!

Gary

Toronto, November 27, 1993

Dear Gary,

When I look back over the substantive nature of the work I've done over the past several years, I see changes. When I look at myself in relation to who I was when I became a full-time faculty member, I see changes. I think the two are not unrelated. I think that I and my work have grown and evolved together, and that is a function of many things including: shifts in my interests, curiosities, and passions; my own development as a teacher educator and university faculty member; and changing needs and demands of the field and the institutions with which I have been affiliated. Some of my early interests have run their course; the needs of the field have changed somewhat — and I do think we have a level of responsibility to respond to issues in the field — and I, as a person and professional, have grown in innumerable ways. The passion I now feel for certain professional issues, I did not necessarily feel ten, five, or even two years ago. But, the work I did then was still imbued with a passion — otherwise I couldn't have done it. With experience and time, I think that I have attained a heightened level of self-confidence, and feel more prepared to see and do things differently. This is a long and roundabout way of saying that I don't think I've sold out.

Ardra

June 1994 — July 1994

As we developed more confidence in our roles as academic writers, we saw increased potential to contribute to the advancement of understanding about teaching and teacher education. However, much of what we wanted to write did not conform to the standards of academic publishing convention, especially, it seemed, in teacher education. We experienced considerable frustration over the conflicting perceptions of what was deemed worthy of publication. While we found considerable value in going public with our self-study analyses and in challenging status quo practices of 'appropriate' forms of knowledge representation, those reviewing our work for publication often did not share our views. Nevertheless, we maintained our conviction about the role of our self-study work in helping us to achieve goals related to the improvement of our own practice as well as to the improvement of teacher education in a broader sense.

Ann Arbor, June 7, 1994

Dear Ardra,

I'm back to talking about the journal review process — again! Journal reviewers have recently called some of my work 'narcissistic', 'self-centred' and 'egotistical', among other things (X?*$%&ZQ%@@$), and I think that I understand where they are coming from — yes, a place very different. I reject their notions, however. . . . I want to tell them that my intentions are to reveal in my writing *my* perspectives on researching, including appropriate 'background stuff', and on the topic at hand as a frame for the rest of the writing to be read and understood. But some see such reflexive writing as solipsistic. I'm reminded of Daphne Patai's [1994] recent article, 'Sick and Tired of Scholars' Nouveau Solipsism', in *The Chronicle of Higher Education*. My point of contention with some reviewers is that my work is discounted — rejected — and I am unable to clarify issues with them directly. How do you deal with this sort of situation and with rejections?

I recollect you showing me reviewers' responses to a manuscript that you recently submitted to an editor (in which you wrote about the research process). Didn't two of the reviewers criticize you for placing the writing lens on yourself, saying that your insights were very naive, and so on, and reflected a neophyte's perspective? . . . They didn't 'get it' about the place of 'the personal' in the research enterprise, the value of reflective intercourse. Can you, as a writer, put this kind of experience in perspective for me?

Gary

Toronto, June 9, 1994

Dear Gary,

You're right. A piece I wrote was harshly criticized recently for being 'self-indulgent', and for giving authority to the subjective voice. One reviewer seemed particularly uncomfortable with the autobiographical nature of the work and, from what I can gather, altogether missed the point of the article. I drew heavily on my own experience in order to both illustrate and argue for reflexivity in research. The reviewer took great issue with my assigning authority to my own experience instead of relying more heavily, perhaps solely, on the authority of existing literature. . . . My account, which I explicitly characterized as 'a reflexive analysis using my theoretical understandings of life history research as a reflective lens for the knowledge derived from my experience of being a participant in a life history study', was criticized by the reviewer for reflecting a 'lack of familiarity with both the literature and tradition [of life history research]'. Placing value on my subjective experience by using it as an important and valid source of knowledge was interpreted as 'a pattern of pervasive ignorance' reflecting a 'novice researcher's' miscalculated attempt to write authoritatively about the topic.

I'd say that this instance was a prime example of reviewers 'not getting it' about the role of the personal in the research enterprise. But, even beyond that, I see in their comments fundamental differences between our epistemological positions. And, I think that is what I am most bothered by — having writing and researching work harshly judged because it reflects a viewpoint that is contrary to that held by those doing the judging. In these instances, reviewers hold and use considerable power over those whose work and writing they evaluate. But, after all, isn't that how dominant positions achieve and maintain their status?

. . . I'm not sure what else to say on the matter. Not too many years ago I would have been devastated by these kinds of review comments about my writing. Now, because I believe I have a better understanding of the subjective and political nature of the review and publication processes, I am less inclined to take every comment to heart. Having said this, I don't wish to imply that I have fashioned a shield to protect myself from criticism. On the contrary, I have found most reviewers' comments and suggestions, regardless of whether they recommend acceptance or rejection, to be very helpful in strengthening my work. Occasionally, though, as in the most recent case when it is clear that the reviewers just fundamentally disagree with the nature, substance, and/or perspective of the work, I respond by seeking opinions of others who, I trust, can judge the work on its scholarly merits and not on the epistemological stance it reflects. . . . Does this help at all?

Ardra

Ann Arbor, July 5, 1994

Dear Ardra,

I agree that, for the most part, reviewers' comments are extremely helpful in refining my writing and ideas. I count many of my published pieces as successful because of the insightful suggestions of reviewers. Switching gears, I want to play with the idea that our personal histories reveal a whole host of compelling foci for our future personal research agenda. Our acknowledged subjectivity is a powerful element in the kind of personal and qualitative research that we do! I want to bring an authenticity to my researching and writing work that transcends the dictates of others and institutions. Such authenticity is derived from 'being' in the midst — in mind and soul — of my work.

Increasingly, I have developed the sense that my writing has to reflect my positions, beliefs, and experiences, my past and present perspectives. I'd like to be able to see a kind of paper trail of my growth, evidence as a series of growth rings on an ancient tree. I made this point in a much earlier letter to you, although I think I couched it in terms of reviewers' rejections, et cetera. Moving from a researcher who employed life history methods (for studying teacher's professional development, as you know) to one who now also employs auto-ethnographic or theoretical autobiographical approaches has, in a sense, meant that I have come full circle. I started with others, then wrote about my own experiences, and am now combining the two. [See Gary's account in our second chapter in this volume.]

Placing myself firmly in the text, whether it be in the voice of a researcher, the voice of a person being researched, the voice of an experienced other, or all such voices, suggests that, as a writer, I embody an alternative scholarly perception of my work and role. Recollect Ruth Behar's [1994] article in the recent issue of *The Chronicle of Higher Education* where, speaking from an autobiographical or life history perspective, she made a case for including the personal in anthropological research. Her position mirrors my own, and I think yours too, although I sense a greater level of caution from you. So then, how has and does this affect my writing? I now find myself unwilling to engage in presenting research about teachers with whom I have worked unless I can tell aspects of my own story as well (perhaps as a teacher or perhaps as a researcher, or both) because my own story provides a perspective and 'reality check' on my researching activities. But the matter is much more complex than that. . . . I am constantly seeking this integration in my writing that I talk about so often.

Gary

Toronto, July 8, 1994

Dear Gary,

For me, authenticity is very closely connected to passion. And, like you, I need both of these qualities in my work. In some ways I think we are both very fortunate. We are working in a time (an era perhaps) that is relatively supportive of the kinds of perspectives we hold and the kind of research and writing we want to do. For example, think back to only a few years ago and the then-prevailing attitudes towards any kind of qualitative research. Compare that to the current zeitgeist. Remember Elliott Eisner's Presidential Address [at the American Educational Research Association's Annual Meeting] in 1993, for instance? There is a much greater sensitivity to issues of (inter)subjectivity, reflexivity, and voice, not only with respect to research participants but to researchers themselves. I don't think the positioning of oneself in one's work is seen as quite the marginal stance it once was. I don't think that 'alternative' is a bad word any more. I think the resistance to explicit self-reflexivity comes when the purpose of it is not clear, when the researcher becomes the central character in the work and upstages the others in the research text. As I have said many times, I believe that we have a responsibility to communicate ideas that will inform future teacher education and education practices. When it is not clear how what we say might contribute to the achievement of that end, we can expect to be criticized for being self-indulgent or narcissistic, or all the other choice terms we have heard. . . . But, I think there is an important distinction to be made between research that is self-indulgent and research that reflects a self-reflexive stance. . . . By the way, the 'level of caution' you say I show — could there be a personal history basis for that? Hmmmm!

Ardra

Themes and issues in our reflective dialogue on writing

Our reflective dialogue evidences themes and issues that mark places in our development as teacher educators, and especially with respect to our roles as scholarly writers. We view writing as *a form of professional development contributing to self-development*, development of teaching and research practices, and to developments in the field of teacher education. We do not claim that our experiences and perceptions are representative of the teacher education community. We expect that the themes and issues embedded in our writings are not unique to our experience. Thus we make them explicit as a set of starting points for further reflection and dialogue on the writing element of professorial practice.

Some starting points for personal inquiry about writing include:

- personal perspectives on writing and the multiple meanings derived from it;
- processes and experiences associated with 'seeing oneself as writer';
- reflections on and observations of one's development as a writer; and,
- high points, low points, motivators, and obstacles associated with the writing process.

Some starting points for inquiry into writing as part of teacher educators' professional work include:

- the role of writing as a form of reflective practice, a vehicle for professional development;
- one's role as writer in relation to enhancing teacher education practice, both specifically and generally;

- one's role as writer and the place of writing in relationship to other academic responsibilities;
- affiliation with the publishing community;
- the review and publication processes especially as they relate to the form and substance of one's work;
- the politics of publishing as it affects professional practice and scholarship activities; and,
- the role and significance of writing to one's self development and within one's institutional context and the academic community in general.

Understanding writing through a personal history lens

Our ongoing efforts to understand ourselves as persons and professionals — either holistically or with respect to particular aspects of our practices — are based on the assumption that who we are and what we do as professionals is powerfully influenced by our personal histories. For us, understanding comes about when a retrospective gaze through the looking glass illuminates points of connection between 'then and now'. As we focus our retrospective lenses on the writing elements of our professional lives and attempt to make sense of our roles as scholarly writers, we seek those connections which will help us trace aspects of our writing selves to their roots in our personal histories.

While it is beyond the scope of this chapter to offer a personal history-based interpretation of the elements of our writing practices evidenced in our letters, we find it useful to offer examples of how we might illuminate our understandings of current practices by examining our lives through some of the themes apparent in our writings. These themes represent points of inquiry that have the potential to reveal considerable insights into our writing practices.

Points for inquiry into Ardra's experience

Much of Ardra's research and writing takes the form of case study, narrative, or life history representations. An exploration of the personal history roots of her research epistemology as well as the roots of her interest in being a writer would reveal the dominant place of storytelling in her early family life and, related to that, the important role of stories in giving meaning to life experiences. Such an exploration would also help to explain some of her difficulties with seeing herself as a writer since, in the context of her early family life, the *telling* of stories and the *reading* of stories, not the *writing* of stories, were central. Additional insights would be gained if Ardra picked up and traced backward the narrative thread highlighting the importance of engaging in non-traditional forms of research, and writing in other than conventional academic styles. Autonomy and individuality were qualities to which she learned to assign high value in her formative years and beyond.

Another theme apparent in Ardra's letters is the importance she places on being able to express her passions for, and investment of considerable time and energy in, her work. A personal history inquiry would lead, among other things, to an exploration of the Protestant work ethic valued and passed down through generations of her mother's family. Ardra's enjoyment of and interest in writing, another theme evident in the correspondence, have both recent and distant roots. As a young person, she was intensely interested in the structural and mechanical aspects of writing — grammar, spelling, vocabulary usage, as well as the actual manual exercise of putting words on paper — and she experienced considerable success in school in both these and the more creative elements of the writing endeavour. Experiencing success in and deriving pleasure from writing were consistent results from Ardra's early attempts at writing, and these seem to have provided the necessary encouragement for her to want to pursue her interests in writing (although not necessarily as a vocation). An exploration of her early and later experiences of writing, both in and outside school, would reveal much about how her current attitudes and responses to writing were influenced by prior experiences.

Points for inquiry into Gary's experience

A life history exploration of Gary's background experiences would provide a basis for understanding some of his lifelong struggles with particular issues. Enduring concerns, such as a need for integration of responsibilities associated with his professional work, are woven consistently through his adult life. Gary's letters also evidence a concern about the 'greater meaning' of his work, as well as for an authenticity of experience and representation of that experience. Such concerns were as relevant when he was an outdoor educator in the dense, rain-sodden jungles of Papua New Guinea as when he was as a beginning teacher educator in the dry, red and mauve, open-skied deserts of Utah. Lifelong concerns are prime starting points for his inquiry into contemporary professional practices. Balance between his personal and professional life is also an ongoing issue for Gary. It is rooted in the powerful habits of his youth and articulation of a strong family- and community-ingrained work ethic. These family patterns of behaviour and ways of viewing the world, laid down in rural Aotearoa New Zealand, are also prime entry points for life history inquiry.

The sense of working or locating himself in an alternative, non-traditional context, professional vocation, or paradigm is also strongly present in the cloth of Gary's prior experiences. It is not merely an artefact of recent experiences and current work responsibilities that he is, by the description of some and his own admission, situated 'on the margins', not unlike being a citizen of Aotearoa New Zealand, a country oceans away from most of the world's populace. Further, growing up in Aotearoa New Zealand — being a New Zealander — and the cultural, physical, and relational artefacts that make up such an experience and identity also offer potential for explorations into Gary's orientation to professional practices and writing. His homeland and his work experiences in other parts of Australasia and South and South-West Pacific island nations profoundly altered his views of landscape, cultures, peoples, and institutions. Inquiry into these experiences is likely to reveal elemental sources for much of his work.

Gary's struggle with writing has been lifelong. As a school pupil, he was labelled 'visual artist' but never really became a proficient creative writer in that context. His artistic creativity cemented certain expectations in teachers' minds about his potential for writing, despite the fact that his parents never expressed great value for reading or writing. Physical work was always more highly prized and rewarded, and his mother still awaits the moment he obtains a 'real job'. Becoming a writer was something that Gary did not expressly set out to do. Gary's concern for the aesthetic, as represented in his artistic endeavours real and imagined, for example, is another thread in the garment of his life. Artistic endeavour and aesthetic sensibilities are woven throughout the professional responsibilities of his adult life, and explorations of them, as well as his writing experiences, are likely to prove illuminating for Gary. Gary's letters reveal concerns about entering the world of publishing and continuing in it, about productivity, about 'selling out', about the pressure of time and its effect on his writing, and about the work of scholars. Each of these topics is a useful place to begin personal history conversations.

Self-study and professional development

Revealing our personal-professional correspondence and writing publicly about our professional work has multiple roles and purposes. It illustrates a process that is part of our ongoing professional development. We demonstrate strategies we have used to explore elements of our own practice and, at another level of significance, we raise awareness of some critical issues with which we, as teacher educators, have been grappling. Writing such as this also serves as a record of some of the elements of our professional thinking and development, a paper trail, important for us over the long term for making sense of the larger schemes of our careers, our contributions to the institutions with which we are affiliated, and to the field of teacher education in general. We say this in the sense that, over the long haul, our thinking and inquiry about our own practices may be more important in our professional development as teacher educators than any of the more traditional kinds of research reports or theoretical positions that we publish.

Through ongoing reflexive analysis of our practices, we extend the boundaries of our thinking about writing, researching, teaching, and teacher education. We become very conscious of the decisions we make regarding our roles as scholars. Exploring and writing collaboratively in tandem, where each of us acts as a lens and a filter for the other, provides the context for us to engage in dialogical, relational learning about our professional experiences and research work. Thus collaborative inquiry and writing serve as a catalyst for our ongoing professional development.

By committing the reflexive process to paper, by making our experiences public, we also provide for those with whom we work a very brief glimpse of the ongoing process of professional inquiry that we urge them to consider and engage. We also provide a point for our students (graduate pre-service teachers and those in masters and doctoral degree programs) to know us at another level, important in the curricular contexts in which we ask them to share elements of their lives through personal history accounts and the like (Knowles, 1993b).

We present our work as dialogue in order to express ourselves as individuals in a collaborative work while making clear our collective positions. This format, we believe, holds promise for making accessible work of this kind. It also resolves some of the problems of collaboratively written text where one person's voice may be submerged by the strength of the other. In 'going public' with the very personal yet professional dilemmas that we face, we forthrightly address issues of professional practice that are commonly experienced yet infrequently discussed in public forums. Our intent is to raise the level of public discussion about such matters. In so doing, we also provide minute snapshots of our professional growth, glimpses of the years spanning the period from our beginnings as teacher educators to the tenure and promotion application process.

Toronto, August 30, 1994

Dear Gary,

What can be more gratifying than completing a piece of writing — filling up blank pages with symbols that work together to communicate ideas, offer interpretations, and invite responses — that reflects our 'real selves'. I love writing, both the process — agonizing as it can be — and the product: watching the pages accumulate; editing the text (playing with words and phrases, and moving them around to make them more vividly capture and communicate intended meaning); discovering where I'm going with an idea or, rather, where it is taking me (since the writing process itself often has a significant role in the creation, not just the communication, of ideas), and liking where I end up; and, finding the 'right' words so that when I stand back and look over what I've written I can say, 'Yes, that's what I meant to say. That's what I think!'

Ardra

[Editors' note: In February, 1995, Gary Knowles learned that he had not been granted tenure at the University of Michigan.]

References

BAKHTIN, M.M. (1981) *The Dialogic Imagination*, Austin, University of Texas Press.

BEHAR, R. (1994) 'Dare we say "I"?: Bringing the personal into scholarship', *The Chronicle of Higher Education*, June 29, pp. B1–2.

COLE, A.L. (1994a) 'I remember . . . : Critical incidents in the thesis journey', in COLE, A.L. and HUNT, D.E. (Eds) *The Doctoral Thesis Journey: Perspectives from Travellers and Guides*, Toronto, OISE Press.

COLE, A.L. (1994b, April) 'Doing Life History Research: In Theory and in Practice', paper presented at the annual meeting of the American Educational Research Association, New Orleans, LA.

COLE, A.L. and KNOWLES, J.G. (1993) 'Teacher development partnership research: A focus on methods and issues', *American Educational Research Journal*, **30**, 3, pp. 473–495.

COLE, A.L. and KNOWLES, J.G. (1994) 'Being "The Researched" in Research on "The Personal": Issues Emerging from our Biographical Work', paper prepared for the Language, Culture, and Schooling Graduate Summer Institute, Faculty of Education, McGill University, Montreal.

DILLARD, A. (1989) *The Writing Life*, New York, Harper and Row.

KNOWLES, J.G. (1991, February) 'Journal Use in Preservice Teacher Education: A Personal and Reflexive Response to Comparison and Criticisms', paper presented at the annual meeting of the Association of Teacher Educators, New Orleans, LA.

KNOWLES, J.G. (1993a, April) 'Experiences of an Intensive, Experience-based, Graduate, Secondary Teacher Education Program: Views of a Professor and Preservice Teacher', paper presented at the National Conference on Alternative Teacher Preparation, Georgia College, Macon, GA.

KNOWLES, J.G. (1993b) 'Life-history accounts as mirrors: A practical avenue for the conceptualization of reflection in teacher education', in CALDERHEAD, J. and GATES, P. (Eds) *Conceptualizing Reflection in Teacher Development*, London, Falmer Press, pp. 70–92.

KNOWLES, J.G. and COLE, A.L. (1994) 'We're just like the beginning teachers we study: Letters and reflections on our first year as beginning professors', *Curriculum Inquiry*, **24**, 1, pp. 27–52.

KNOWLES, J.G. and COLE, A.L. with PRESSWOOD, C. (1994) *Through Preservice Teachers' Eyes: Exploring Field Experiences through Narrative and Inquiry*, New York, Merrill.

KNOWLES, J.G. and COLE, A.L. (1995) 'Researching the "good life:" Reflections on professorial practice', *The Professional Educator*, **17**, 1, pp. 49–60.

KNOWLES, J.G. and HOEFLER, V. (1989) 'The student teacher who wouldn't go away: Learning from failure', *Journal of Experiential Education*, **12**, 2, pp. 14–21.

MAGER, G.M. and MYERS, B. (1983) *Developing a Career in the Academy: New Professors of Education. Technical Report No. 143, Society of Professors of Education*, Washington, DC.

MEAD, G.H. (1934) *The Social Psychology of George Herbert Mead*, Chicago, University of Chicago Press.

PATAI, D. (1994) 'Sick and tired of scholars' nouveau solipsism', *The Chronicle of Higher Education*, February, p. 23.

SAMPSON, E.E. (1993) *Celebrating the Other: A Dialogic Account of Human Nature*, Boulder, CO, Westview Press.

6 Returning to the Physics Classroom to Re-think How One Learns to Teach Physics

Tom Russell

Introduction

This is the story of a personal action research project in which I took a leap of faith, as a teacher of physics teachers, and returned to the physics classroom to see if I could still be a successful physics teacher myself. I also wanted to see how the experiences of daily high school teaching would affect my ways of thinking about my regular work with people learning to teach physics. Fresh from a year's sabbatical leave in England in 1990–91, I approached the physics teacher at my son's high school and he agreed to an exchange of services. I took full responsibility for one class of Grade 12 physics (75 minutes each day) in the fall semester of 1991, and he came to Queen's once a week to teach a two-hour class with the physics method students in the Bachelor of Education program. We repeated the same arrangement in the fall of 1992.

In the UK there is a formal requirement that teacher educators have 'recent, relevant, and successful' classroom experience. I did not have such experience before the fall of 1991; I had not taught in a high school for more than twenty years. Now that I may correctly be characterized as having recent, relevant, and successful experience, I have also come to ask, 'So what?' and 'Is that enough?' By making myself a data source for my continuing study of teachers' development of professional knowledge — a research program that Hugh Munby and I began in 1985 — I was able to begin to answer those questions. I believe that my teaching in a school was and will continue to be an appropriate and valuable activity, both personally and for those learning to teach physics.

Teaching the Ontario Grade 12 physics course once from start of finish could never have been enough. I felt this way immediately after the first experience, and virtually every day of the second experience confirmed that opinion. I cannot help but wonder why there is no literature of the second-year teacher to match that about the first-year teacher; teacher education deserves a literature of celebration to accompany the familiar literature of turmoil and exhaustion. When one repeats courses taught the previous year, the familiarity with text materials and with typical student difficulties with new concepts leaps out like an old friend shining a light to show the way along the path that initially seemed so complex. Thus I would now argue that just one 'recent, relevant, and successful' teaching experience may not be enough. I can now say with confidence to the beginning physics teacher, 'I understand the turmoil of the first year, and it gets much better in the second year' — better, but no less complex, for as some problems fade, others that have been neglected can be given the attention they deserve. My personal 'first year' in 1991–92 was similar to that of a beginning teacher in the sense that I did not have daily firsthand knowledge of the specific textbook being used or the laboratory equipment available in the school. Of course, my first year back in the classroom was also different from that of a beginning teacher because skills of planning, management and evaluation do, thankfully, transfer from one level to another.

Two groups of B.Ed. students experienced this collaborative arrangement, and I have learned a great deal by listening to their reactions to the experience of the B.Ed. program and my course within it. Interestingly, the reactions of the two groups of physics method students were quite different. The first group seemed impressed that a professor was actually teaching every day; the second group found it interesting, but not significant. I thought I was in a better position in the second year to build and develop links between my time in the school and their experiences at Queen's. I arranged for some of them to tutor students in my class, and each week I held one method class in my school classroom where I had finished teaching. The second group also took much more advantage of my open invitation to observe my teaching, appreciating the opportunity to visit a high school before practice teaching began.

This chapter includes data provided by members of the second group, whose more complex reactions prompted me to collect data that I was too busy to collect with the first group. I may never know why the second physics method group did not seem to value my daily physics teaching in the fall semester as the first group did. The second group had classes with me at the school while the first group did not, and what was intended to provide a practical context seems not to have had the desired effects. As I saw their reactions and worked to understand them (Munby and Russell, 1994), I noted particularly their difficulties during the first five weeks of their B.Ed. program, before they had any practice teaching experience. In hindsight it is not surprising that they showed little ability to find 'pedagogical meaning' when they observed my classes, met with me in my classroom at the school, or participated in discussions about their forthcoming first practicum. Kagan and Tippins' (1992) comparison of pre-service and in-service teachers' responses to observation of teaching, points to important differences:

> In general, the pre-service teachers defined good teaching from a student perspective: in terms of fun, student involvement, positive reinforcement, and affective elements of a teacher's personality. The inservice teachers defined good teaching from a teacher perspective: in terms of clear lesson structure and readily identifiable components (explicit objectives, definition of terms, examples, guided practice).
>
> The inservice teachers were able to render spontaneous functional

interpretations of teacher behaviors, often ignoring the specifics of the behavior itself and citing only the underlying purpose. . . . In contrast, the preservice teachers invariably described specific teacher behaviors and only occasionally noted their functions. (Kagan and Tippins, 1992, p. 156)

Without teaching experiences of their own, the method students could only observe, listen, and discuss from their very familiar perspective of 'student'. Without teaching experiences of their own, they could not see or listen from the perspective of 'teacher'. Why should they be able to? Is it not a fundamental role of experience to alter our perceptions of others' experiences? No program of teacher education could omit the student teaching practicum, and I now see more clearly that the practicum is essential not for perfecting teaching skills (as those learning to teach would like) but simply for coming to understand what it is they must learn in their early years of teaching.

This chapter begins with a series of questions indicating how I interpret my experiences in an action research framework. This is followed by an outline of the concept of 'authority of experience' in relation to learning to teach (Munby and Russell, 1994). This sets the stage for presentation of data from students in my physics method class in 1992–93, at the mid-point of their eight-month program and at the conclusion of their pre-service studies. The chapter closes with a summary of these rich and intensely personal experiences and an account of my associated personal development as a teacher educator.

Action research in physics teaching and teacher education

Jack Whitehead (Bath) has taught me to frame a cycle of action research with the following questions:

- What is my concern about my practice?
- What am I going to do about it?
- What evidence will I gather to enable me to judge my own actions?
- How will I validate the claims I make about my actions?

The following are brief responses to these four action research questions, set in the context of the introductory discussion:

What is my concern about my practice?

I had two practices to be concerned about. First is the practice of teaching people to teach physics. I have always wanted to be seen as a teacher educator who attended to reality as well as theory, as one who could practice what he preached. My immediate concern with physics method work is whether 'recent, relevant and successful' experience will make a difference to those I am trying to help enter teaching. Second is the practice of teaching Grade 12 physics. Here I wanted to demonstrate to myself that I can still be successful in the role of physics teacher. Yet I also wanted to be seen as special in some small sense — a feeling that I think is shared by many other teachers. The rhetoric for teaching science has changed in twenty years, and again my concern reduces to 'Can I practice what I preach?' and 'Can I do in my own teaching what I ask of those entering the teaching profession?'

What am I going to do about it?

At the simplest level, I decided to engage in both activities at the same time. If I could hang on long enough and keep thinking at both levels, I hoped to make progress on two fronts: understanding better what my physics method students are learning to do, and finding out the realities of today's physics teaching. I committed myself to keeping notes as extensively as possible. In 1992–93, I was particularly successful in generating a daily record of each lesson in the physics class. This was remarkably helpful, both as a record and as a process for analyzing each day's work with a view to that of the next day. It has become something I can share with future method classes.

What evidence will I gather to enable me to judge my own actions?

I have always relied extensively on written comments from my students as a guide to what is happening to them and as a strategy for bringing out issues that require attention. I always collect such evidence as free responses to open-ended questions, at times in the form of 'Strengths, Weaknesses, Suggestions' and at times in the form of more specific areas that I am interested in hearing about. With the physics method students, I gathered further evidence by asking each to come to my office for a 30-minute interview just after the halfway point of their B.Ed. program, and also by requiring each person to write as a final assignment the story of the year's experience learning to teach.

How will I validate the claims I make about my actions?

This is the hardest question. Judging the effects of teaching may be the most complex and least developed aspect of teaching and teacher education. Because teaching has been judged for so long on evidence from tests and examinations, neither teachers nor students are comfortable with many other types of data about the effects of teaching. When I ask for written responses from students in either setting, I rarely have an opportunity to engage them in discussion of their responses, for two reasons: such discussion is unfamiliar and often uncomfortable, and it takes time from the 'expected' curriculum. This paper is itself incomplete because a detailed analysis of the story written by each B.Ed. student in physics in the last two years remains to be undertaken. I take encouragement from the fact that the stories show clear signs of progress for many, in the very last days of their program.

In the remainder of this chapter, I present evidence from the physics method students' written 'backtalk' and final stories to indicate some of the relevant tensions that they experienced. Through this extended inquiry into the process of 'learning to teach' in which my own actions played such a central role, I have come to see more clearly that one personal goal is to engage students (either in physics or in learning to teach physics) in a dialogue about how physics and teaching-learning are being understood as they go through the familiar and traditional educational forms: in physics, the units on light, sound, mechanics, electricity, and electromagnetism; in learning to teach physics, the courses in methods and foundations and the all-important practice teaching assignments.

Jack Whitehead always challenges me to go further by posing the question, '*How can I help my students improve the quality of their learning?*'. This may be the ultimate question of pre-service teacher education, because the learning that happens in a pre-service program must be so different from that which has occurred in earlier formal school experiences. Those who are learning to teach cannot clearly describe or recognize what it is that they need to learn, beyond the most obvious realization that time must be spent in schools at the front of a classroom. The teacher educator faces the further challenge of modelling as well, so that the question takes on two levels: 'How can I help my students to improve the quality of their learning, so that they may improve the quality of the learning of those they teach?'

To set the stage for the statements student teachers made about learning to teach as I was returning to the classroom myself, I describe what Hugh Munby and I are calling 'authority of experience'. For us, this phrase has become an important addition to the familiar but poorly understood concept of 'learning from experience'. The phrase 'authority of experience' was suggested by the 1992–93 physics method students' mid-program conversations and by Anna Richert's (1992) arguments for the importance of voice in learning to teach.

The authority of experience in learning to teach

The authority of *reason* is rooted in argument and the scholarly virtue of rigour. Claims to know how teaching should occur can be grounded in educational theory or in educational research. This authority is very familiar to those learning to teach, for it has been the basic value in all their education. When a professor speaks, one writes and studies in anticipation of the examination. The authority of reason is weakened in pre-service teacher education because education is not seen by the outsider as a rigorous discipline, because attending education courses does not have the force of new knowledge that we associate with the arts, sciences, engineering, law or medicine, and because it is so very easy for teachers in schools to dismiss teacher education courses as weak or irrelevant or simply unrealistic: 'It won't work'.

When experienced teachers say, 'That won't work' and 'Forget everything they taught you at Queen's', they are relying on the authority of *position*, rather than the authority of reason. Any teacher can display the force of authority of position to students with statements of the form, 'Do it because I said so', but this authority usually substitutes for that of reason only temporarily. Yet when the experienced teacher meets the inexperienced student teacher, the authority of position can also play a very significant role. 'Do it this way because I've struggled with this problem for twenty years and I know this is the only way that works', is an argument rooted in the authority of extensive personal experience. The inexperienced new teacher has little or no recourse. The logic of reasoned argument cannot challenge the position of one who has far more experience.

Our research since 1985 has focused on 'learning from experience' but it is only recently that we have come to see the importance of suggesting that personal *experience* has an authority of its own that should be contrasted directly with the authority of educational argument and the authority of other people's experiences (Munby and Russell, 1994). In hindsight, Richert's (1992) words may have helped us see the way:

> Listening to yourself as an authority on your own experience . . . is an important part of learning. In fact listening to your own words and attempted explanations is fundamental to reflective practice that results in learning to teach. While the power of speaking lies in part in the fact of being heard, being heard is not something that can be taken for granted in teaching. For one thing, being heard implies that someone is listening and there is no norm for listening to teachers within the professional community of schools. Beyond the norms of the profession, the demands on teachers' time preclude much reciprocal conversation among colleagues; teachers are too busy to listen to themselves let alone listen to one another. (p. 193)

We are not suggesting that reason and the experience of others should be dismissed or even minimized. Our goal is to have the authority of experience recognized by those learning to teach, so that it takes a significant place beside the familiar authorities of reason and position. The physics method students in 1992–93 seemed to show more clearly than their predecessors that they find it very difficult, as beginning practitioners in a short professional program unlike any previous educational program, to trust in personal experience or to place confidence in their own voice. Yet from the first day of their first year of teaching, they will only have their own experiences and voices to guide them; gone are the professors, and the experienced teachers in nearby classrooms can describe their experiences but cannot transfer them. We believe that new teachers should be shown how to recognize and develop the authority of personal experience. This would involve listening to one's self in relation to students' experiences of one's own teaching. It requires an openness to student 'backtalk' and a trust in the importance of one's own voice. It requires a willingness and an ability to listen to one's own experiences as one also listens to the wisdom of those with more experience and of those who have explored educational issues analytically and empirically.

Student teachers' views of learning to teach and learning from experience

Mid-year comments about learning to teach

The following are comments about the teacher education experience made in January, 1993, just after the midpoint of the pre-service program at Queen's. Curriculum/method courses in physics and mathematics are the only two courses in the program that extended over the entire eight-month period. These comments show the tensions that pre-service teachers can experience between the familiar authorities of reason (in university coursework) and position (in teachers' extensive experience of what works). It is also possible to infer, by its absence, their unwill- ingness to trust their own voices and initial experiences. Sadly but understandably, some conclude that teaching is no more than a matter of personal opinion.

Paul: If an institution puts money or staff where something is important, then I think the students start to see it's something that is important and worthy. . . . The Faculty of Education hasn't really thought out — they don't have an overall focus of what teacher education is supposed to be, or it's very willy-nilly. They're trying to cover all the bases but they're not worrying about the game.

Hope: It just depends on what your view of this year is. I mean, do a lot of people think that you can only really learn by actually teaching, so then any time that we're actually spending here in classes is just like a filler? It's another hurdle that you have to jump in order to be certified.

Bill: A lot of the time I don't know why I have to go to classes here. It doesn't seem to relate to teaching in a classroom. Some specific classes are teaching something that's really interesting, and I appreciate that and that's great. And sometimes I go to class and I'm not interested in what's going on, and I don't see how it could possibly help me when I go to teach it.

Don: I got so frustrated there just before Christmas . . . that I wrote out . . . my idea of how teachers' college should be. . . . I was just so sick of all these classes. To be honest, so many of them end up being so similar, and you end up feeling that you are taking three classes that are all the same. Like all my foundations classes; they've all ended up having the same feel to them. They've all been, like, big discussion classes. . . . The curricu- lum classes were usually more nuts and bolts. [Tom: And is that where you'd like to see them?] It's nice to get a variety, and that's — I know you tend to want to promote thinking about your teaching, and I have no problem with that, but I want something of everything.

Al: In a lot of these issues I don't think that there is any answer or absolute, and I think that's what most people should take out of this program is that, if you come in thinking you're going to get an answer, you're going to be shown the way, I think that perhaps that's the main change people will go through — perhaps they'll go through with it — they'll realize that that isn't available in education. . . . In the curriculum, in the mathematics course, it is somewhat more catering to what some people are asking for: 'I want some information. I want to be taught to teach'. And I think that's valuable. I think it makes the students feel more comfortable and, as I said before, it exposes you to different ideas and ways of approaching things.

Mary: The comments I've been hearing a lot are, 'I'm expecting to be told how to be a teacher'. I'm expecting that to a certain extent too, but it seems like — I'm almost afraid for them when they go out and start teaching and have to hang on to everything by themselves?

Matt: Our [physics] class opens a lot of discussion, which is good, and I like to hear what other people have to say, and their ideas on topics. And it kind of helps me form how I feel, and sometimes what I feel is changed, after hearing other people's arguments. And you get to see the different sides of things, and that's good, so I appreciate that.

End-of-year comments about learning to teach

By the end of their program, perspectives had shifted somewhat. Earlier themes continued, but there are signals of moderation and closure as well. The frustration with coursework persists; students dread the suggestion of a longer program. This can be interpreted as frustration with the absence of any certainty or firm conclusions and the general tone of personal opinion and 'Anything goes'. I find it hard not to conclude that more time — particularly in longer practice teaching assignments — would give a better sense of just what has to be learned and how courses and experience contribute to that learning. Here the students-soon-to-be-teachers are identified by different pseudonyms; no attempt should be made to link these comments to those at mid-year.

Kyle: Many of the courses have been saying a lot without really saying much. I feel that the time spent at the faculty could easily be reduced to a few months of studies. There seem to be a lot of little unnecessary assignments that mean nothing to many. All they are is a source of aggravation. Our time in the field should be increased. That is not to say that every course was a waste of time. The curriculum courses, for the most part, were extremely helpful. I actually enjoyed the media lab assignments. But there really isn't a whole lot else out there to compliment. I may be a little off, but this is how I feel at the present time.

Kyle continues with unusual comments that reveal disappointment with some observations made during time in schools and a questioning of the authority of some teachers' extensive experience.

> *Kyle*: I've been told on more than one occasion that the theory doesn't work, out in the field. I think it is more a question of 'Do you try to make it work?' It's easy to say, 'Oh it doesn't work', but was a real attempt made? Did you believe it would fail before you started? I guess I have become a little disillusioned with the attitude of some of the know-it-all teachers out there. The theory doesn't work because it's not applied. Teachers are not supposed to scream at their students to the point of making them cry. Teachers are supposed to be open to new ideas, like destreaming, and not crucify the idea before attempting to see if the theory will work. Teachers are not supposed to centre out students, make them feel small, talk about them behind their backs. But I have observed all of these, on more than one occasion. Teachers aren't perfect, but that should be their ultimate goal. They are role models, holding important positions in the public's eyes, and should act accordingly.

Steve commented directly about what I was trying to do by teaching in a nearby school, and an aside shows that there were not enough opportunities for dialogue about my goals and intentions:

> *Steve*: One last thing which I would like to comment on is what I think Tom tried to do with our physics method class this year. This is my interpretation, which may be wrong. I think that Tom was trying to give us the freedom and responsibility to decide what we wanted to learn. It was left up to us to question things and to ask questions. Our fate with the course was put into our own hands. I think Tom was trying to get us to question what is being done and to explore different options, to come up with our own ideas. I think Tom was trying to get away from the typical 'This is how it is, accept it and like it' class. I think a lot of the students had a hard time adapting to this approach to teaching. We are so used to having all of the information spilled out for us and all we have to do is soak it up like a sponge. No one has taught the majority of us to question things. This is something which I feel is definitely lacking in the field of science. We tend to just accept things for what they are without any questioning. It took me awhile to see it but I now appreciate what I think Tom was trying to do.

Detailed and plausible comments by Helen show an overall level of comfort that was not apparent earlier in the program:

> *Helen*: So, how has the year stacked up? It has given us a lot to sink our teeth into from the psychology and philosophy standpoints. A lot of questions

have been raised in our foundation courses that we really do need to ponder before we can establish our own personal convictions about who we are as a teacher. The curriculum classes have opened my thinking to the option of using activities and co-operative learning in both the mathematics classroom and the science classroom. The use of activities in the mathematics classroom is something that I was never exposed to as a mathematics student so this exposure has been valuable. A lot of time was spent in our physics class looking at improving our teaching and how we can continue to do that. These types of discussions were very useful because they made me realize that there are a lot of things to think about when we teach and the only way we will improve is to continually think about what it is we are doing, and to talk to others. Should we expect in eight months that a Faculty of Education can teach us to be great teachers? In September I would have thought 'Yes'. Now I realize that this is not likely because it will take our lifetimes to become great teachers.

Dave captured the style of a story to create a very readable account of his year, one that shows a high degree of introspection and personal responsibility for the year's events.

Dave: Back at the Faculty for the remainder of the [first] term, the rush was on again. Nothing that needed to be done was difficult. It seemed that the reason for giving so much work was simply to keep us busy. I was very frustrated at this point. If they couldn't find something more useful for us to do, why not give us the time to debrief ourselves? I guess it is easy to say that I would have done that, but perhaps the time would have been used less profitably by socializing instead of thinking. In either case, little of value was accomplished during the final two weeks of term. I again felt a little cheated that the professors at the Faculty could not find better ways of using our time here. There was a rumour at one point that it would be beneficial to teachers in training to extend the B.Ed. program to two years. This is possibly the silliest idea I've heard this year if the things we did this year represent the best that the Faculty can come up with. I understand that teaching someone how to teach is difficult at best, but I believe that quality outweighs quantity by far in this endeavour. Trying to cover up a lack of quality with quantity will not solve any problems. My last two teaching rounds went pretty smoothly. Both placements were at the same school, which allowed me to create one combined Mathematics and Science placement which lasted the entire four weeks. This gave me the opportunity to get a better feel for what it would be like to have a class for a whole month. In almost every class, I was just starting a unit when I arrived at the school. The extended time made it possible for me to complete the units and do the testing as well. I was very depressed when my Grade 10 Science class did very poorly on their test. It made me see two things. One, that Grade 10s are not terribly self-motivated, and two, that it must remain the job of the teacher to get students to motivate themselves, something that I obviously failed to do. I think that part of the problem also lies in the fact that I was a little too easy on the students during the placement. I was a little too quick to give them the answer when they didn't know it right off. Other things along the same line also contributed to the situation. It was now time for the last three weeks at the Faculty. It was not a very appealing thought. It was very tempting to just not come back, but there was the little matter of a degree, so I got in the truck and made the four hour drive back to Kingston. I feel better now that most of my assignments are out of the way, and I can take a look at what has transpired over the past months. In retrospect, I think I have really changed over my year at Queen's. It is not a simple task to pinpoint when or how the change took place. While I sat in my plastic chair at graduation last year, I was a little frustrated at how hard they had made it for me to be there. I realize now, however, that most of the blame for this lies on my shoulders. I should have worked harder, and things would have been easier. I know that this June I will be sitting in a similar plastic chair, wondering why I didn't get as much as I had expected out of this year. This time, the rules had changed so much that it took me the whole year just to figure them out. Again, I am very tempted to blame myself for this, however, one thing I did learn is that motivation ultimately does come from the teacher. If the teachers do not take what they are doing seriously, it is not likely that students will create their own motivation.

Excerpts from Dave's story and the comments by Kyle, Steve, and Helen show that an eight-month pre-service teacher education built on relatively traditional assumptions can be a frustrating experience that sends new teachers off to begin their careers without a sense of closure. No program element — method courses, foundations courses, or practice teaching — is automatically relevant or convincing. Taking the method course to the school where I was teaching every day for the first term of the B.Ed. program did not ensure relevance in the eyes of those learning to teach. In the absence of program coherence that might permit various elements to be seen as complementary, those learning to teach react in ways that reflect their existing attitudes to coursework and experience. My teaching in a school and encouraging them to analyze personal experience were useful to some but 'a waste of time' to others.

Conclusion

Before returning to the initial topic of re-thinking how one learns to teach physics and the role of the authority of experience in that process, it seems appropriate to review my personal stance toward the topic of 'reflective practice', which was the perspective that started me along the path to these explorations. Schön's *The Reflective Practitioner* was published in 1983, and I immediately began using his perspective on the development of professional knowledge as a frame for interpreting my teaching and research experiences. Five years later, I had explored Schön's arguments and related them to experiences to the point that I felt I understood that 'the reflection is *in* the action' (Munby and Russell, 1989): professional learning occurs when a new perspective on personal practice arises from experience and is then expressed in new actions. Our interest has always had two broad directions: improvements in science teaching, and improvements in the experiences of those learning to teach science.

Now, a decade later, I have drawn on a number of sources as I have also extended my own personal practice to the physics classroom. Jack Whitehead's (Bath) unique and persistent ways of framing questions in action research have been both supportive and generative. Bob Bullough's (Utah) accounts of new directions in his own practice of teacher education have encouraged me to believe that action research and writing about experience can be meaningful to beginning teachers (Bullough, Knowles, and Crow, 1991). John Baird (Melbourne), Ian Mitchell and Jeff Northfield (Monash) have pioneered the direct involvement of secondary school students in their own learning processes and extended the results to the professional learning of teachers (Baird and Mitchell, 1986; Baird and Northfield, 1992). Karen Guilfoyle (Idaho), Mary Lynn Hamilton (Kansas), Stefinee Pinnegar (Brigham Young), and Peggy Placier (Missouri) have shown the courage to critique (individually and collectively) their own initial experiences as untenured assistant professors of education (Russell and Pinnegar, in press), and Beth Hamilton has organized an AERA special interest group on the self-study of teacher education practices. Anna Richert's (Mills College) call to recognize the importance of voice in teacher development rang clearly as I considered my own voice in teacher education. Throughout this period, Hugh Munby has been the most supportive and encouraging research colleague I could ever hope to work with.

I have always sensed important parallels between action research and the 'epistemology of practice' suggested by Schön's accounts of 'reflection-in-action'. I believe Schön's work has contributed to shifts in what we are willing to accept as knowledge claims about professional practice, and that this has supported the climate for action research. Had I returned to the physics classroom before 1983, I would not have interpreted my experiences in the ways I have in the 1991–93 period. The phrase 'authority of experience', which emerged as Hugh Munby and I struggled to listen to the voices of my physics method students, takes our work forward by focusing the contrast that is essential in learning to teach. Those enrolled in pre-service programs are determined to learn from the theory, research, and maxims shared by their professors, and they are even more determined to learn from the decades of teaching experience embodied in the teachers who receive them for practice teaching. Most pre-service teachers appear not to recognize the authority of experience: personal voice and values are undervalued in their previous educational experiences and by the standard assumptions of most pre-service programs. Similarly, the voices of their own students (temporarily, in practice teaching; more permanently, in their early years of teaching) are undervalued. Action research requires and facilitates recognition of the authority of experience. Action research cannot thrive in the climate that my physics method students experienced, a climate of competing but misunderstood authorities with little development of attention to the voices of beginning teachers and their students. Teacher education for 'lifelong professional learning' needs action research, the perspective of 'reflective practice', and recognition of the authority of experience in relation to other authorities about teaching.

Two basic perspectives implicit in Schön's (1983) work are central to my initial attraction to that work: the gap between our beliefs and our practices is much more pervasive than we normally admit, and professional practice cannot evolve unless we apply to our own practices the perspectives we recommend to others. My two semesters of Grade 12 physics teaching have convinced me that teacher educators must always look for parallels between what we advocate as good learning for students in schools, what we advocate as good learning for new and experienced teachers, and what we advocate as good learning for ourselves. Even so, looking is not enough. We must assume that we are living contradictions, and use the strategies of action research and the perspective of reflective practice to identify contradictions, change our practices, and gather data to show the consequences of our changes.

By returning to the physics classroom, I recognized anew the significance of personally learning the details of a science textbook's problems and ways of organizing curriculum content and the challenge of learning to use the equipment available in a particular classroom. Real professional learning in the second year of teaching proceeds from the base of intense, often chaotic, experiences in the first year. I would never have understood this without returning to the classroom for my own 'second year'. At the same time, my real professional learning was only possible with the support of an experienced teacher willing to share his domain with me, with the support of action research and reflective practice perspectives, with the support of external research funding, and with strong beliefs in the importance of greater involvement of students in their own learning processes.

Always in the background, often lost in the frustration of the pressure to cover the curriculum, was the *authority of reason*: the literature of science education challenged me to attempt different teaching strategies, although I do not believe I ever wandered far from the norms of the school where I taught. Always in the background, often distanced by my determination to do it my own way, was the *authority of position*: my teacher partner had begun his teaching career in the school in the same week that I began my pre-service teacher education career at Queen's, and he had natural and appropriate inclinations to assume that I would conform to some of his practices. In my second year, the *authority of experience* moved to the foreground as I used a daily computer-based journal to record and analyze my teaching, to trace the evolving puzzles of practice, and to invent modest variations to address those puzzles.

Teaching physics as action research

My two half-year, full-course school teaching experiences are recent, relevant, and (apparently) successful. But there is more. I have come to recognize the authority of personal experience as a vital ingredient in my own redevelopment as a teacher. I did not interpret my initial years of physics teaching in this way and, importantly, I did not interpret my initial years of physics method teaching in this way. The task ahead is to examine my own method teaching, as I have my recent physics teaching, from the authority of experience perspective. By posing the 'quality of student learning' question, I also intend to explore various ways of helping new teachers recognize and develop the authority of experience. In my excitement and enthusiasm about being a teacher as I was also a teacher educator, I moved too quickly for some of the pre-service teachers in my physics method course, just as I moved too quickly through the physics curriculum for some of the Grade 12 students. Only late in the 1992–93 year did I realize just how I was moving too quickly, and next year I will adjust the pace, accepting the student teachers' initial need for fine details of the physics curriculum they will teach. I will also accept their need to be trained in strategies for coming to recognize the authority of their own experiences against the backdrop of the familiar authorities of educational theories and maxims and of other teachers' extensive experience.

As I work to understand how one learns to teach and how the teacher of a physics method course contributes to that goal, I am struck by the eternal gaps between coursework at Queen's and practice in schools, and by the related willingness of those learning to teach to criticize both universities and schools, but only when situated in one and talking about the other. It is astonishingly difficult to get students to 'talk back' publicly about their frustrations and dissatisfactions with university courses, in part, of course, because they fear punishment in the form of lower grades. Similarly, they cannot 'talk back' to teachers in schools because they realize that 'theory' taken on board in a university course is no match for a teacher's confidence grounded in years of experience.

I am grateful to the physics method students who have engaged me in various levels of dialogue about their experiences learning to teach. I have succeeded in getting many of them to 'talk back' on paper as their eight-month program is ending, but the closure remains partial and incomplete. I hope that these two years will be useful to future physics method students now that I better understand both the type of dialogue that is required and the extent to which I must provide training in the skills necessary to recognize the authority of experience. How different would pre-service teacher education programs be if courses and practice teaching experiences were framed by the question, 'How can I help these student teachers to improve the quality of their learning?' Richert's (1992, p. 192) statements about voice pose the challenge:

> Voice is a vehicle for reflective practice which results in ongoing learning
> in teaching. Knowing how to speak, including how to frame questions,
> how to grapple with answers, how to identify problems and focus on

solutions, how to use theory to inform practice, and so on, is as important as knowing what to speak about. Programs of teacher education must have a structured expectation of voice; they must provide ample opportunity and a safe and supportive environment for the voiced conversations to be exercised.

Acknowledgments

The chapter is from the 1992–1995 research project, 'Case study research in teachers' professional knowledge' (Hugh Munby and Tom Russell, principal investigators), funded by the Social Sciences and Humanities Research Council of Canada. An early version was presented at the meeting of the Canadian Society for the Study of Education, Ottawa, June, 1993. It was also the focus of discussions at Monash University and the University of Melbourne in July, 1993. I am grateful to the B.Ed. physics students at Queen's in 1991–92 and 1992–93 for their attention to and comments about my efforts to improve my teaching by returning to the classroom setting. I am grateful to the following people for e-mail conversations about teaching, research, and reflection: John Baird, Ruth Davis, Moira Laidlaw, John Loughran, Allan MacKinnon, Stefinee Pinnegar, Anita Roychoudhury, and Jack Whitehead. Jan Carrick transcribed tapes and offered excellent editorial suggestions.

References

BAIRD, J.R. and MITCHELL, I. (Eds) (1986) *Improving the Quality of Teaching and Learning: An Australian Case Study — The PEEL Project*, Melbourne, Monash University.

BAIRD, J. and NORTHFIELD, J. (Eds) (1992) *Learning from the PEEL Experience*, Melbourne, Monash University.

BULLOUGH, R.V., JR., KNOWLES, J.G. and CROW, N.A. (1991) *Emerging as a Teacher*, London, Routledge.

KAGAN, D.M. and TIPPINS, D.J. (1992) 'How US pre-service teachers "read" classroom performances', *Journal of Education for Teaching*, **2**, pp. 149–158.

MUNBY, H. and RUSSELL, T. (1989) 'Educating the reflective teacher: An essay review of two books by Donald Schön', *Journal of Curriculum Studies*, **21**, pp. 71–80.

MUNBY, H. and RUSSELL, T. (1994) 'The authority of experience in learning to teach: Messages from a physics methods class', *Journal of Teacher Education*, **45**, 2, pp. 86–95.

RICHERT, A. (1992) 'Voice and power in teaching and learning to teach', in VALLI, L. (Ed) *Reflective Teacher Education: Cases and Critiques*, Albany, State University of New York Press, pp. 187–197.

RUSSELL, T. and PINNEGAR, S. (Eds) (1995), 'Becoming a Professor of Teacher Education' [special issue], *Teacher Education Quarterly*.

SCHÖN, D.A. (1983) *The Reflective Practitioner: How Professionals Think in Action*, New York, Basic Books.

Part 4

Ways to Study Practice in Teacher Education

7   Educative Relationships with the Writings of Others

Jack Whitehead

Introduction

My aim is to show how action research can contribute to the professional development of reflective teachers and teacher educators by helping them to create their own, new forms of living educational theory. By 'living educational theory' I mean their descriptions and explanations of their own educational development. I begin by locating action research within a search for an educational question of the kind, 'How do I improve my practice?' or 'How do I live my values more fully in my practice?', or 'How do I help my pupils to improve the quality of their learning?' I now want to draw your attention to the need for creating new forms of educational theory and to the different contributions from action research communities, groups and networks from around the world. The groups and networks I have in mind include those influenced by critical and other forms of social science in Australia (McTaggart, 1992; Kemmis, 1993; Henry, 1992; Smyth, 1993; Zuber-Skerritt, 1991), self-study in America (Herrmann, 1994; Hamilton, 1994; Pinnegar, 1994; Austin, 1994), the authority of experience in Canada (Russell, 1994 a&b; Munby & Russell, 1994), living and other forms of theory in Europe (Altrichter, 1990; Whitehead, 1989, 1993; McNiff, 1991, 1994; Lomax, 1994; Elliott, 1993) and participatory action research in developing countries (Fals-Borda, 1994).

The need for new forms of educational theory

When I began teaching in London in 1967, the view of educational theory that dominated teacher education courses was that it was constituted by the philosophy, psychology, sociology and history of education. By the 1980s, this view had broken down because the theory could not be related directly to the process of improving educational practice. On a study visit to Eastern Europe in 1984, I could see a clearly defined Marxist ideology constituting educational theory on teacher education programs. Since November 1989, with the collapse of the Berlin Wall, there has been a decisive rejection of the view that educational theory is constituted by Marxist ideology. With the ferment in Europe, in the movement towards European integration, no clear European educational theories have yet emerged. There appears to be little intellectual activity in the American Educational Research Association that is focused on the nature of educational theory. Fenstermacher (1994) has argued that the systemics of schooling are being emphasized at the expense of the educative purposes, suggesting that more pre-service teacher education should take place in schools. Whilst Shulman (1992) is working on the development of pedagogical content knowledge and a case-based approach to teacher education, there is a lack of clarity about the nature of the explanations for the professional development of teachers that is emerging from this approach.

My case, that there is a need to create new forms of educational theory, rests upon the assumption that teachers and teacher educators need educational theory in order to understand and explain our professional practice. I am also assuming that a characteristic of an educational theory of teacher education is its capacity to explain the professional, educational development of a teacher educator. But what kind of educational theory would you and I accept as having the capacity to produce a valid explanation for our professional, educational development? Let me suggest an answer that requires a radical break with traditional, conceptual forms of theory. I am thinking of those theories that are presented in general terms as sets of determinate relations between variables in terms of which educational phenomena are explained. The break I am suggesting is to think of educational theory as being constituted by the descriptions and explanations — the personal educational theories — that you and I produce for our own educational development in enquiries of the form, 'How do I improve my practice?' or 'How do I live my values more fully in my practice?' Because action research is distinguished from other forms of research by the fact that researchers are investigating their own practices, I am suggesting that we should look at the different action research approaches below to see which may offer the most appropriate approach to the above questions and to the possibility of creating new forms of educational theory.

Action research approaches around the world

One approach to action research has been influenced by the critical theory of Jürgen Habermas (Carr and Kemmis, 1986). A seminal paper by Brian Fay (1977) offered an 'educative' model of action research grounded in critical social theory. One aim of this model, and an evaluative criterion to test its adequacy, is to provide some understanding of the ways in which those enlightened by the theory can overcome the opposition of those in power. Thus an analysis of recent work of McTaggart (1992), Henry (1992), Kemmis (1993) and Smyth (1993) should reveal to what extent the educative model of action research, grounded in critical social science, has been integrated into their lives as teacher educators in a way that provides some understanding of how they have engaged in overcoming opposition. I find their conceptual theories helpful in illuminating the way in which political and economic power relations influence schooling, education and society. However, I believe their contributions would be strengthened by analyses of their own learning and educational development as they explored the practical implications for their own lives of believing their own theories and engaging with the political, economic and educational relationships in their workplaces and societies.

The work of Zuber-Skerritt (1991) in Australia has a different theoretical base to critical theory. I find her work helpful in her descriptions of a variety of models of learning drawn from the work of Lewin, Kolb and Piaget. However, her readers are not provided with a demonstration of how she has integrated the models into an explanation of her own professional development in higher education. As one of the central tenets of action research is that the action researcher is studying her or his own practice, I wonder if a study of her own educative relationships would help to show how to overcome a gap between theory and practice. This is what I am trying to do in this chapter. I suggest that the creation of living educational theories by practitioners, as they try to improve the quality of their practice, will show how the gap between conceptual forms of theory and practical experience can be overcome.

In America, educational researchers have recently formed a special interest group on the 'self-study of teacher education practices' within the American Educational Research Association. Some members of this group have already offered impressive accounts of their own lives as teacher educators (Guilfoyle, 1994; Hamilton, 1994; Herrmann, 1994; Pinnegar, 1994; Placier, 1994; Russell, 1994c). The strength of this group is in its use of story and vivid metaphors in accounts of their own professional lives. Their work is grounded in self-study, in their own learning from experience and in collaboration within a community. The contribution of the group may be strengthened by heeding Noffke's (1994) call to consider how their knowledge claims are to be addressed. An epistemological question that might be helpful is, 'What are the standards of judgment that can be used to test the validity of the knowledge claims produced through the self-study of teacher education practices?' Connelly and Clandinin (1988) have emphasized 'personal practical knowledge' and Koren's (1994) recent work on 'body knowledge' may offer a way forward in understanding the nature of the new criteria in an epistemology of practice.

In Europe a number of action research approaches can be defined. Working with Zuber-Skerritt and others, Altrichter (1990), from Austria, has defined the characteristics of action research. It will be interesting to see if he offers an account of his own work as a teacher educator or moves on to another project where theory is separated from an account of his own practice. John Elliott (1989) has been very influential in the development of action research in teacher education in England and throughout the world. In numerous publications he has developed a view of action research as a practical educational science. He has recently applied this idea in a proposal for the reconstruction of teacher education (Elliott, 1993). I wonder if the idea of a practical educational science is going to be able to include the art of classroom inquiry (Hubbard and Power, 1993) and the spiritual dimension of good quality educative relationships (Newby, 1994). As Elliott lives, and researches, the implications of his proposal, it will be interesting to see if it is possible to include the spiritual, aesthetic and ethical dimensions of educational explanations in a practical educational science.

Feminist researchers have offered analyses that show the way in which patri-archal power relations have acted to suppress women's voices, and explain how these might be overcome (Weiner, 1989; Noffke, 1994; Hollingsworth, 1994; Richert, 1994). In a particularly powerful analysis, Weiner claims that feminist researchers appear to share several, or all, of the following assumptions in planning their work:

- that women in society are subordinated and oppressed in relation to men;
- that changes need to be made in the social/economic/political position of women;
- that gender and gender divisions are important in social science and edu-cational research;
- that women and their experiences should be made visible;
- that feminist research need not necessarily be about but should be for women;
- that feminist research should be concerned with improving the situation of girls and women.

In this work and elsewhere (Whitehead 1991, 1993), I hope that I have shown an understanding and acceptance of these feminist assumptions. As a male researcher I know that I may unwittingly be supporting the oppression described by Weiner. In my work with Moira Laidlaw and Dawn Bellamy, which I describe below, I have consciously attempted to live my value of equal opportunities in my educative relationships in a way that enables women's voices to be heard and respected and in a way that promotes these feminist interests.

The participatory action research (PAR) movement had its genesis in commu-nity action in developing countries. Fals-Borda and Rahman (1991) have set out the theoretical basis of PAR, with its commitment to dialogue and to supporting its emancipatory potential. In his view of postmodernity and social responsibility, Orlando Fals-Borda (1994) warns that the postmodern discourse is for the most part silent on questions of political strategy. He acknowledges that there is merit in challenging 'meta-narratives' such as Marxism, development principles, and liberalism. How-ever, he sees problems arising when postmodernists confine themselves to applying discursive constructs and metaphors to complex realities like the city, feminism or the class structure. He argues, for example, that when ideologies are criticized to the point of decreeing the end of history and the end of utopias, a door is open for neo-Liberals to discard egalitarian values and to reject the adoption of redistributive mechanisms of wealth and property, even when these are obviously urgent and necessary. He asks that we teachers and researchers be more careful and specific in recognizing that postmodern discourse does have political effects and that there is a danger in some of this discourse that we might be undermining whatever we are trying to build.

With such talent and resources of the international educational research com-munities at work, why do we lack explanations for the educational development of teacher educators? Why is it that research into teacher education rarely shows the educative influence of a teacher educator on the professional and educational development of a teacher? It may be that self-study by teacher educators is of such recent origin that the research has not had sufficient time to show the influence of teacher educators on the teachers they are helping to educate. In my own case, I have no such excuse. I have been working as an educational action researcher at the University of Bath since 1973. Having offered accounts of my own educational development as an educational researcher in the context of the politics of truth and power relations of my workplace (Whitehead, 1991, 1993), I have begun to study my professional practice as a teacher educator and to offer evidence from my colleagues and students on the quality of my educative relationships. In 1994–95, I am tutoring two groups of students for the educational and professional studies component of their course. Dawn Bellamy was in one of the 1993–94 groups that I tutored. Before I show some of the influences of my ideas on a colleague and novice teacher, I first extend my understanding of the six criteria I use to distinguish my action research approach to my work as a teacher educator.

Six criteria of action research as a teacher educator

My first criterion concerns enquiry. As already noted, an enquiring mind is fundamental to being a teacher educator. Questions of the kind, 'How do I improve what I am doing?' and 'How do I help my students to improve the quality of their learning?' are central to my approach to action research. I agree with Hubbard and Power (1993) in their book, *The Art of Classroom Inquiry*, where they say, 'Try to Love the Questions Themselves'. They highlight the importance of enquirers speaking from the authority of their own experience. Hugh Munby and Tom Russell (1994) have recently called researchers' attention to the importance of recognizing the authority of experience in teacher education. A question that Tom and I believe may be the ultimate question of pre-service teacher education is, 'How can I help my students to improve the quality of their learning?' This is the kind of question I also find teachers and novice teachers love to pose. Dawn Bellamy (1994) in the study described below, asks, 'How can I help Thomas to increase his flexibility as a learner so that he shows the same assuredness in his writing as in his speaking?'

The nature of 'I' in such questions brings me to an original idea and the second criterion of *'I' as a living contradiction*. I think the originality of placing your own 'I' as a living contradiction (Whitehead, 1993) in your own enquiry and educational theory has powerful appeal because it corresponds to your experience when you recognize that you hold certain values whilst at the same time you experience their denial or negation in your practice. I have been particularly struck by teachers' responses as they acknowledge experiencing themselves as living contradictions on viewing videotapes of their classroom practice. I am suggesting that the experience of existing as a living contradiction is a very powerful motivator in your life as you try to resolve the tension of this experience by trying to live your values as fully as you can in your educative and other relationships.

My third criterion is that, as a reflective teacher educator who is undertaking an action enquiry into the process of improving the quality of learning for your students, you *include your own 'I' as a living contradiction* in your use of the common-sense form of the action/reflection cycle below (Whitehead, 1985):

- I experience a concern when my values are negated in practice;
- I imagine a way forward;
- I so act and gather data to enable me to make a judgment on the quality and effectiveness of my actions;
- I evaluate my actions in terms of my values and understandings;
- I modify my actions in the light of my evaluations.

However, you may need some support, such as that offered by the Marino Institute of Education (McNiff and Collins, 1994), to transform your everyday professional practices into a form of research-based professionalism that recognizes and legitimates the disciplined nature of your enquiry. For example, Marion Fitzmaurice (1994) shows how, with the support of staff from the Marino Institute, she followed the systematic action plan of identifying problems, imagining solutions, implementing solutions, evaluating solutions and modifying practice as she answered her question above.

My fourth criterion is based on the idea that as a reflective teacher educator you can help to transform what counts as educational knowledge and educational theory in the academy by constructing descriptions and explanations of your professional life, testing your accounts for validity in an educational community and seeking their legitimization in a university context (Whitehead, 1989, 1994; McNiff, 1991). The work of Lomax (1994) and Clarke *et al.* (1993) on the standards of judgment for critiquing and testing the validity of action research reports bears witness to the transformation in understanding that needs to take place in universities if these new forms of educational knowledge are to be legitimated as original and scholarly contributions to existing forms of knowledge. The originality in this idea is that a new form of living educational theory is being created in the descriptions and explanations that individuals produce for their own educational development (Whitehead, 1989, 1994). This idea has been further developed by Jean McNiff and Una Collins (1994) at the Marino Institute of Higher Education in Ireland. Thus my fourth criterion for judging the action research of a reflective teacher educator is that a description and explanation for one's own educational development be presented within a form and content that can be publicly tested for validity. This criterion raises questions about appropriate forms of representation for action research accounts.

In his Presidential Address to the American Educational Research Association, Eisner (1993) gave powerful support to the search for more appropriate forms of representation for educational research. He argued that we should be exploring the significance of the forms of understanding that poetry, literature, dance, mathematics and literal language make possible. It may be a little unnerving to accept the challenge of creating one's own living educational theory in enquiries of the kind, 'How do I live my values more fully in my practice?', but action research is nothing if not challenging!

My fifth criterion highlights a limitation in *judging an action research approach solely on the above criteria*. This concerns educative communities and their role in cultural renewal and in improving social order (McNiff *et al.*, 1992). With its emphasis on the practitioner researching his or her own practice, there is a danger that the 'I' of the individual researcher might be seen as separated from the social context and relationships in which the enquiry is located. This danger has been overcome in participatory action research, PAR. One of the strengths of the PAR movement (Fals–Borda and Rahman, 1991) is its stress on community issues and problems. In her analysis of a participatory project with Battered Families' Services in New Mexico, Maguire (1987, 1993) explains how she worked at resolving the tensions between her roles as organizer, educator and researcher. She shows how she retained her sense of individual integrity whilst working in a community to support a group of formerly battered women. Here is her conclusion:

> The primary lesson for me is that the redistribution of power, among and between the world's women and men, is a long-haul, collective struggle in which there is work for each of us. Participatory research is but one tool in that struggle. However, transformation, social and personal, is not an event, it is a process that we are living through, creating as we go. It is dangerous to compare our modest beginnings and exhausting middles to the successful, documented endings of others' work. For we never know when we begin where the work will take us and those involved. Perhaps that is what allows us to even begin. Learn from others' work, but don't be intimidated by it. It is too easy to be seduced into comparing, then trivializing or discounting your efforts. The point is to learn and grow from doing, and to celebrate the doing, no matter how flawed, small-scale, or less than ideal.

What I think is shared in action research communities is a form of question in which the questioner is studying his or her own practice in an attempt to help to improve the quality of his/her own life and that of others. Action researchers working in widely different parts of the world have demonstrated a capacity to study themselves in a systematic form of enquiry that is aimed at helping their fellows. They have also provided public accounts of their learning. These are often in the form of stories that include a description and explanation of their educational development in a way that shows their dialogical or conversational engagement with the power relations of an existing social order. This brings me to my sixth criterion, to *dialogue*. In the form and content of an action research account from a reflective teacher educator I expect to hear dialogue both internal and with others in which evidence of learning can be seen.

Having set out what I see as six characteristics of the action research of reflective teachers and teacher educators I now want to focus on my own practice to give more detail of the values and ways of working that reflective teacher educators might employ in their own action research.

Researching my work as a teacher educator

Whilst I am attracted to term 'teacher educator' because of its focus on education, I am puzzled by its meaning. What does it mean to be a teacher educator? If I make a claim that I am one, should I be able to show the evidence that demonstrates that I have influenced the education of a teacher or teachers? What kind of evidence can I offer you that shows that I am a reflective teacher educator who is researching his own practice? I want to answer this last question by showing you something of my educative relationships through the words of Moira Laidlaw, a colleague whose Ph.D. research program I supervise, and through those of Dawn Bellamy who, whilst a novice teacher during 1993/94, was tutored by both Moira Laidlaw and me. Dawn shows that she has integrated the above criteria into her own living educational theory as she helps Thomas to improve the quality of his learning.

Whilst I do not want to impose my own frameworks on my students, I believe that readers would be wise to question the extent to which the ideas above have been used freely by others. I believe the ideas are significant for helping others to create their own educational theories, and I do want to share them, *but only in a way that permits another to freely choose whether or not to use them.* Bearing this in mind I now offer evidence of my influence in my work with a teacher educator and a novice teacher. In 1993–94, Moira Laidlaw worked as a part-time lecturer and teacher educator in the School of Education. She asked me to supervise her M.Phil. research in 1991 and successfully transferred to a Ph.D. research program in November, 1992. Moira has already published her reflections on my tutoring and her views on action research (Laidlaw; 1993, 1994), showing how she integrated my ideas into her own enquiry.

I now want you to hear the voice of Dawn Bellamy as she embraces the above ideas in an action research approach to her practical educational enquiry of the kind, 'How do I help my pupils to improve the quality of their learning?' I have asked Moira to introduce Dawn's work to you. In the remainder of this section of the chapter, the voice alternates between Moira and Dawn, as Moira provides background and describes her role in Dawn's action research inquiry.

Moira: Dawn was a member of a student group placed on teaching practice in Wootton Bassett School in the South-West of England. This school has developed an action research approach to staff development and has an action research group that meets several times a month. Here is an extract from Dawn's account of her educational development (Bellamy, 1994) as she reflects on her experience and embraces the action-reflection cycle with the inclusion of 'I' as a living contradiction.

Dawn: On January 27, 1994, I attended a meeting of the Wootton Bassett Action Research Group, hoping to find out a bit more about the collaborative aspect of action research. The meeting inspired me. In my journal I wrote:

> I want to believe in action research. I want it to work for me in my professional development and want the research that I do to benefit my learners. My educational values are as real as anyone else's and now I have

the chance to share them, to live them and to reflect on their effects within my classroom. I have a feeling of power, a sense of control. Will it last?

The idea of becoming a teacher-researcher certainly appealed to me. In the midst of the confusion that was the PGCE [course], I seemed to have found something that would help me regain an element of control over my learning and that would put me into contact with people who shared similar values and a commitment to education.

Whatever it was that was luring me could not be ignored if I wanted to remain true to myself and consequently true to those people with whom I would interact as an integral part of the world. If I expected authenticity from the pupils in the classroom, if I wanted the people around me to feel free to be themselves and not to hide behind facades, then I had to be prepared to do the same. I had to search for the freedom that existed in the unmasking. I was feeling quite flustered at this stage, wondering if I would ever find the means to move beyond my self. I knew that my enquiry had to involve other people — a self-centred enquiry would not be enough — but I was unsure whether I could make that move.

When I wrote in my journal on February 22, I was at quite a different stage in terms of developing my own action research enquiry:

I worry about my ability to complete an enquiry. It all seems too self-centred at the moment. Will I be able to complete an enquiry that will be of value to anyone other than myself? So, the story so far is confusion, panic, despair, anger, frustration, disappointment, bitterness, doubt; what is it that keeps me going? Sometimes the light switches on and I catch a glimpse of the future and I feel as if everything will be all right. The existence of the constant dialectic means that this positive feeling cannot last forever. The negative, the questioning, will inevitably start to chip away at the image. So can I do it? Who knows?

Two days later I was still feeling the pressure:

So it looks like I'm stuck with this bloody journey. I'm beginning to wish I'd turned back before the beginning. I really hate myself, the way I'm thinking, the way I'm feeling, the way I'm behaving towards the people around me. If only I could get rid of this self I seem to have developed — the self that wants to challenge, to question. All the time I'm writing this, there's a voice inside my head screaming that I can't give up. It keeps telling me that the only way for me to go on living any sort of life that will be in any way worthwhile is to get back on my journey, hold on tight and hope that things improve soon.

My growing awareness of the ways in which I had deceived myself, and therefore others, in the past was incredibly disturbing. What sort of a life had I been leading? Before these entries, on February 18, I had written:

It is harshly disturbing to realize that everything that has gone before has been a mere facade. The paradoxical juxtaposition of joy and pain is integral to the human condition. It is part of our becoming and, as such, should be recognized and not denied. By refusing to acknowledge the whole it seems to me that the full potential of our existence will never be realized.

I suppose that in the two later journal entries I was acknowledging the pain, although I am not sure that I was accepting it as calmly as I was suggesting that people should, in the entry dated February 18. Whatever the discomfort, I could not turn back. I returned to my search for a question . . .

I knew that I had to wait until I got back into the classroom for my inquiry to begin in any practical sense. My 'complementary school' assignment for my second teaching practice in the spring of 1994 was an 11–16 mixed comprehensive in Swindon, and until I got there I could not know anything about the future of my inquiry. I did not even know if English was taught in mixed ability groupings; perhaps the focus of my enquiry would have to change immediately. In order to produce a valid study, I would have to conform to the principles of an action enquiry as first set out by Jack Whitehead in 1980:

1 I experience a problem because some of my educational values are negated.
2 I imagine a solution.
3 I act in the direction of the imagined solution.
4 I evaluate the actions.
5 I modify my actions/ideas in the light of my evaluations.
   (Whitehead, 1993, p. 38)

I knew that to begin with I would have to discover myself to be a 'living contradiction', to hold educational values but to negate them in my practice. If, as it seemed, one of my values is that all pupils should be given the opportunity to learn within an environment that stretches them and enables them to realize their full potential, and, in particular, that the exceptionally able should not be left to fend for themselves, then I would have to find myself in a situation in which there was a possibility that I might negate such values within my practice. From my experiences in education, I was aware that classrooms cannot be engineered to fit the requirements of a researcher and, even if they could, I would not want that to happen. I wanted to follow McNiff's (1991, p. 68) definition: 'Action research is research WITH rather than ON other people'.

That had been one of the problems with the PGCE course requirements. The university seemed to expect things to happen in schools at particular times, and it was not a situation I wanted to revisit. I was conscious of the need for flexibility from the start, and I prepared myself to adapt to my new context, ready to work towards the fulfilment of any dream under the dream umbrella that asks the question, posed by Jack Whitehead: 'How do I improve this process of education here?' (Whitehead, 1993, p. 69). I was still slightly unsure of my ability to complete a valid enquiry. The whole thing still seemed a bit daunting. But I set off for my complementary school undeterred and full of curiosity.

Moira: I draw your attention below to the way in which Dawn takes on ideas, from Jack's work, of *herself as a living contradiction*. She is able to show what it means to her own practice to come to terms with such a contradiction and includes her own 'I' within an action-reflection cycle. In terms of my own tutoring of her enquiry, her full document shows many examples of the dialogues we engaged in, which reveal how seriously she considers the ideas of others before coming to her own synthesis (Bellamy, 1994) as her living educational theory. One of the most significant values I try to bring to any educative relationship is the importance of students and pupils being facilitated to speak in their own voices about concerns that have moved them to try to improve their practice. Here is an example of a conversation following a lesson I observed where I experienced a dichotomy between the way Dawn related to her pupil, Thomas, as an individual and within a group.

> **Dawn:**   I don't think I'd ever have picked up about the sort of difference between me with individuals and me with the class as a whole.
>
> **Moira:**   It was really striking.
>
> **Dawn:**   I think it was probably more striking today but I'm sure it exists all the time, but I've never been conscious of it. Never ever. . . .
>
> **Moira:**   It was so striking and I really would like to talk about this in a sense, I mean in terms of your enquiry, because I think there are some issues underlying everything we've talked about before the tape was turned on that are to do with power and control — power and control over others, and also power and control over yourself. And I think that there was such a dichotomy between the way that you treated Thomas as another human being and an individual on a one-to-one with the way that you treated him institutionally, in other words with the group, that is at the heart of what Foucault writes about: when power is institutionalized it becomes, can become, abusive. Is that a fair comment?
>
> **Dawn:**   Definitely. When I looked back at the way I had behaved in the lesson (21/4/94), I could see myself, as the person who was exercising power, caught up in its machinations without even realizing that that was what I was doing. I had lost sight of myself as a human being in interaction with other human beings and had become a teacher with a desire to control, to manage a classroom. So, once again, it seemed that I was a 'living contradiction'. The educational values that I hold have nothing to do with controlling pupils, making sure that they are doing what I want them to do. That is not the way that I believe learning, effective learning, happens and yet it seemed that I had become exactly the sort of teacher that I had hated at school, the one who barked orders with no concern for the pupils. Looking into the mirror held up by action research does not always produce the most pleasant reflections. So instead of letting the pupils collaborate with me to produce a flexible learning environment in which

the needs of individuals are taken into account, I had led from the front, refused to interact with pupils' input if it did not conform to the way in which I perceived the lesson to be progressing, and become a character from one of my own educational nightmares. What had happened to the dreams?

At her teaching practice school, Dawn experienced a problem with one of her pupils, Thomas. This is how Dawn described her concern:

> Thomas appeared to have a preoccupation with the technical features of his writing, such as handwriting and spelling, and often reacted quite violently to being asked to produce a piece of written work. When he started to bang his head on the table and refused to do any writing, I was horrified and wanted to do something to help him to alter his perceptions of the writing process so that such an extreme reaction would not occur again.

It is difficult to communicate concisely the efforts Dawn made to understand how to help Thomas. Her action research report (Bellamy, 1994) contains a detailed analysis of her work with him over some six weeks of teaching practice in March and April, 1994. Her report gives evidence of her recognition of her experience as a living contradiction. It shows her disciplined action/reflection approach to her enquiry of the form, 'How do I help Thomas to improve the quality of his learning?' It shows her capacity to produce her own living educational theory and ends with the following evaluation of her work in encouraging Thomas with his writing of a poem he called 'Khare'.

Dawn: When I met him (Thomas) for another taped conversation (14/4/94), my plan was to give him the space to talk about anything he wanted, but as a catalyst for discussion I handed back his 'Khare' poem, wondering if he might like to talk about it. The conversation was quite magical. It was as if Thomas began a process of becoming right there before my eyes. He was quite wary of me to begin with, but it was not long before he was immersed in his enthusiasm for the background to the poem and seemed to lose sight of the curricular aspect of our relationship altogether. We were talking about a part of the poem in which the lines of a spell have to be arranged in the correct order to avoid death:

> **Dawn:** And how do you know which way to put it together? Is it just chance?
> **Thomas:** No. I've read it before.
> **Dawn:** No, but, so the person has to put this spell together?
> **Thomas:** Yes. If you're reading the book.
> **Dawn:** Right.
> **Thomas:** You put the spell together.
> **Dawn:** O.K. But that's just guess work, isn't it? When you do it first of all?

Thomas: Yes.

Dawn: So you could have put one, two, four, which might have been the logical way, mightn't it? And if you do it that way, that would have been wrong and you'd have died?

Thomas: Yes.

Dawn: Oh. So you put it together and then you turn the pages to find out what your fate is?

Thomas: Yes. As I was saying, 'back to the serpents . . .'

Dawn: Oh, I'm very sorry. Did I interrupt you?

Thomas: (Laughs) . . .

Although we were ostensibly talking about Thomas' poem (the curricular), our dialogue was more prominently an interchange between two unique human beings, in which Thomas felt at liberty to chastise me for interrupting him, could laugh at my sarcastic apology, and in which he was the expert, helping me to clarify my understanding.

Within this conversation I believe that I resolved both of my 'living contradictions'. I was no longer guilty of dominating the discourse, bulldozing Thomas into claiming to understand things from my point of view. I believe that we were engaged in true dialogue in which my original questions had encouraged Thomas to consider the wider ramifications of his poem, as a result of which he was able to teach me about what had inspired him to write so well. I also believe that I resolved the contradiction that led to his original feelings of being controlled. I gave him the room to be a person rather than just my pupil. I let him talk about something that interested him, rather than restricting our dialogue to my concerns. In doing so, I think I demonstrated the way in which the curricular and the human can be seen to touch each other in the continual ebb and flow of a dual unity. His interests had directed his writing, and now his writing, annotated by my responses, was touching his humanity, allowing him to talk about his interests in a different way and to take on the responsibility of communicating his enthusiasm to another human being.

After this conversation, the nature of our relationship changed once again. He was no longer distrustful of my motives (I have to assume that he would have said if he was), he felt able to question me about his academic work (it was as if he no longer felt threatened by my power as his educator), and I began to view him as a whole, rather than an aspect of a whole.

When, in a subsequent lesson, Thomas decided that the extension work I had planned was not what he wanted to do, my action was governed by a concern for him as a person in an educational environment, attempting to take some responsibility for his own learning. I asked him what it was that he wanted to do and he chose to write a poem. I believe that by giving him the choice I have shown an aspect of professional development: I no longer needed to feel in control completely; I delegated some of the educational responsibility to Thomas. Entwined within my professional development is Thomas' ability to choose to write a poem. I had given him the space to make a choice and he had responded in a way that seemed to me to exhibit a respect for me in having given him the space to take some responsibility. He might have chosen to do nothing, or he might have chosen to draw a picture, but he chose to write. This took me back to one of his comments in our first taped conversation, and reminded me of the impact that a caring educator can have upon a human learner:

Dawn: So tell me the sort of things you like doing in English, then, generally.

Thomas: Well . . . um . . . drawing and poem–writing. It was just drawing, but now it's poem–writing and drawing.

Conclusion and action plan

In the 1994–95 school year, Dawn Bellamy is a newly qualified teacher at Wootton Bassett School in Swindon, England. She intends to register for an advanced program of action enquiry at the University of Bath during 1995. My hope is that we will continue to work together to extend our views on the nature of educational theory and its value in helping to improve the quality of learning.

I began to tutor a new cohort of students in September 1994. As last year, I am tutoring thirty-four students in two groups for the educational and professional studies component of their PGCE course. One of my failings in last year's course was my lack of insight and emphasis on the creation of a sense of an educative community with my students, of the kind so described by a group of twenty-two of Tom Russell's students at the University of Waterloo, who were also registered for the teacher education program at Queen's University. They have compiled a document of teaching experiences and classroom practices, in a spirit of group-sharing and reflection, and they called their text, *The Experience Book. . . . The Roots of our Ever-branching Tree* (Russell, 1994b). To help me to improve the quality of my work, I have accepted Ruth Hubbard's (1994) invitation to explore the concept of community with the contributors of *Teacher Research — The Journal of Classroom Inquiry* to enter into the dialogue on how my enquiry is changing and evolving as I work with others in and out of schools.

I have tried to show here the value of action research in constructing an individual's educational theory in the descriptions and explanations of reflective teachers and teacher educators with their students and their pupils. In emphasizing the importance of teachers, teacher educators and pupils speaking in their own voices, whilst acknowledging the influence of the ideas of others, I have tried to show how a teacher educator might answer a question of the kind, 'What evidence do you have that you have influenced a teacher's education and that this influence is being expressed in the educational development of a pupil?'

As is often the case, I begin an enquiry with a question of the kind, 'How do I help my students to improve the quality of their learning?' only to find that my students have helped *me* to improve the quality of *my* leaning. I am grateful to

Moira Laidlaw (1994) and Erica Holley (1993) for bringing the significance of educative relationships to the forefront of my enquiry. I am indebted to Terri Austin (1994) for drawing my attention to the ways in which the Alaskan Teacher Research Network celebrate and sustain their sense of being an educative community that can welcome and embrace pupils, parents and others from the wider community. They have inspired me to seek to make a greater contribution to educational communities by joining with others in researching and creating educational knowledge as part of the process of improving the quality of learning of the next generation. Part of this endeavour is a request to the readers of this chapter to see if the above ideas have value for your own professional lives and commitments. Are these ideas of any value in helping you to research your own practice as you work at helping your students, community and society to improve the quality of their learning, as well as your own?

References

ALTRICHTER, H. *et al.* (1990) 'Defining, confining or refining action research?', in ZUBER-SKERRITT, O. (Ed) *Action Research for Change and Development*, Brisbane, Griffith University Press, pp. 13–20.

AUSTIN, T. (1994) 'I'm only in Wasilla', in WESSEL, K. (Ed) *The Far Vision, The Close Vision — A Collection of Writings by Alaska Teacher Researchers*, Fairbanks, University of Alaska.

BELLAMY, D. (1994) *How Can I Help Thomas to Increase His Flexibility as a Learner So That He Shows The Same Assuredness In His Writing As In His Speaking?*, University of Bath, England, Action Research in Educational Theory Research Group.

CARR, W. and KEMMIS, S. (1986) *Becoming Critical: Knowing through Action Research*, Geelong, Deakin University Press.

CLARKE, J. *et al.* (1993) 'Ways of presenting and critiquing action research reports', with CLARKE, J., DUDLEY, P., EDWARDS, S., ROWLAND, S., RYAN, C. and WINTER, R., *Educational Action Research*, **1**, 3, pp. 488–489.

CONNELLY, M. and CLANDININ, D.J. (1988) *Teachers as Curriculum Planners: Narratives of Experience*, Toronto, OISE Press.

EISNER, E. (1993) 'Forms of understanding and the future of educational research', *Educational Researcher*, **22**, 7, pp. 5–11.

ELLIOTT, J. (1989) 'The professional learning of teachers', *Cambridge Journal of Education*, **19**, 1, pp. 81–101.

ELLIOTT, J. (1993) *Reconstructing Teacher Education*, London, Falmer Press.

FALS-BORDA, O. and RAHMAN, M.A. (1991) *Action and Knowledge*, New York, Apex Books.

FALS-BORDA, O. (1994) *Postmodernity and Social Responsibility: A View from the Third World*, keynote address to World Congress 3 on Action Learning, Action Research and Process Management, University of Bath, 6–9 July 1994.

FAY, B. (1977) 'How people change themselves: The relationship between critical theory and its audience', in SMYTH, J. (Ed) (1986) *Reflection-in-Action*, Geelong, Deakin University Press, pp. 55–92.

FENSTERMACHER, G. (1994, April) 'Why, When and How Professors of Education Should Be Teacher Educators', paper presented at the annual meeting of the American Educational Research Association, New Orleans.

FITZMAURICE, M. (1994) 'The junior certificate history course and the less able pupil', in McNIFF, J. and COLLINS, U. (Eds) *A New Approach to In-Career Development for Teachers in Ireland*, Bournemouth, Hyde Publications, pp. 69–76.

GUILFOYLE, K. (1994, April) 'Finding Out More Than I Wanted To Know: Using Teacher Research and Critical Pedagogy in Teacher Education', paper presented at the annual meeting of the American Educational Research Association, New Orleans.

HAMILTON, M.L. (1994, April) 'A Teaching Odyssey: Sailing to the Straits of Teaching through the Gales of Academia', paper presented at the annual meeting of the American Educational Research Association, New Orleans.

HENRY, C. (1992, July) 'The Human Face of Critical Social Science: Orlando Fals-Borda and the Praxis of Participatory Action Research', paper presented at the Second World Congress on Action Learning, Action Research and Process Management, University of Queensland, Brisbane.

HERRMANN, B.A. (1994) 'Building professional contexts for learning for preservice and inservice teachers and teacher educators', in LAIDLAW, M., LOMAX, P. and WHITEHEAD, J. (Eds) *Proceedings of World Congress 3 on Action Learning, Action Research and Process Management*, University of Bath, England, pp. 82–85.

HOLLEY, E. (1993) 'I can speak for myself', in WHITEHEAD, J. (1993) *The Growth of Educational Knowledge: Collected Papers*, Bournemouth, Hyde Publications, pp. 141–145.

HOLLINGSWORTH, S. (1994) 'Feminist pedagogy in the research class: An example of teacher research', *Educational Action Research*, **2**, 1, pp. 49–70.

HUBBARD, R.S. (1994) 'Note from the editors in teacher research', *The Journal of Classroom Inquiry*, **1**, 2, pp. iii–v.

HUBBARD, R.S. and POWER, B.M. (1993) *The Art of Classroom Inquiry: A Handbook for Teacher Researchers*, Portsmouth, NH, Heinemann.

KEMMIS, S. (1993) 'Foucault, Habermas and evaluation', *Curriculum Studies*, **1**, 1, pp. 35–54.

KOREN, B. (1994) '"A concept of a body knowledge" and an evolving model of a movement experience: Implications and application for curriculum and teacher education', *American Journal of Dance Therapy*, **16**, 1, pp. 21–48.

LAIDLAW, M. (1993) Chapter 15 in WHITEHEAD, J. *The Growth of Educational Knowledge: Collected Papers*, Bournemouth, England, Hyde Publications, pp. 149–164.

LAIDLAW, M. (1994) 'The democratizing potential of dialogical focus in an action enquiry', *Educational Action Research*, **2**, 2, pp. 223–241.

LOMAX, P. (1994) 'Standards, criteria and the problematic of action research within an award bearing course', *Educational Action Research*, **2**, 1, pp. 113–126.

MAGUIRE, P. (1987) 'Participatory Action Research: A Feminist Perspective', unpublished manuscript, School of Education, University of Massachusetts.

MAGUIRE, P. (1993) 'Challenges, contradictions, and celebrations: Attempting participatory research as a doctoral student', in PARK, P. (Ed) *Voices of Change: Participatory Research in the United States and Canada*, Wesport, Connecticut, Bergin and Garvey.

McNIFF, J. (1991) *Action Research: Principles and Practice*, Routledge, London.

McNIFF, J. and COLLINS, U. (Eds) (1994) *A New Approach to In-Career Development for Teachers in Ireland*, Bournemouth, Hyde Publications.

McNIFF, J., WHITEHEAD, J. and LAIDLAW, M. (1992) *Creating a Good Social Order Through Action Research*, Bournemouth, Hyde Publications.

McTAGGART, R. (1992) 'Reductionism and action research: Technology versus convivial forms of life', in BRUCE, S. and RUSSELL, A.L. (Eds) *Transforming Tomorrow Today*, Brisbane, Action Learning, Action Research and Process Management Incorporated, pp. 47–61.

MUNBY, H. and RUSSELL, T. (1994) 'The authority of experience in learning to teach: Messages from a physics methods class', *Journal of Teacher Education*, **45**, pp. 86–95.

NEWBY, M. (1994) 'Towards a Secular Concept of Spiritual Maturity', unpublished manuscript, Kingston University, England.

NOFFKE, S. (1994) 'Action research: Towards the next generation', *Educational Action Research*, **2**, 1, pp. 9–22.

PINNEGAR, S. (1994, April) 'Negotiating Balance Between Context, Colleagues, Students, Families and Institutions: Responding to Lived Experience in the Second Year', paper presented at the annual meeting of the American Educational Research Association, New Orleans.

PLACIER, P. (1994, April) 'An Action Research Approach to a Contradiction in Teaching: Reconciling Grades with Democratic Education', paper presented at the annual meeting of the American Educational Research Association, New Orleans.

RICHERT, A. (1994, April) 'A Naming and A Voice in Learning to Teach', paper presented at the annual meeting of the American Educational Research Association, New Orleans.

RUSSELL, T. (1994a) 'Reconstructing educational theory from the authority of personal experience: How can I best help people learning to teach?', in LAIDLAW, M., LOMAX, P. and WHITEHEAD, J. (Eds) *Proceedings of World Congress 3 on Action Learning, Action Research and Process Management*, University of Bath, England, pp. 195–198.

RUSSELL, T. (1994b) Foreword to *The Experience Book. . . . The Roots of our Ever-Branching Tree*, Waterloo-Queen's Co-operative Science Education Program, Kingston, Ontario, Queen's University Faculty of Education.

RUSSELL, T. (1994c, April) 'Returning from the Field: Did Recent, Relevant and Successful Teaching Make a Difference?', paper presented at the annual meeting of the American Educational Research Association, New Orleans.

SHULMAN, L. (1992, April) 'Knowledge Integration and Application in Teacher Education: Development of Cognitive Flexibility in Complex Domains', address to the annual meeting of the American Educational Research Association, San Francisco.

SMYTH, J. (Ed) (1993) *A Socially Critical View of the Self-Managing School*, London, Falmer Press.

WEINER, G. (1989) 'Professional self-knowledge versus social justice: A critical analysis of the teacher–researcher movement', *British Educational Research Journal*, **15**, 1, pp. 41–52.

WHITEHEAD, J. (1985) 'The analysis of an individual's educational development', in SHIPMAN, M. (Ed) *Educational Research: Principles, Policies and Practice*, London, Falmer Press.

WHITEHEAD, J. (1989) 'Creating a living educational theory from questions of the kind, "How do I improve my practice?"', *Cambridge Journal of Education*, **19**, 1, pp. 41–52.

WHITEHEAD, J. (1991) 'How do I improve my professional practice as an academic and educational manager?' in COLLINS, C. and CHIPPENDALE, P. (Eds) *Proceedings of the First World Congress on Action Learning, Action Research and Process Management, Vol, 1*, Australia, Acorn Press.

WHITEHEAD, J. (1993) *The Growth of Educational Knowledge: Collected Papers*, Bournemouth, Hyde Publications.

WHITEHEAD, J. (1994, April) 'How Teacher Researchers are Creating a New Form of Educational Knowledge', paper presented at the annual meeting of the American Educational Research Association, New Orleans.

ZUBER-SKERRITT, O. (1991) *Professional Development in Higher Education: A Theoretical Framework for Action Research*, Brisbane, Griffith University.

8   Methods and Issues in a Life History Approach to Self-Study

Ardra L. Cole and J. Gary Knowles

The purposes of this chapter are to present methods and a rationale for a life history approach to self-study of teacher education practice, and to discuss issues in self-study and life history research that have arisen from our work. There is considerable value in turning the research camera inward to better understand some of the life and career history influences we bring to our professional practices, and how these influences intersect and interact with contemporary institutional and societal realities. We lay out a framework for self-study work grounded in a life history perspective, and we present reflective accounts that illustrate the place and influences of our own personal histories on our thinking and research. We consider how teacher educators might study their own practices, as individuals and in tandem with others, and how they might engage in a broader program of self-study. Because there is the potential for considerable tension within the thinking and actions of individuals when they study their own practices, especially in relation to others, we raise for discussion a number of technical, procedural, ethical, political, and educational issues and questions associated with self-study and life history inquiry.

A self-study framework

Our approach to self-study is grounded in experience. Our self-study framework is similar to the one we advocate for pre-service teachers and experienced practitioners. It is based on certain assumptions about professional practice and professional development. First, we believe that becoming a teacher or teacher educator is a lifelong process of continuing growth rooted in the personal. Who we are and come to be as teachers and teacher educators is a reflection of a complex, ongoing process of interaction and interpretation of factors, conditions, opportunities, relationships, and events that take place throughout our lives in all realms of our existence — intellectual, physical, psychological, spiritual, political, and social. Making sense of prior and current life experiences in the context of the personal as it influences the professional is, in our view, the essence of facilitating professional development. Thus we situate professional inquiry in the context of life or personal histories. As Ardra said in a life history interview:

Teaching is part of who I am. Understanding teaching is my work. . . .
Knowing myself as person is very much part of knowing myself as professional. The better I understand myself as teacher and teacher educator, the
better I understand myself as person, and vice versa. . . . My whole practice
as teacher, professor, and teacher educator is integrally connected with who
I am as a person. (Interview, July 6, 1993)

Second, we believe that professional development is facilitated by opportunities for
ongoing critical reflection on and inquiry into the broad spectrum of experiences
that influence professional lives and careers. We, therefore, place emphasis on the
importance of being professionals who engage in critical analysis of practice with
attention to the multiple roles and contexts that comprise it.

In some respects our work has elements of a theoretical autobiography
(Middleton, 1993) or an auto-ethnography (Denzin, 1989, Diamond, 1992). It is
also informed by the collaborative autobiography work of Butt, Raymond, McCue,
and Yamagashi (1992), Clandinin and Connelly's (1994) work in the area of narrative
inquiry, and by the work of others such as Ayers (1989) and Smith (1994) who place
biographical inquiry at the centre of personal and professional understanding.

In our self-study program we seek to understand the multiple roles, contexts
and relationships that comprise our practices, and how the many facets of our
professional work relate to one another. We focus on our professional roles as
learners, teachers, researchers, writers, supervisors, colleagues, and faculty members.
We reflect on teacher education in general and on what it means to be a teacher
educator, both within the institutions with which we are affiliated and in the
broader teacher education and education communities. To explore aspects of our
practice, we keep professional journals, record some of our conversations and class
sessions, keep field notes on visits to each other's classrooms and work settings, and
record discussions on collaborative teaching ventures. We engage in dialogue via
postal service and electronic mail, follow student evaluations of our teaching and
coursework, and even solicit written or audio-tape recorded commentaries by support staff with whom we work. More recently we have each worked with other
life history researchers who facilitated our self-study through life history interviews,
classroom observations, and discussions of our practice. With these perspectives and
rationales in our thinking, we engage in self-study activities grounded in a life
history framework. Given that much of our individual and collaborative research
activities employ life history methods (e.g., Cole and Knowles, 1995; Goodson
and Cole, 1994; Knowles, 1988, 1991, 1992, 1994; Knowles and Cole, with
Presswood, 1994), the transition from life history studies of others, to life history
studies of self was not difficult, and the boundary between the two is blurry indeed.
It is in this regard that our work resembles a theoretical autobiography or an auto-
ethnography.

We have presented outcomes of our ongoing quest for professional self-
development and reflection on our own practice — analyzing and representing, in
various forms, elements of that practice — in publications, paper presentations,
formal and informal seminars and discussions, and collaborative research group

meetings. Our research program has proven to be personally and professionally rewarding, and continues to challenge us and extend the boundaries of our thinking about our individual practices and the contexts in which we work, and about teaching, researching, and teacher education more generally.

Examples and methods of self-study

Gary's autobiographical narrative

We begin with an account developed by Gary to elucidate connections between his personal and professional life, much as he has advocated pre-service teachers do as they explore their assumptions about being teachers (see, Knowles and Holt-Reynolds, 1991; Knowles, 1993; Knowles and Cole, with Presswood, 1994). This account is an example of a focused autobiographical narrative created through a reconstruction based on a particular set of critical incidents in Gary's career life. Shaped into an autobiographical or personal history account, these remembrances become a research text (Clandinin and Connelly, 1994) that illustrates how his fundamental assumptions and positions are represented in and grew out of some very disparate experiences.

> The journey to my present profession and location began in New Zealand, where I grew up. As a young architecture professional I was asked to help design a new school. The project architect was content to follow the design briefs as negotiated by the school's administrators. I was alone in noting the absence in the design brief of teachers' and students' voices and the inattention to the intimate connections between pedagogy and design. Against the recommendations of project colleagues I immersed myself in the life of a school; I tried to uncover the essence of teaching and the crucial ingredients of empowering school design representative of progressive pedagogies. Thus began an excursion into places of learning. I cautiously explored lives in context. Without being able to name what I was doing, and as undeveloped as my activities were, I now recognize my work in the school as participant observation and life history exploration.
>
> I tried to uncover connections between lives as lived and spaces as constructed. I observed teachers and children at work and engaged them in conversations. I explored teachers' career histories and pedagogical practices, trying to disclose their experiences of school spaces; I inquired into children's experiences of space and form, their sense of place and space within the structure of the school. The outcome of this engaging work, however, was less than satisfying. Insights into the needs of teachers and students, and my voice, were eventually buried on the drawing board by layers of design sketches and opposing perspectives of more senior, authoritarian colleagues. The project was completed, my input was minimal, but I maintained a special interest in education.

Several years later, disillusioned with the prospects of autonomy in the field of architecture, I determined to become an educator. After graduating from a baccalaureate degree teacher preparation program in Australia, I became a classroom teacher and principal in public, quasi-public, and private schools in Australia, New Zealand, Fiji, Papua New Guinea, and other South Pacific islands, before moving to the United States of America. In these various multi-cultural educational settings — from a small, suburban community school, to large, urban, single-sex schools, to a rural, alternative, residential, self-supporting school — my teaching rested on principles of experiential learning and notions about the value of alternative education and pedagogies. The work of Goodman (1964), Illich (1970), and Holt (1969, 1976), for example, influenced my thinking because they too challenged the status quo in schools. More powerful for its lasting impact was the work of my compatriot, Sylvia Ashton-Warner. Her autobiographical account, *Teacher* (1963), presented her pedagogy in the context of her life and the lives of her students, experiences of teaching Maori children to read and write. Cognizant of the considerable inconsistencies and incongruities some observers have associated with Ashton-Warners' life and teaching (see, Hood, 1988, 1990), I nevertheless discovered a level of authenticity not often found in teaching texts. Yet, like many teachers, my practices were grounded in personal experiences and I lacked a philosophical framework to locate those practices. At this time, as a mentor to prospective teachers working in my classrooms and schools, I first thought of myself as a teacher educator.

Seeing myself as a teacher educator brought an awareness of the need to highlight and formulate the unique elements of my pedagogy. I became intent on articulating the rationales for my practice as a geographer, as a social studies teacher, as a teacher of architectural drawing and other subject matter. More than anything, as I tested the assumptions on which my work rested, I tried to ameliorate the conflicting perspectives in my teaching. Sometimes this resulted in clear directions for furthering my work. Other times, I was unable to distinguish the differences between the fine details associated with conflicting pedagogical assumptions.

Later, when developing an experiential, international education program in Papua New Guinea, regularly teaching in remote and mountain jungle villages, I worked closely with anthropologists who reinforced and enhanced my earlier experiential groundings in ethnographic research methods. Then, wanting to extend my philosophical understandings of experiential and alternative education, I moved to the USA eleven years after becoming a teacher. Initiating the move from teacher of cultural and physical geography through fieldwork in Papua New Guinea to graduate student in the USA was very difficult. The programs I first entered in the USA did not meet my heartfelt needs or long-term intellectual goals, although they did help ground my perspectives.

Eventually, after some floundering around trying to locate an intellectual home in which to fit, I entered the doctoral program in cultural foundations of education at the University of Utah. Beginning at this point, and continuing for some time, were three interlocking experiences, each of which become background or foreground depending on various rather oblique circumstances. One was directly related to my teaching work at the university, another to obligatory coursework in positivistic research orientations and methods, and the third to prior and emerging interests in 'home education'.

Early in my university work I became heavily involved as a pre-service teacher educator and found that my pedagogical perspectives, while valued, were imbedded in vastly different life experiences than those of my colleagues. My orientations, while compatible with some of the faculty, were nevertheless grounded quite differently. Looking to make sense of my pedagogical perspectives, I came upon the notion that autobiographical writing might facilitate the exploration of my prior experiences in the context of present practices.

About the same time (1983), I became intrigued by the public following and mass media representations of a prominent Utah Supreme Court case in which the widow of a Mormon, polygamist home educator (John Singer, who was killed by the police) argued the right to home-educate her children. Living in a remote area of Fiji where there was no elementary school available I, too, had home-educated my children. The connection between my own experience and the issues represented in the Utah media caught my attention. On reading the scant research literature available, and advocacy writings, I recognized the dissonance between public and private conceptions of home-education and between parents' and researchers' rationales for home-educating.

My gut response to reading about home education was that an in-depth look at parents' lives in context might reveal something substantially different than the relatively superficial views represented in published survey studies. I engaged a group of parents in an exploration of their teaching practices in relation to their experiences of formal education, learning, and simply being members of families and neighbourhoods. Through extensive autobiographical/life history inquiry, I gained an in-depth understanding of home educators that pointed to much more than the superficial rationales for their practices that the media and survey research revealed. As I experientially learned more about life history research, the potential to understand home educators' rationales and pedagogies in relation to their lives became apparent.

While the interest in both my own pedagogy and the pedagogies of parent-educators was growing exponentially, I suffered from serious intellectual schizophrenia. Unable or unwilling — I am not quite sure — I did not reach into the recesses of prior experiences and revive the essence of the informal research activities in which I had participated. I regarded them as atheoretical. Nor did I question the foundations on which traditional educational research was grounded. In a sense I was paralyzed by the power of subtle and obvious suggestion and by socialization pressures and thus accepted and learned to understand and employ positivistic, statistical research methods. During this intense time my being cried out at the dissonance. My thinking was in disarray. I continued to deny that the dissonance and intellectual conflict were anything other than *my* failure to master the intricacies of mathematical and statistical frames of reference. These feelings came despite achieving high grades in coursework. Only after six advanced courses in statistics and survey research, and ultimately not feeling that these approaches vaguely felt like mine to employ, did I seriously consider that there were other frames, other lenses, to view the world of teaching and classrooms.

The turning point in my thinking came from reading survey research associated with home education. Not only was most of the research poorly conceptualized, but there was dissonance between the results and methods reported, and my own, much earlier, experiences in architecture and with anthropologists. Further, there was a level at which I found myself questioning the basis of the method and the value of the statistical devices. Perhaps it was simply because, for the first time, I read research reports that purported to examine something about which I could claim direct involvement and knowledge. All the other positivistic educational and sociological research I had read was beyond the realm of my experience and I was, at that time, intellectually unprepared to refute it.

After my initial work with parent-teachers, I located my developing understandings about the place of exploring lives in context within the principles of symbolic interactionism (Blumer, 1969). Life history theorists and researchers such as Plummer (1983), Bertaux (1981), and Denzin (1984), were influential because they philosophically and practically grounded the method. This new-found knowledge opened my eyes further to the possibilities of researching. Further, Goodson (1980–1, 1983) and Ball and Goodson (1984) showed the utility of life history research for understanding teachers' lives within historical, political, institutional, and social milieu.

As I neared completion of the initial life history study of parent-teachers, I developed a professional relationship with Bob Bullough that resulted in intense work with beginning teachers as, separately and together, we explored their professional development. Most of this work centred on new teachers' self identities as emerging professionals and drew on life history approaches. I also specifically explored elements of teachers' life histories in relation to their teaching strategies. These connections are increasingly made explicit in my teacher education pedagogy, one grounded in personal knowing and the foregrounding of pre-service teachers' personal history-based and contemporary experiences. In 1989, I completed my dissertation on beginning teachers' biographies and coping strategies. *Emerging as a Teacher* (Bullough, Knowles and Crow, 1991), which explores the experiences of several first year teachers, was completed soon after.

My researching and teaching go hand-in-glove. Since my appointment to The University of Michigan in 1989, I have continued to develop qualitative research skills and refine the focus of my work. While I continue to study home-educating parents, my energy is mostly directed to teacher education, especially issues of teacher development and socialization. This focus is reinforced by my teaching responsibilities; I have endeavoured to blend my teaching with my researching, just as I have worked to make meaningful the practice-theory link for prospective teachers. Life history research, therefore, has played a major part in my own professional development and its growth in my work was not happenstance but a direct result of some powerful experiences. But, more than that, there is a degree of resonance between my learned world view and sense-making, and the interpretive paradigm broadly conceived — there is a kind of 'ring of truth' that sounds loudly in my mind's ear.

Gary's purpose in writing this chronological overview was to raise for awareness and further reflection some of the key personal history influences on his research epistemology. Issues relative to his developing pedagogy remain in the background in this account. He seeks to make clear the threads of continuity and congruity in his researching life. Gary's narrative, like all narratives, is a reconstruction that reflects contextual, personal, and temporal biases, producing one of many reconstructive possibilities. There are many other ways he could have represented the relationship between his past experiences and his present research practices. In preparing this public account, however, Gary made decisions about the form and the focus that are at once both educational and political. Despite such considerations of the potential usefulness of the form of the account for others and the kinds of interpretations others may make from it, the primary value of the personal, reflective representation rests in the private domain. Both the writing of the account and the account itself have helped Gary address issues of his professional practice and amplify his quest for congruity within those practices.

Ardra's self-study analysis

Ardra's account represents a different life history approach to self-study. Her research text was created through analysis of information gathered in a life history study of her practice conducted in collaboration with another researcher. The research activities spanned a period of one year, during which time she participated in a series of life history interviews and reflective conversations based on observations of her teaching and other activities associated with being a professor, and engaged in autobiographical writing about her practice. This is one example of the kind of analysis she has brought to bear on her professional practice as a result of extensive and systematic record-keeping and information-gathering. In the following account, Ardra uses excerpts from some of the life history interviews and reflective conversations following classroom observations, as well as journal entries, to show how the theme of *responsibility*, a value rooted in her personal history, plays out in aspects of her teaching and research practice, and in her overall commitment to professional work.

The first excerpts from transcriptions of the life history interviews give a sense of the meaning I give to responsibility in research.

I talk a lot in the doctoral level qualitative research methods class that I teach about the critical role of experience in understanding oneself as researcher. As a researcher, I think you need to experience and think about what it means to do what you are asking research participants to do. It is one thing for me, as teacher, to talk about that, however, and quite another to do it. So, today in class, placing myself in a position of 'the other', in an authentic way, was important. I talked about my experiences of being 'the researched', in the life history project, and, in so doing, I believe I was able to communicate, in a very real way, some of the issues associated with researching the personal that we as researchers need to attend to. . . .

The issue of confidentiality when having interviews transcribed is an important issue, for example. From my perspective as 'the researched', I had the unusual advantage of choosing whom I might invite to do the transcribing. We don't often think about how the identity of individuals might or might not be revealed to those who are transcribing. . . . How much time do we really spend thinking about the information once it leaves our hands? We take care to look at things such as maintaining anonymity by using pseudonyms in the written text but, if we do not do the transcribing ourselves, how much care do we take when we employ others to do that work for us? (Interview, November 2, 1993)

Excerpts from an earlier discussion of research issues further elucidate the value I place on the researcher's responsibility in research. These excerpts allude to connections between my sense of professional responsibility as a researcher and the theme of responsibility as rooted in my personal history.

Knowing how to handle appropriately issues of self-disclosure is an on-going challenge for the researcher. This kind of interviewing, as in life history conversations, is a significant departure from some of the more traditional interviewing roles a researcher might play. Clearly, with this kind of personal research that intrudes into people's lives, the challenge and responsibility for the researcher is great.

As researchers, it is really important to be aware of how we represent people's lives. I seem to have a penchant for heightened responsibility in research. There are really strong connections between being responsible to others in our daily lives and being responsible to those whom we research. . . . Because of different experiences, expectations, and responsibilities that we have felt throughout our lives, we bring that value of responsibility, and of feeling responsible, to our professional work — in this case, research. Being responsible is a value I have developed throughout my life but I am very aware of bringing that value to my work as a researcher. I feel very passionate about it. (Interview, July 6, 1993)

The connections I alluded to in the previous excerpt were repeatedly evidenced in my life history interviews. To make explicit the roots of my 'penchant for responsibility', I present excerpts from several life history interviews.

I was born in December. My mother always said that I was her 'Christmas present' — more than she could have hoped for. All her life she had wanted to have a baby girl and she finally had me — at a time when she thought she wouldn't have any more children. To deserve the special status assigned to me by my mother was a great responsibility. (Interview, May 27, 1993)

I always accepted the fact that assuming responsibility for others was very important, and I assumed a lot of responsibility — sometimes, perhaps more than I even care to think about. That feeling of responsibility interfered with my making some decisions and, certainly, interfered with the decision-making process. I spent, and still do spend, a lot of time feeling responsible to others when perhaps I should not. As a child, always feeling this tremendous sense of responsibility was a burden although it was also an expression of commitment, and love, and caring, and so on. I don't regret in any way the kinds of responsibility I assumed and carried out with respect to my family. I am very pleased and proud of the level of responsibility that I assumed and the kinds of things that I did but I am very, very aware of the influence that value, or quality, has had on my character, on my life.

On the one hand, although much of what I have done in my life has been my own thing, I wonder, sometimes, that if I did not have this very strong sense of responsibility, if my own thing would have been much different. Whatever I did I kept on a path that was acceptably defined. I am happy with the decisions I made, though, and I think they are a reflection, in some way, of the responsibilities I have always felt toward others in my life. (Interview, July 6, 1993)

This tension between duty to self and duty to others, that has been so prevalent in my personal life, plays out as well in my professional life. The following journal entry and segment of a subsequent discussion are illustrative.

I am frustrated, shocked, angry, disappointed and, I think, hurt. Towards the end of class today, a few of the students raised concerns about their being able to complete their final assignment to *my* satisfaction when I am not going to be here. They said they wanted me around 'in case they need me'. 'Who will we go to if we have a problem?' they asked, reminding me that my study leave would begin before their assignments were due. 'Who would you go to any other time?', 'Who have been your resources and support all term?', I asked, as I surveyed the twenty-five others in the room who have acted in that capacity since the beginning of the year.

I don't know if my disappointment was over their interpretation of the assignment, or their response to my going on study leave — maybe both. The implication that the assignment they were doing was merely another academic exercise completed for a professor — for me, not them — for purposes of satisfying a course requirement, rather than the more meaningful and personally relevant exercise I had tried to define it as, makes me think that I haven't been able to successfully communicate my perspective to some. 'This is for *you*, an opportunity for you to articulate and make sense of *your* understandings about qualitative research. You have to see the assignment as part of *your* thesis process. It has to be worthwhile and meaningful to *you*' has been my chant for ten weeks now.

Was I, and am I, so upset because some obviously missed my point? Or, are my feelings in response to their expressed attitude toward my going on study leave? Is this a gender issue? Would they respond similarly to a male faculty member, junior or senior? Would they expect one of my senior male colleagues to be around 'just in case'? Do they feel that I am abandoning them by leaving before they feel ready? Why am I reacting so strongly to this, especially when I know the concerns expressed are those of a very small minority of the class members? (Journal, November 11, 1993)

In retrospect, it became clear that students thought that I was shirking my responsibilities to them, and that is what cut to the quick. . . . I am still very angry about it because I think that I probably give about 200 per cent and I saw their questioning of my availability while on study leave as a statement that I was not living up to expectations and responsibilities. It angered me and, of course, underlying anger there is always something else that I think, in this case, is hurt.

I was talking with a very influential woman in my life the other night about a personal matter that had upset me. Her response was, 'You have to get over this feeling of responsibility and being responsible for everyone. You have to be responsible for yourself. Connected with and exacerbated by that', she said, 'is the fact that you are so easily hurt'. I think those two things were showing up in my response to the students' comment. It should have rolled off my back. (Interview, November 25, 1993)

The following statement is another example of how my personal history influences play out in my professional commitments.

I can recognize now times when the amount of work I take on is just ridiculous. I always insist that I can do it and, 'Yes, I can', but now I am starting to think, 'At what cost?' Before, I never even thought about the cost. It was not as obvious to me. I recognize it as the continuation of a pattern I established even as a young child. I always took on so much, so much, so much. Finally, I would just reach a point where I would be in tears and would say, 'What can I do? What can I do? I have to get this thing done. I said I was going to do it so I need to'. I would get through that situation and vow *never* to take on so much responsibility again but, then, I would do it again. It is a pattern. . . . I still do the same kinds of things. (Interview, June 7, 1993)

Life history explorations also allowed me to understand elements of my teaching. In the following segment, the tension of responsibility to self and others is evidenced again.

I spend a lot of time worrying about trying to balance, or trying to address, the tension between responding to individuals' expectations in a learning situation and abiding by my own values, beliefs, and principles. . . . To teach the way I believe I need to teach, and the way that I think is most meaningful and conducive to students' learning, is to challenge traditional ways of doing things. To do that is to invest a lot of time and effort and to take a lot of risk. There are costs associated with that. For many people, teaching is just something that you go and do because you have to. For me, it occupies a whole lot more of my time, and that is time that is taken away from other things that are perhaps valued more in the academic community. So my challenge is to try to integrate my work so that I am not investing a whole lot of time in something that I believe in very strongly but that places me at risk of not attending to other things that are considered by the academic community to be more important than teaching. (Interview, October 6, 1993)

In the final two segments I articulate another dilemma presented by my 'penchant for responsibility', this time in the context of my dual commitment to teaching and to self-study.

I see it as a responsibility to make an ongoing commitment to improvement of my teaching that means an ongoing commitment to sensitivity and responsiveness to the needs of learners. I think that requires me to be a learner as well. (Interview, November 25, 1993)

To be a learner means that I engage in research on my own teaching. People who are part of my teaching are not involved in my research as willing participants. They are involved as students and they have an understanding and expectation that the learning context that we have created together is a safe place for them. Once they become part of my research agenda, what is my responsibility toward them and the promised safety of that group and the confidentiality of what they say? Now, clearly, I am not going to share specifics about things that happen; however, what responsibility do I have as a teacher-researcher to students . . .? While they are the basis for the information that I gather, *they* are not involved in my research. They have not given me their informed consent to participate in *my* research. They are students, and does that then give me the right to draw on their contributions in the class even though it is with the express purpose of understanding my own teaching and my own practice? What kind of sensitivity do I have to have toward these people in the group? (Interview, October 20, 1993)

This analysis of Ardra's practice, though viewed within a life history context and therefore, we believe, more holistic and meaningful, still represents but fragments of experience interpreted through one of many possible lenses. Like Gary, Ardra could have used other themes or arrangements to illustrate links between elements of her personal history and professional practice. For example, from the many themes that emerged from an analysis of her life history data, she could have chosen to explore: the role of context in the teaching-learning enterprise, especially the importance of 'safe' learning contexts; the notion of independence as a life- and career-shaping influence; the personal history roots of questioning as a pedagogical tool (Knowles and Cole, 1994); the personal history basis for her pedagogical commitment to experiential learning; the place and value of story telling in her family history, and how that has influenced her epistemological stance on research methodology; or, the roots of feminism in her experiences of growing up in a matriarchal family. And she could have chosen other ways in which to represent these themes. For example, because autobiographical writing played such a significant role in the research, she could have written an autobiographical narrative similar to Gary's, or used illustrative stories of experience as a basis for interpretation and representation. She might have conducted a more detailed and focused analysis of instances of classroom or research practice to more distinctly elucidate the theme of responsibility. Also, she could have used other examples from the data that would have cast the representation in a slightly different light. We see this kind of work — the interpretation of practice within the context of one's life — as an ongoing autobiographical project.

The self-study of teacher educators' lives

We see a life history framework as appropriate for the study of teacher educators' lives and work. Life history approaches have a long and reputable history in the fields of psychology (Allport, 1942; Dollard, 1935; White, 1963), sociology (Bertaux, 1981; Denzin, 1989; Plummer, 1983), and anthropology (Langness, 1965; Watson and Watson-Franke, 1985) as a way of understanding life as lived in the present and influenced by personal, institutional and social histories. More recently, life history approaches have been adopted by educational researchers to study teachers' lives and careers, teaching, schooling, and curriculum (e.g., Ball and Goodson, 1985; Beynon, 1985; Casey, 1993; Goodson, 1980–1, 1988, 1991, 1992; Goodson and Cole, 1994; Knowles, 1992, 1993; Measor and Sykes, 1992; Smith, Dwyer, Prunty and Kleine, 1988; Woods, 1987). Middleton (1992, 1993), a feminist sociologist and teacher educator in New Zealand, has written autobiographical and life history accounts focusing on New Zealand feminist educators. Within those accounts, Middleton's personal history and emerging conceptions of education and teaching are a central lens through which she articulates several theses. Apart from Middleton's work (and our own) we are unaware of examples of research where life history approaches are the central vehicle for the examination of teacher educators' lives, let alone the lens for self-study.

The life history method is suited to gaining insights into the confusions, contradictions, and complexities of everyday life. It is particularly useful for locating critical incidents or epiphanies in lives, the points of profound change and influence (Denzin, 1989; Measor, 1985; Plummer, 1983). Gary's autobiographical narrative illustrates how the identification and interpretation of critical life incidents can provide insights into some of the complexities of professional practice. As Plummer

(1983) asserts, 'Life history research advocates, first and foremost, a concern with the phenomenal role of lived experience, with the ways in which members interpret their own lives and the world around them' (p. 67). Goodson (1980–1, 1988, 1991, 1992) argues for a life history approach to understanding teachers, teaching, and schooling: 'Studying teachers' lives will provide a valuable range of insights into the new moves to restructure and reform schooling [including teacher education] into new policy concerns and directives' (Goodson, 1992, p. 11). Thus we assert that the argument for studying teachers' lives and the contexts in which they work also applies to the study of teacher educators.

Ardra's account, presented earlier, was based on information gathered using three methods typical of life history research: extensive, in-depth interviews; observations within classroom and other institutional contexts; and examination of institutional and personal artifacts, documents, or autobiographical writing. Of primary importance in life history explorations are the meanings that people give to their experiences, and these meanings are central to understanding the place of social, cultural, historical, and political influences and constraints (Becker, 1986; Denzin, 1989). Through systematic contextual analysis it is possible to gain insights into individuals' lived experiences within contexts of personal and institutional histories. Uncovering the theme of responsibility as a narrative thread running through and connecting Ardra's personal and professional life histories provided such insight for her.

As Denzin (1989) claims, citing Reimann and Schutze (1987), the outcomes of life history research are likely to contain 'Theoretical generalizations . . . which may emphasize any of the following: 1) career models, 2) structural processes in the life course, 3) models of social worlds, 4) relational models of biography . . .'. (p. 56). Theoretical generalizations begin when teacher educators themselves begin to theorize about their lives. Gary's narrative text illustrates the beginnings of this process. We maintain, therefore, that the exploration of our own lives and the lives of others around us, in the context of institutional and societal influences, will provide important insights into elements of professional socialization and career development in academe. For teacher education and teacher educators, this is a potentially illuminating task.

Issues and questions: A framework for proceeding

Life history research, on one's own or another's practice, has a personal and intrusive nature that is wrought with potentially perplexing issues. We caution researchers to proceed with sensitivity and care, and to be mindful of the many issues and concerns inherent in self-study and life history work. As a vehicle to raise awareness of pertinent research issues we borrow from an organizing construct developed for an earlier publication (Cole and Knowles, 1993). In that article, 'Teacher Development Partnership Research: A Focus on Methods and Issues', we discussed issues arising from our research with teachers in: planning and preparation, information gathering, interpretation and representation, reporting and use. In considering issues associated with these phases we raised questions relating to technical, personnel (which we now prefer to call interpersonal), procedural, ethical, political, and educational concerns as a way to inform prospective collaborative research enterprise.

Throughout our self-study work, we have emphasized the power of relational knowing, the power of being involved in self-study with another or others; yet, there are many issues to be addressed in both tandem and solitary arrangements for self-study and life history research. The self-study process is similar to other kinds of research; there are similar phases in which to operate and processes in which to engage, and there are numerous issues to address. At each phase of the inquiry process — from planning to reporting — one meets difficult and sometimes perplexing issues that require attention so that the inquiry process can be mutually beneficial and collaborative, reflective of learning in relation.

We use a framework presented in the previously mentioned work as a mechanism to discuss some of the issues and questions related to self-study and life history inquiry. The framework is a four-by-five grid in which the four columns have the headings:

- Planning and preparation
- Information gathering
- Interpretation and representation
- Reporting and use

and the five rows have the headings:

- Technical issues
- Personnel and interpersonal issues
- Procedural issues
- Ethical issues
- Political issues
- Educational issues

We invite you to use the framework and to pose these and other questions *at each phase of the inquiry*. We define the issues broadly so that there may be considerable overlapping between them.

Technical issues

Technical issues present themselves at every phase of self-study research. They are essentially issues that revolve around the initial facilitation and ongoing continuance of the inquiry process. While technical issues may seem mundane or superficial when compared to other issues, they can substantially influence the manner and direction in which the research proceeds. Time and technology have been the main origins of technical issues we have faced in our own self-study work.

In life history and other forms of self-study work, information is usually gathered through various combinations of autobiographical writing, interviewing, observing, and collecting artifacts — all of which are time- and energy-consuming. Because technology (such as audio- and video-tape recorders, computers, facsimile equipment, and so on) sometimes impedes rather than facilitates progress, time and energy are often spent in unanticipated ways.

Given the work pressures and demands of academic institutions and the priority given to non-teaching responsibilities, the following questions are significant:

- How can we find time to engage in self-study?
- How much time is required for substantial and beneficial self-study inquiry?
- How can roles and responsibilities be adjusted to allow time for self-study as part of professional practice?
- If fiscal support is required for self-study and life history research, where will it be found? What are the available technological supports for facilitating self-study? And further,
- How can collaborative self-study work with others be facilitated?

Personnel and interpersonal issues

The satisfactory resolution of personnel and interpersonal issues associated with life history research are essential. We, along with other feminist researchers, place interpersonal relationships at the centre of the research process. So, too, with self-study work in relation. Mutual explorations of others' lives and career histories within societal and institutional contexts lay bare much that is usually hidden from view. This work is very personal and potentially revealing. Thus, there needs to be a strong relational foundation before even agreeing to proceed.

From our experiences in participating in collaborative self-study research, we have reaffirmed our beliefs about the importance of attending to the research relationship, and about the need for ongoing negotiation of both interpersonal elements of that relationship as well as elements that define how those involved conceptualize and carry out their roles and responsibilities in the study.

Researching is a dynamic process, and so too are the relationships that make up the collaborative inquiry process. Central in our thoughts about relationships within the research process are questions such as:

- Is the research relationship based on mutual respect, interests, intents and a potential for mutual benefit?
- How are responsibilities to be shared throughout the inquiry?
- How are differences in emphasis and expectations to be addressed?
- How are individual differences in professorial roles and responsibilities, rhythms, and patterns of work to be accommodated?
- How are the strengths of research partners identified and considered, and to what extent are they complementary?
- Are the research partners comfortable with the planned process and the responsibilities of relational self-study?

- Are others (such as secretarial staff) to be involved in the research process? How? Why?

Procedural issues

Procedural issues rest in the relationship of method to context, and emanate from decisions about how the research, including writing and reporting, is actually carried out. Among the many issues that have arisen for us during self-study and life history research are those concerning conceptualization of the work, project time frames, location of interviews, and the role and use of the audio- or video tape recorder. Attention to matters related to the manner in which the research proceeds — the inquiry framework and methods used, the time frame, the needs of all participants, the site of the research, and so on — is essential for mutually beneficial and satisfying research. Assuming that technical and personnel issues are resolved, for example, questions central to procedural issues include:

- How is the self-study work related to other personal research, scholarly foci, or agenda? What are the obvious and not so obvious links? Can potential links be formed?
- How, when, and where should the inquiry process proceed?
- What is the inquiry framework? What is the focus of inquiry?
- What methods of data collection and analysis are appropriate? How is information transformed (e.g., from audio-tape to printed text)?
- How might the inquiry process interfere with established routines? What allowances need to be made? For example, what steps need to be taken to enable an observer to be present during some professional activities such as teaching, advising, or committee work?
- And, as elements of the inquiry are completed, who has access to the information and ongoing analysis? Where are materials stored?
- How will (or even, should) the reporting process proceed? How are decisions about reporting made?

Ethical issues

We see research focused on people's lives as a moral act and, therefore, infused with ethical responsibilities. Self-study and life history research are potentially highly intrusive and involve making public disclosures of elements of personal and professional lives. Concerns range from making decisions about who is to transcribe tapes, to where and how information will be stored, to how anonymity and confidentiality will be respected, to how to respond to conflicting interpretations of data, and to whose voice is heard in the reported accounts. Issues related to access to and 'ownership' of data throughout and beyond the life of a study reflect myriad ethical as well as procedural, personnel and interpersonal, and political concerns. Some of the many ethical questions that need to be considered throughout are:

- How will confidentiality be assured prior to data analysis? In other words, for example, who will transcribe interview tapes? Who will have access to the research information?
- How can information be presented or reported in a way that does not place research participants at risk?
- What happens in the case of collaborative research when there are conflicting impressions and interpretations? Whose voice is heard? How are decisions to be made?

Political issues

Political issues, like ethical issues, are central to self-study and life history research. Within contexts that value product over process, and where the competitive nature of the academy militates against disclosure of other than 'best practices', analyses of practice within their institutional contexts can be risky business. Many times in our self-study work — in the process of self-disclosing certain information, or when reading transcripts and realizing anew the personal nature of what we had said, or when considering the implications of 'going public' with some of what we had articulated — we have stopped to think about some of the personal and professional ramifications associated with personal research. Many times we have deleted self-disclosing text. Negotiation of voice and representation of our lives present considerable challenges for both of us. Among the questions to be considered in relation to political issues are:

- Who will be the audience of the research?
- How will participation in this kind of inquiry be viewed by others in the university community? by members of public school communities?
- What potential impact might there be on the participant's role and status within the academic institution? within other education institutions? within the field in general?
- To what extent will peers view this work as valuable, as contributing to individual scholarship and to the collective scholarship of the institution and the field? Or, how will self-study work be articulated as research contributing to individual scholarship? And how will it be evaluated by peers in formal tenure and promotion application proceedings?

Educational issues

The main purpose of self-study research, and research in teacher education more broadly, is to inform and enhance teacher education and professional practice. Our view is that in-depth explorations of the teacher education professoriate have the potential to substantially contribute to the understanding and improvement of teacher education at individual, institutional, and more global levels. For individuals involved as participants, personal studies of professional practice are a form of reflective inquiry similar to the kind of reflective practice widely advocated for teachers. At a broader level, personal and contextualized studies of the teacher education professoriate provide much needed knowledge about who teacher educators are and how they carry out their professional lives within various institutional contexts. Such studies also provide insights into important elements of professional socialization and development in academe.

Some of the central questions regarding educational issues that need to be addressed are:

- How can the process and outcomes of self-study best serve the inquirers? students of teaching? the local institutional community? the profession of teacher educators? the field of teacher education?
- How can understandings from self-study illuminate the various conditions of the professoriate and of institutions? How can this work contribute to educational change and modification of the status quo?

We also ask a question that constantly lingers in the back of our minds:

- How can self-study, and therefore the ongoing improvement of practice, be institutionally and professionally validated as an integral part of our professional roles?

Self-study and professional development

We engage in self-study work because we believe in its inherent value as a form of professional development. We are not sufficiently naive, however, to think that everyone else in our institutions and in the broader academic community shares our enthusiasm and belief. While doing research *is* an expectation in our respective institutions, it is typically assumed that we do research as researchers, *not* participants. The merit structure of the university, especially research institutions, typically places greater value on researching and writing activities than on other kinds of professional work. The currency of academe is essentially based on a system of quantification — the number of publications, the amount of research money gained, the number of student enrolments, the number of students graduating, and the number of doctoral dissertation advisees and completions. The qualitative dimensions of university life and professional practice are given lesser value, it often appears, perhaps because they are so difficult to grasp cleanly. Issues related to the quality of teaching, quality of students' learning experiences, and quality of institutional life for faculty and students in general are not often given much overt attention. As we engage in studies of our own work and that of other untenured professors like us, we face certain dilemmas, some of which we have resolved, at least temporarily, and others which remain unresolved.

Whether doing this kind of work is a 'good' thing is an issue we have resolved. From a pedagogical standpoint, and based on our beliefs about the importance of understanding ourselves as persons and professionals in the contexts within which we live and work, there is no question that we need to continue to commit ourselves and our time to self-study work, which includes being part of others' research agenda. As a way of responding to institutional standards and expectations regarding our 'performance' we have turned our self-study work into a relatively successful and rewarding program of writing and publishing. What we do not know yet, however, is whether our currency of self-study has a sufficiently high exchange value. In other words, in the eyes of institutional evaluations and assessments, are the publications viewed by those who work with us as contributing to the institution and field? Is this work published in 'the best' journals? Do funding agencies have sufficient interest in the kind of work we do? How does it contribute to work within the local institutional context? Will it contribute to 'institutional recognition' for the employing body?

Life history, self-study, and the enhancement of teacher education

Our broad intent in this chapter is to extend elements of our ongoing conversation to other teacher educators who are interested in pursuing, or who already engage in, life history based self-study work. We think that teacher educators who engage in self-study through personal history explorations stand to benefit in the same ways that pre-service and experienced teachers benefit from reflexive inquiry on *their* practice. Ongoing reflexive examination of professional practice challenges thinking about teaching and teacher education, and raises awareness of curricula and pedagogical decision-making. Apart from advantages to daily professional practice, we see benefits that are much larger.

Reflexive inquiry facilitates understanding and articulation of the links between initial and formal teacher education and the career-long professional development of classroom teachers and university teacher educators. It also provides a vehicle for discussion of professional practice and the ongoing improvement of teacher education. With self-understanding, which is contextually defined within careers as well as institutional and societal milieu, comes an understanding of the teacher education professoriate. Thus an understanding of the backgrounds, experiences, attitudes, intellectual and praxis perspectives, knowledge, and career aspirations of those involved in teacher education, of ourselves in relation to others, as well as of individual and institutional commitments to teacher education, can provide insights into the future of teacher education.

Our focus on the future is not happenstance. We see a need for considerable reconceptualization of the goals of teacher education and the work of teacher educators, and we see life history reflexive inquiry as future-oriented. Understanding past experiences can provide valuable insights into current practice and future directions of teacher education. As individuals and as a collective of teacher educators, we may be better able to reform teacher education by better understanding our own positions and the paths we have taken to those positions.

References

ALLPORT, G.W. (1942) *The Use of Personal Documents in Psychological Science*, New York, Holt, Rinehart and Winston.

ASHTON-WARNER, S. (1963) *Teacher*, New York, Simon and Schuster.

AYERS, W. (1989) *The Good Preschool Teacher*, New York, Teachers College Press.

BALL, S.J. and GOODSON, I.F. (1984) 'Introduction: Defining the curriculum: Histories and ethnographies', in GOODSON, I.F. and BALL, S.J. (Eds) *Defining the Curriculum: Histories and Ethnographies*, London, Falmer Press, pp. 1–14.

BALL, S.J. and GOODSON, I.F. (Eds) (1985) *Teachers' Lives and Careers*, London, Falmer Press.

BECKER, H.S. (1986) *Doing Things Together: Selected Papers*, Evanston, Northwestern University Press.

BERTAUX, D. (Ed) (1981) *Biography and Society: The Life History Approach in the Social Sciences*, Beverly Hills, CA, Sage.

BEYNON, J. (1985) 'Institutional change and career histories in a comprehensive school', in BALL, S.J. and GOODSON, I.F. (Eds) *Teachers' Lives and Careers*, London, Falmer, pp. 158–179.

BLUMER, H. (1969) *Symbolic Interactionism: Perspective and Method*, Englewood Cliffs, NJ, Prentice Hall.

BULLOUGH, JR., R.V., KNOWLES, J.G. and CROW, N.A. (1991) *Emerging as a Teacher*, London, Routledge.

BUTT, R., RAYMOND, D., McCUE, G. and YAMAGASHI, L. (1992) 'Collaborative autobiography and the teacher's voice', in GOODSON, I.F. (Ed) *Studying Teachers' Lives*, London, Falmer Press, pp. 51–98.

CASEY, K. (1993) *I Answer With My Life*, New York, Teachers College Press.

CLANDININ, D.J. and CONNELLY, F.M. (1994) 'Personal experience methods', in DENZIN, N.K. and LINCOLN, Y.S. (Eds) *Handbook of Qualitative Research*, Thousand Oaks, CA, Sage, pp. 413–427.

COLE, A.L. and KNOWLES, J.G. (1993) 'Teacher development partnership research: A focus on methods and issues', *American Educational Research Journal*, **32**, 3, pp. 473–495.

COLE, A.L. and KNOWLES, J.G. (1995) 'Extending boundaries: Narratives on exchange', in JOSSELSON, R. and LIEBLICH, A. (Eds) 'The Narrative Study of Lives', **33**, pp. 205–51.

DENZIN, N. (1984) 'Interpreting the Biography and Society Life Project', *Biography and Society Newsletter*, **2**, pp. 5–10.

DENZIN, N. (1989) *Interpretive Biography*, Newbury Park, CA, Sage.

DIAMOND, C.T.P. (1992) 'Accounting for our accounts: Autoethnographic approaches to teacher voice and vision', *Curriculum Inquiry*, **22**, 1, pp. 67–81.

DOLLARD, J. (1935) *Criteria For the Life History*, New Haven, CN, Yale University Press.

GOODMAN, P. (1964) *Compulsory Mis-education*, New York, Horizon.

GOODSON, I.F. (1980–81) 'Life histories and the study of schooling', *Interchange*, **11**, 4, pp. 62–76.

GOODSON, I.F. (1983) 'The use of life histories in the study of teaching', in HAMMERSLEY, M. (Ed) *The Ethnography of Schooling*, Driffield, UK, Nafferton, pp. 27–53.

GOODSON, I.F. (1988) 'History, context, and qualitative methods in the study of curriculum', in GOODSON, I.F. (Ed) *The Meaning of Curriculum*, London, Falmer Press, pp. 121–150.

GOODSON, I.F. (1991) 'Teachers' lives in educational research', in GOODSON, I.F. and WALKER R. (Eds) *Biography, Identity and Schooling: Episodes in Educational Research*, London, Falmer Press, pp. 137–140.

GOODSON, I.F. (1992) *Studying Teachers' Lives*, London, Routledge.

GOODSON, I.F. and COLE, A.L. (1994) 'Exploring teachers' professional knowledge: Constructing identity and community', *Teacher Education Quarterly*, **21**, 1, pp. 85–105.

HOLT, J. (1969) *The Underachieving School*, New York, Dell.

HOLT, J. (1976) *Instead of Education: Ways to Help People Do Things Better*, New York, E.P. Dutton & Co.

HOOD, L. (1988) *Sylvia: The Biography of Sylvia Ashton-Warner*, Auckland, New Zealand, Penguin.

HOOD, L. (1990) *Who Is Sylvia?: The Diary of a Biography*, Dunedin, New Zealand, John McIndoe.

ILLICH, I. (1970) *Deschooling Society*, New York, Harper Colophon Books.

KNOWLES, J.G. (1988) 'A beginning English teacher's experience: Reflections on becoming a teacher', *Language Arts*, **65**, 7, pp. 702–712.

KNOWLES, J.G. (1991) 'Parents' rationales for operating home schools', *Journal of Contemporary Ethnography*, **20**, 2, pp. 203–230.

KNOWLES, J.G. (1992) 'Models for understanding preservice and beginning teachers' biographies: Illustrations from case studies', in GOODSON, I.F. (Ed) *Studying Teachers' Lives*, New York, Routledge, pp. 99–152.

KNOWLES, J.G. (1993) 'Life-history accounts as mirrors: A practical avenue for the conceptualization of reflection in teacher education', in CALDERHEAD, J. and GATES, P. (Eds) *Conceptualizing Reflection in Teacher Development*, London, Falmer Press, pp. 70–92.

KNOWLES, J.G. (1994) 'Metaphors as windows on a personal history: A beginning teacher's experience', *Teacher Education Quarterly*, **21**, 1, pp. 37–66.

KNOWLES, J.G. and COLE, A.L. (1994) 'Researching the "good life": Reflections on professorial practice', *The Professional Educator*, **17**, 1, pp. 49–60.

KNOWLES, J.G. and COLE, A.L., with PRESSWOOD, C. (1994) *Through Preservice Teachers' Eyes: Exploring Field Experiences Through Narrative and Inquiry*, New York, Merrill.

KNOWLES, J.G. and HOLT-REYNOLDS, D. (1991) 'Shaping pedagogies against personal histories in preservice teacher education', *Teachers College Record*, **93**, 1, pp. 87–113.

LANGNESS, L.L. (1965) *The Life History in Anthropological Science*, London, Holt, Rinehart and Winston.

MEASOR, L. (1985) 'Critical incidents in the classroom: Identities, choices, and careers', in BALL, S.J. and GOODSON, I.F. (Eds) *Teachers' Lives and Careers*, London, Falmer.

MEASOR, L. and SYKES, P. (1992) 'Visiting lives: Ethics and methodology in life history', in GOODSON, I.F. (Ed) *Studying Teachers' Lives*, London, Routledge, pp. 209–233.

MIDDLETON, S. (1992) 'Developing a radical pedagogy: Autobiography of a New Zealand sociologist of women's education', in GOODSON, I.F. (Ed) *Studying Teachers' Lives*, London, Falmer, pp. 18–50.

MIDDLETON, S. (1993) *Education Feminists: Life History and Pedagogy*, New York, Teachers College Press.

PLUMMER, K. (1983) *Documents of Life, an Introduction to the Problems and Literature of a Humanistic Method*, London, George Allen & Unwin.

REIMANN, G. and SCHUTZE, F. (1987) 'Some notes on a student research workshop on "Biographical Analysis, Interaction Analysis, and Analysis of Social Worlds"', *Biography and Society Newsletter*, **8**, pp. 54–70.

SMITH, L.M. (1994) 'Biographical method', in DENZIN, N.K. and LINCOLN, Y.S. (Eds) *Handbook of Qualitative Research*, Thousand Oaks, CA, Sage, pp. 286–305.

SMITH, L.M., DWYER, D.C., PRUNTY, J.J. and KLEINE, P.F. (1988) *Innovation and Change in Schooling: History, Politics, and Agency*, London, Falmer Press.

WATSON, L.C. and WATSON-FRANKE, M. (1985) *Interpreting Life Histories: An Anthropological Inquiry*, New Brunswick, NJ, Rutgers.

WHITE, R.W. (Ed) (1963) *The Study of Lives*, New York, Atherton Press.

WOODS, P. (1987) *Inside Schools*, London, Routledge.

Part 5

Broader Perspectives on Teacher Educators' Work

9 Themes, Processes and Trends in the Professional Development of Teacher Educators

Lya Kremer-Hayon and Ruth Zuzovsky

Introduction

This chapter explores themes, processes and trends in the professional development of teacher educators who are directly involved in the pedagogical preparation, guidance, and supervision of student teachers. Teacher educators in these categories often share two main characteristics: 1) they have a professional career that started with successful teaching of youngsters, and 2) they have no formal and specific preparation for their role as teacher educators.

The professional development of teachers has received much attention from international researchers and policy makers; many studies, reviews and books have been published on the topic (Huberman, 1989; Burden, 1990; Fessler and Christensen, 1992). However, only a small part of this literature looks at *teacher educators* (Diamond, 1988; Ducharme, 1993; Moore, Lalik and Potts, 1993). As university teachers who have recently started a new program for teacher educators, we set out to shed more light on the inner world of teacher educators' professional development. The scarcity of studies on teacher educators on the one hand, and their impact on teachers' professional development on the other, inspired us to carry out this study. The themes, processes and trends of teacher educators' professional development were derived from content analyses of interviews conducted with a group of teacher educators in Israel.

Theoretical framework

A review of the literature on the professional development of teachers yields two approaches: a life cycle or chronological approach and a mental/structural one. The life-cycle approach focuses on changes that occur along a time axis of age and experience. Teachers' careers are viewed as a sequence of periods or phases characterized by typical events, roles, concerns, and motivation. Moving from one phase to another along their career path, teachers accumulate experience and construct their professional knowledge and repertoire of professional behaviours and attitudes. The life-cycle approach is influenced by models of general development (Erickson, 1959; Super, 1957, 1981, 1985). Erickson offers a life-span model divided into eight developmental phases corresponding to conflicts and crises experienced by the individual. Super defines career as a combination and sequence of roles played in the course of one's lifetime. Role changes are described in relation to age and to general developmental patterns such as growth, exploration, establishment, maintenance, and decline. Building on these models, researchers in the life-cycle tradition have described typical phases in the professional life of a teacher. Although they may differ on the number of phases, those using life-cycle approach agree on the general sequence of development that includes entry and exploration, stabilization, diversification and stock-taking, a mid-career phase, and disengagement and exit (Watts, 1982; Burke, 1987; Fuller and Bown, 1975; Fuller, 1969; Cohen and Klink, 1989; Sikes, 1985; Adams, 1982; Fessler and Christensen, 1992; and Huberman, 1989).

The structural approach considers teachers' professional development, not from its observable, phenomenological aspects, but from an inner perspective. It focuses on mental changes and mental structures through which professionals perceive reality. Such changes are qualitative in nature; they involve simple to complex, global to differentiated, and sporadic to integrated cognitive structures. This pattern of development differs from the life-cycle phases by presenting a qualitative hierarchy rather than a chronological sequence. In order to differentiate between life-cycle and structural approaches, we use the term 'stages' to describe the latter and 'phases' to refer to the former.

Studies employing the life-cycle approach describe either significant periods in the teaching career — beginning with teaching, moving toward mentoring and higher (tertiary) education — or the transition from one period to another (Ducharme, 1993; Moore, Lalik and Potts, 1993). Studies employing the structural approach concentrate on cognitive changes such as conceptual level [CL], self-concept, principled reasoning [PR], modes of thinking, and ego structures (Reiman and Thies-Sprinthall, 1993). While some researchers in the structural tradition address cognitive elements (Piaget, 1963; Perry, 1970; Hunt, 1987; Harvey, Hunt and Schroder, 1961), others study broad, comprehensive structures (Loevinger and Wessler, 1970; Sprinthall and Thies-Sprinthall, 1983; Glassberg and Sprinthall, 1980).

Comprehensive models that fit into the structural framework and deal with structural changes in teachers' professional lives are offered by Weatherby (1981) and Diamond (1988). Weatherby describes the professional development of faculty roles, and identifies three main developmental shifts: from acting as agents of socialization, through being role models or interpreters of good teaching, to becoming partners with their students in a process of mutual growth. Diamond's model, like Weatherby's, sketches parallels between teachers' and students' professional growth. Using Kelly's (1955) personal construct theory, Diamond developed a stage-by-stage theory of teachers' professional development. He focuses on the distinctive qualitative differences in the construction, content, and mode of teaching and learning at various points in time along the career path, and clearly identifies with the structural approach: 'a progression from being concrete, undifferentiated, simple, structures of individuals to becoming more abstract differentiating, complex and interdependent collaborators' (p. 134). There follows a description of Diamond's five-phase model.

First is a *pre-conjectural stage*, when the teacher responds to students' low conceptual levels, viewing them as passive learners, and knowledge as a commodity that can be imprinted on docile minds. At this stage, teachers consciously build and clone their own theories. The next two stages are characterized by *dogmatism* and *decision-making*. During these stages, teachers tend to complete their advanced degrees, usually to enhance their promotion. They supervise practising teachers, conduct research, and adopt rigorous attitudes toward the 'knowledge base of teaching' at the expense of relevance. They tend to cherish top-down research findings that are offered to guide their student teachers' practice. Competency-based approaches are popular among educators at this stage. Another top-down way of justifying prescriptive teacher-education is to rely on the results of expert-novice research findings and to use them as a model of good teaching. The fourth stage is described as *inventive or conjectural*. At this stage, teachers are involved in supervising practising teachers who are studying for advanced degrees. At this stage, the students are perceived as theory constructors. Their education is meant to help them make their tacit theories more explicit and amenable to criticism and refutation. At this stage teachers play the role of partners or facilitators of the process of constructing their students' views. The last stage is termed *emancipatory*. Here the teachers act as *conversational scientists*, concerned with transforming education in consultation with teachers and students, the two forging collegial rather than vertical relationships (Diamond, 1988, p. 138). The teachers act as critical conduits, helping their students to evaluate their own meanings (*ibid.*, p. 139). This stage is also characterized by mutual learning, or synergy, of teachers and their student teachers. The latter are perceived as striving toward self-direction, assisted by teachers.

In light of such developmental models as Diamond's, the aim of this chapter is to identify the types of changes that reflect major structural changes during the professional careers of teacher educators. Being aware of Diamond's stages, but not captive to them, this chapter classifies narratives relating to the professional development of teacher educators in accordance with emergent themes, the processes through which these develop, and the trends that characterize these processes.

Rationale and participants

A review of literature on research methods guided us to interpretive modes of research and, within those, to interviews as appropriate tools for the purpose of our study (Erickson, 1986). Our rationale for selecting interpreted and analyzed interviews as the source of information rests on the hermeneutic approach that 'involves holistic and integrative interpretations that seek to understand the whole in light of its parts' (Moss, 1994, p. 7). This tool is intended to yield interpretations that reflect the original intent inherent in the analyzed content. Bruyn's (1966, p. 22) position that 'to understand the inner world of teachers, the researcher must approach it from the subject's perspective and view their culture just as the people he is studying view it', was an additional element of the rationale for using interviews as data sources. Narratives as a research tool for revealing personal meaning constituted a third element of the method employed in this study. Based on our own and others' experience, teacher narratives offer much promise for capturing life experience and development (Pinar, 1975; Connelly and Clandinin, 1990).

We interviewed eight teacher educators, all with prior experience as teachers. All eight are teaching courses on teaching methods and supervise student teachers in their practicum. Four of them have two or three years of experience and the other four have sixteen to twenty years of experience as teacher educators. Four prepare student teachers for teaching in elementary schools, and the remaining four prepare for teaching in secondary schools. Thus there are four pairs of teacher educators in our study: two novice-elementary, two experienced-elementary, two novice-secondary and two experienced-secondary. We included novice teacher educators with the expectation that these interviews would shed additional light on the first years of experience, which might have been 'washed out' from the memory of the experienced teacher educators. Moreover, this selection allows a comparison between novice and experienced teacher educators, and thus is likely to highlight the characteristics of both groups and to enrich what we learn about their professional development.

Procedure and data analysis

After a brief introduction in which the interviewees were informed about the study goals, the interviewer began by posing the following open-ended request: 'Please reflect and think aloud upon your professional development as a teacher educator'. The interviewees were encouraged to say whatever came to their minds, and their flow of talk was not interrupted. When they stopped, the interviewer went back to topics that needed more elaboration and asked for clarification by posing probing questions. Finally, the interviewees were asked whether they could detect any distinct developmental stages in the course of their careers. This question was posed only to the experienced teacher educators who had a time perspective and could reflect on their development in retrospect.

Following Marton's suggestion (1981), the data were analyzed from two perspectives, a first-order perspective that is more amenable to statistical analysis, and a second-order analysis that lends itself more to qualitative analysis (Powney and Watts, 1987). In employing the first-order perspective, as suggested by Marton, key concepts were derived from each unit of analysis. These data were then placed into broader classes of reference. The frequencies were transformed into percentages to allow for comparison between the two groups of teacher educators. The second-order perspective consisted of in-depth content analyses and interpretations, based on two questions:

1   How do teacher educators perceive the processes through which their professional knowledge develops?

2 What are the most apparent trends that characterize their professional development?

The interviews were transcribed verbatim and analyzed independently by two individuals who, after a short period of training in analyzing the qualitative data, reached 88 per cent agreement on the themes as well as on their classification into the broader groups of reference.

Themes of reference

Results are reported in the order of the data analysis, beginning with the first-order perspective that yields themes of reference. The first-order content analysis revealed the following themes: (1) Professional Knowledge; (2) Teaching Concerns and Dilemmas; (3) Ideological Concerns; (4) Confidence; (5) Personal Development. Not all the themes were discussed by both novice and experienced teacher educators. For instance, Ideological Concerns emerged only in the interviews with experienced teacher educators, and Self-Confidence emerged only in the interviews with the novices. Table 1 presents the distribution of themes for both groups of teacher educators as obtained through the qualitative data analysis. The specific content of each theme is discussed in the sections that follow.

Table 9.1: Themes in the references to professional development

Themes	Experienced	Novice
1 Professional Knowledge	45%	35%
2 Instructional Concerns and Dilemmas	30%	45%
3 Ideological Concerns	20%	0%
4 Confidence	0%	15%
5 Personal Development	5%	5%

Professional knowledge

Both novice and experienced teacher educators referred to professional knowledge. The novice teacher educators expressed some frustration resulting from not having the professional knowledge needed to fulfil their roles as teacher educators. They realized that their knowledge, which had served them well as teachers, was not sufficient for coping with the problems inherent in teacher education: 'Success in teaching does not necessarily predict success in educating teachers', said one interviewee, who went on to suggest that 'teacher educators need to have specific preparation including a period of internship'. Another interviewee's difficulty was expressed as follows:

I encounter problems which I did not anticipate. The university courses which I attended were too theoretical. I have some difficulties in translating theory into practice.

A third novice teacher educator said:

This is my second year as a teacher educator. Having had some experience as a co-operating teacher, I thought I was well prepared for the job. On the job, however, I realize that I do not have the necessary knowledge to cope with the problems I face.

Similar ideas were expressed by experienced interviewees:

I was very excited and flattered when I was offered the job, but at the same time full of anxiety as I had no specific preparation in the field of teacher education. My previous experience as a co-operating teacher was not sufficient. As a teacher educator I was expected to help students place their experiences in theoretical frameworks, make linkages between theory and practice, fill in gaps in pedagogical knowledge, create sequences, and suggest meanings based on sound rationales. How to do this was beyond my knowledge.

These references, made by both groups of teacher educators, may be summed up as a call for specific preparation of teacher educators for the role of educating teachers.

Instructional dilemmas and concerns

Instructional dilemmas and concerns constituted another group of themes that emerged in the references made by both groups of teacher educators. A characteristic dilemma of the novice pertains to the desired sequence of topics in the teaching and learning processes:

Is it more effective to start with discussions on theories and models of teaching and continue with field observations, or is it rather more effective to derive topics of discussion from observations of teaching? What is the optimal proportion of study between theory and practice?

I can use direct as well as indirect styles of supervision. I am aware of the advantages and disadvantages of both styles, and I certainly prefer the latter. My student teachers, however, prefer a direct style and express this preference in an assertive manner. Shall I stick to mine or to their preferences?

Experienced teacher educators appear to be concerned with ways of facilitating their students' learning and making it relevant to their practicum, as well as with difficulties in helping students make linkages between theory and practice: 'How can I help students in understanding the relevance of theories to their practice and help them apply their knowledge into practice', was a common concern expressed by experienced teacher educators. 'I would like to be exposed to models of supervision, but at the same time develop my own practical knowledge.'

Ideological concerns

It is not surprising that the novice teacher educators did not relate to ideology, probably because they were absorbed in the daily problems of 'here and now', which have more to do with survival in their new roles. The experienced teacher educators were concerned with issues that are beyond daily routines, and a major part of their relation to professional development focuses on ideology and on ethical and moral issues. The next quotations from interviews present several ideological concerns:

> I should like to know that teacher education does not remain on the level of teaching competence, that it deals with issues of ethical and moral behaviour, and humanistic values.
>
> There is today a tendency to be takers rather than givers. I try to have an influence on changing this tendency.
>
> Value education should be a major goal of teacher education, especially humanistic education in a computerized world. I thought I would change the world by preparing good teachers for the next generation. I had a vision of my own and expected to facilitate the development of a vision in my student teachers, but was disappointed when this did not happen. In retrospect I realize how foolish and unreal this expectation was. I wanted things to happen fast and I thought I failed when changes did not occur as fast as I expected them to. Now I know that I was a little unrealistic.

The ideological concerns of experienced teacher educators tend to be perceived in retrospect as unrealistic and sometimes result in disappointment and frustration.

Self-confidence

> I wish I could get some feedback on my teaching, so that I know if what I am doing is O.K. I feel like I am walking in the dark not knowing whether I am walking in the right direction.

These and similar references were made over and over again by the novice teacher educators. It is only natural that problems related to self-confidence would emerge in interviews with novice teacher educators. It is rather surprising, however, that the experienced teacher educators did not mention this topic at all. Lack of self-confidence may be viewed from two angles. In some cases it can be a disadvantage, because it may result in frustration; in other cases it can be an advantage as it may result in motivation to learn and grow professionally and thus overcome the uneasiness related to the lack of self-confidence.

Personal development

Along with the themes that emerged in the professional area, several aspects of development that transcend this area were apparent. One such aspect concerns the development of personal traits, especially in the field of human relations, and this was expressed mainly by the experienced interviewees:

> I became a better and more perceptive listener with family and friends.
> I often ask myself what each encounter with students contributed to me as a teacher and as a human being.
> My development as a teacher educator has been integrated into my whole being. My professional development is strongly related to my development as a person in general. These two aspects nurture each other.

The perception that professional and extra-professional development nurture each other in a mutual way is of special interest and is worthwhile of further investigation (see the chapter by Cole and Knowles in this collection).

These five themes of reference were obtained from the first-order analysis, which considered the question, 'What are the teacher educators' perceived themes that constitute their professional development?' We turn now to the results obtained from the second-order analysis, which are based on in-depth content analysis and interpretation (Marton, 1981), and which shed light on the question, 'How does the professional development of teacher educators occur and what trends does it follow?'

Results: Processes and trends in professional development

Processes

The first question in our second-order analysis was: 'How do teacher educators perceive processes through which their professional knowledge develops?' The responses to this question point to a general process as well as to more specific ones. Generally, the acquisition and construction of knowledge is viewed by teacher educators as a dynamic process fraught with difficulties, but also as satisfying. Their professional knowledge accumulates and develops in a continuous effort of coping with the problems that they encounter in interactions with student teachers. This process occurs in spiral cycles: each solved problem generates new ones, which call for additional solutions. The more experienced one becomes in this process, the more one recognizes subtle problems and gaps in knowledge, which in turn call for more sophisticated elaborations and solutions.

> I view my development as a dynamic system of vectors in motion, as a continuum of problems, difficulties and frustration, on the one hand, and as a search for solution and satisfaction on the other. My development moves in a cyclic process of problems and solutions; each difficulty which I overcame nurtured my maturity.
>
> Development is a dialectical process, it is a process of absorption from outside sources and an elaboration in the inside.

For one interviewee this was a difficult process of unfreezing former beliefs and attitudes:

> It shakes you, it takes you off your balance, but when you get your balance back, you are different, more mature, sometimes more confident and at other times more sceptical.

In addition to this general process, there are several more specific processes that constitute this acquisition and knowledge construction:

Trial and error constitutes one aspect of knowledge construction. Not having the necessary pedagogical knowledge regarding teacher education, the novices — and, in retrospect, the experienced teacher educators — express their urgent need to develop such knowledge. In their narratives they tell how they struggled to construct their own knowledge by employing a strategy of trial and error. This strategy, they claim, proved to be helpful in building their own personal and practical knowledge.

> By trial and error I put to test a variety of ways which I myself went through as a student teacher. Sometimes these ways work, and at other times they don't. I hope that by gaining more experience I can find a way out of this labyrinth.

The labyrinth metaphor suggests an interesting back-and-forth movement to finding one's way.

Intuition and past experience as students were also reported as constituting the process of acquiring professional knowledge.

> In facing difficulties, I tried to remember what my school and university teachers did, and I employed the same ways.

It happened that in cases with which I had no former experience, I acted on the spur of the moment. Later, when I reflected upon this situation, I could not explain to myself why I acted as I did. I was not aware of any thinking process that preceded my actions.

Introspection and reflection-in- and -on-action were described as processes of learning by looking deeper into situations, by thinking about and analyzing present and past experiences, and by in-depth analysis and evaluation of one's own growth.

Looking at my encounters with student teachers from the angle of an outside spectator provides me with some important feedback. I can play two roles at the same time: one is the role of an actor and the other is one of a spectator.

In retrospect I realize now that I was imprisoned in phraseology. Now I stay away from slogans and inquire into the meanings of the concepts I speak about; I test everything I study in view of my experience. This deepens my introspection and enriches my thinking and feelings.

Developmental Trends

Next we analyzed the developmental trends that could be identified in the narratives of our interviewees. Five trends were developed from the differences between novice and experienced teacher educators, as well as from the narratives of the latter group who looked at their professional development in retrospect.

Expansion: Moving from a narrow view of 'Here and Now' towards a broader view of 'Then and There' emerged as a clear developmental trend, starting with a focus on daily matters, such as classroom management, and moving towards ultimate educational goals. This shift in focus was well reflected in the interviews:

I have made big steps on the pathway which leads to professional knowledge of teacher education. This was a pathway fraught with difficulties. As a beginning teacher educator I focused on specific daily matters. Over time, the focus changed in the direction of more remote educational issues, such as educational policies and the quality of professionals' life. Now I perceive educational problems in a broader context, beyond specific situations.

While the 'here and now' matters pertain to concrete and narrow topics concerning knowledge, the 'then and there' relate more to the abstract and broad nature of knowledge. Another excerpt illustrates this same shift:

My knowledge developed from a rather narrow focus on preparing student teachers for daily classroom management and teaching towards a wider circle of interest that includes humanistic perspectives and values.

Diversification: From uniformity towards pluralism and from positivism towards relativism in the perception of professional knowledge. This trend was illustrated by a metaphor:

> I changed directions from walking in one well paved avenue towards searching for varying and new avenues.

The same shift was expressed in another way:

> In the course of time I realized that my supervision style was too structured and did not leave much space for student teachers' initiatives. I used to guide them towards one way of teaching. I know now how wrong I was.

A similar trend of diversification emerged in ways of coping with dilemmas. Experienced teacher educators welcome dilemmas and coping with them is viewed as a vehicle leading to professional development. Moreover, relating to dilemmas in a positive manner may also be viewed as an aspect of professional development.

> When encountering a dilemma I used to push it under the carpet and I tried to ignore it. I could not tolerate multiple avenues. Now dilemmas present me with a challenge to think, to inquire, and accept the idea that there is no single best way to go by.

A movement from disregarding or trying to avoid dilemmas toward an open and critical approach that tolerates and even welcomes educational dilemmas and ambiguities is clearly apparent.

Dependence-independence: In parallel, and looking in retrospect upon their own teaching, the experienced teacher educators described a change in focus that started with dependence upon models and developed into their own inquiries:

> In the beginning I needed structure and exact directions. Later on I started to find my own way, I looked in different directions, my perspective widened, I became an inquiring teacher educator, and my repertoire of supervision styles grew.
>
> The struggle with dilemmas and contradictions results in professional maturity. Now I welcome gaps in knowledge and contradictions between theory and practice. Such situations are an intellectual challenge for me.

From formalism towards practicality: The sources of knowledge used in problematic situations changed from *formal* and rather *rigid* to *practical* and *personal* types of knowledge. Two main sources of knowledge were noted in the narratives of the beginning teacher educators. Formal knowledge acquired in university courses and professional literature constituted one source. Intuition and reflexive inquiry constituted another. In both cases, the teacher educators developed their personal knowledge, built through a long series of reflections on practice. Characteristic of the novices' narratives were the following comments:

I cannot apply the knowledge I had been acquainted with in college, some of it is irrelevant to my work. I often rely on intuition.

The experienced teacher educators, having gone through the first stages of induction into their role, relied on their practice as a main source of knowledge.

If I find that theory does not help, I have the courage to disregard it. I keep testing my theory to find out where it helps and where it hinders, where it works and where it does not, and then I try to apply it into practice. As a beginner I fenced myself behind models of supervision which I tried to apply. In the course of time I became more sure of myself and dared to act according to my experience.

Another interviewee offered a similar view:

I rely on my practical knowledge which developed in the course of the years, based on a long series of trial and error. I became my own teacher, and I learnt from my student teachers, through them and through intuition.

From a task and rigid orientation towards a personal and flexible orientation: From a focus on supervision styles towards a focus on students' idiosyncrasies emerged as a change in the realm of instructional and supervisory concerns. This change was reported clearly by one novice teacher educator who said:

I spend much time on my own study of supervision techniques. I want to be sure that I am doing the right things.

The experienced teachers' narratives were different:

My thoughts focus now on students. I try to find out what their needs are, and plan their student teaching accordingly. I accept them as they are, and start from there. I encourage them to build upon their own experiences.

My main problem now is how to help student teachers become independent in their pedagogical thinking. I try to understand the reasons that underpin their actions, their inner world. I adapt my expectations to students' rhythms of development so as to understand their inner worlds and become a better listener to their inner voices and needs.

Discussion: Themes, processes and trends

Based on the results of the content analysis of interviews with novice and experienced teacher educators, the discussion of their professional development can be summarized under three broad headings: themes, processes and developmental trends. Although these are intrinsically intertwined, for purposes of in-depth analysis they are discussed separately. The data analysis and discussion are presented through the lenses of the chronological and constructivist frames of reference that make up our theoretical framework.

Themes that captured the attention of teacher educators

Professional knowledge, and its sources and ways in which it is generated and accumulated, emerged as the most dominant theme that captured the attention and concerns of both novice and experienced teacher educators. This is not entirely surprising considering that knowledge is a basic element that can guide supervision behaviours, and upon which teacher educators can rely. Moreover, knowledge constitutes an important element of professionalism; hence the feeling of lacking such knowledge easily leads to frustration and to reduced confidence in one's professional activities.

Most references to professional knowledge relate to the insufficient preparation of teacher educators to fulfil their new roles. This raises a significant question: Is there a knowledge base upon which specific programs for teacher education can be developed, and without which teacher educators cannot function on a professional level? If such a knowledge base does exist, why are teacher educators not acquainted with it? Have they been exposed to such knowledge without recognizing its relevance? Conversely, if such a knowledge base does not exist, should teacher educators be prepared not to expect it, as unfulfilled expectations may lead to frustration?

A related question was raised by Beyer (1987, p. 19): 'What knowledge is of most worth in teacher education?' While elaborating on this question he claimed that teacher education still relies on linear thinking, on instrumental reasons, and on technical rationality. This phenomenon has been noted in our study as more characteristic of the novice teacher educators. The reliance of novice teacher educators on structure and technical rationality that emerged in our data may well be understood in the context of the uncertainty that most beginners report. However, this is not the case with the experienced teacher educators we interviewed. These individuals viewed their professional knowledge as improvised, and as constructed in a 'bottom-up' manner. Their narratives reflect a relatively high level of reflection and professional maturity.

Another theme emerged only in the interviews of the more experienced teachers. Having coped with initial problems, and having a broader time perspective, these interviewees compared present with past encounters with student teachers. In doing so, they perceive a deterioration in value orientations of student teachers. They are disappointed, especially since they feel they can do little about it. Such disappointment is probably a common phenomenon that transcends the world of professionals. The feeling of experienced teacher educators that their vision failed to be actualized results in dissatisfaction.

The time element, inherent in reference made with regard to ideology by the experienced teacher educators, was related not only in comparing past with present value orientations, but also in trying to construct images of the ideal teacher for the future. The uncertainly resulting from having to prepare teachers for unknown future conditions is challenging but may also be frightening, especially considering the growing call for accountability in teacher education.

Processes of knowledge acquisition

Professional development is perceived as a slow, continuous and evolutionary process, its main constituent being professional knowledge. The perceived lack of professional knowledge essential for effective education of teachers resulted in the need to construct such knowledge. The processes through which teacher educators acquired their professional knowledge constituted a trial-and-error strategy in which individuals relied on their intuition. Trial and error and intuition appeared as a 'bottom-up' style of knowledge acquisition. The continuous search for better actions, the cycles of never-ending processes of problem solving, and the reflective investigation clearly point to an inquiry-oriented approach, to a style of knowledge acquisition characterized by the construction of personal and practical knowledge.

Developmental trends

The results, although not identical to the five stages suggested by Diamond (1988), point to several continua along which the professional development of teacher educators occurs. In most cases, the career of a teacher educator is preceded by some experience in teaching children. Having no specific formal preparation for teacher education, teacher educators begin with a period of exploration characterized by uncertainty and by focusing thought and activities on methods and styles of supervision. After gaining some confidence, they focus on their students. In this respect they are similar to all teachers (Fuller and Bown, 1975). This period of diversification also involves high expectations in the realm of values and ideology, followed by a more realistic look, sometimes with disappointment and discouragement, and at other times with an acceptance of reality.

References to the construction of professional knowledge yield clear differences between novice and experienced teacher educators. The novice seems to perceive professional knowledge as existing 'somewhere — out there' and expects to be exposed to it; this perception is in line with a technical rationality view. The experienced teacher educators see professional knowledge as self-constructed in a bottom-up manner. The general trend can be characterized as a development from technical rationality to reflection. We identified five broad continua on which teacher educators can place themselves.

- Expansion — from a 'here and now' concrete orientation toward a more abstract 'there and then'
- Diversification — from uniformity and dogmatism to pluralism and relativism
- From dependence on models toward independence and emancipation

- Formalism-Practicality — from formal to personal and practical use of sources of knowledge
- From focus on methods, technicalities and rigid styles of supervision towards a focus on students, values and flexible styles of supervision

These continua can be used as a tool for teacher educators' introspection and self-diagnosis regarding their development of professional knowledge. It may also serve educational policy makers and university professors in planning curricula for programs preparing teacher educators. Our findings can be summarized in the following way:

Teacher educators' professional development revolves around:

Themes of	in processes of	following trends of
Knowledge		Expansion
Dilemmas	Trial And Error	Diversification
Ideology	Intuition	Dependence-Independence
Self-Confidence	Reflection	Formalism-Practicality
Personal Development		Rigidity-Flexibility

Figure 9.1: A map of teacher educators' professional development

Do these themes, processes and trends apply to all teacher educators? Probably not. In order to arrive at any generalization and disclose commonalities and idiosyncrasies in teacher educators' professional development in various contexts and environments, further investigations are needed. We are grateful to the eight participants in our study for providing such rich data that have enabled us to better understand the professional development of teacher educators in Israel.

References

ADAMS, R. (1982) 'Teacher development: A look at changes in teachers' perception across time', *Journal of Teacher Education*, **23**, 4, pp. 40–43.

BEYER, L. (1987) 'What knowledge is of most worth in teacher education?' in SMYTH, J. (Ed) *Educating Teachers: Changing the Nature of Pedagogical Knowledge*, London, Falmer Press.

BRUYN, S. (1966) *The Human Perspective in Sociology: The Methodology of Participant Observation*, Englewood Cliffs, NJ, Prentice-Hall.

BURDEN, P.L. (1990) 'Teacher development', in HOUSTON, R. (Ed) *Handbook of Research on Teacher Education*, London, Macmillan, pp. 311–328.

BURKE, P.Y. (1987) *Teacher Development: Induction, Renewal and Redirection*, London, Falmer Press.

COHEN, M.W. and KLINK, B. (1989) 'Career development: A longitudinal approach for fostering inquiry in preservice-teacher education', *Journal of Teacher Education*, **40**, 2, pp. 3–8.

CONNELLY, F. and CLANDININ, P. (1990) 'Stories of experience and narrative inquiry', *Educational Researcher*, **19**, 5, pp. 2–14.

DIAMOND, C.T.P. (1988) 'Constructing a career: A developmental view of teacher education and teacher educator', *Journal of Curriculum Studies*, **20**, 2, pp. 133–140.

DUCHARME, E.R. (1993) *The Lives of Teacher Educators*, New York, Teachers College Press.

ERICKSON, E. (1959) 'Identity and life cycle', *Psychological Issues*, **1**, 1, pp. 119–161.

ERICKSON, F. (1986) 'Qualitative methods in research on teaching', in WITTROCK, M.C. (Ed) *Handbook of research on teaching*, New York, MacMillan, pp. 119–161.

FESSLER, R. and CHRISTENSEN, J.C. (1992) *The Teacher Career Cycle: Understanding and Guiding the Professional Development of Teachers*, Boston, Allyn and Bacon.

FULLER, F.F. (1969) 'Concerns of teachers: A developmental conceptualization', *American Educational Research Journal*, **6**, pp. 207–226.

FULLER, F.F. and BOWN, O.H. (1975) 'Becoming a teacher', in RYAN, K. (Ed) *Teacher Education*, 74th Yearbook of the National Society for the Study of Education, Part 2, Chicago, University of Chicago Press, pp. 25–52.

GLASSBERG, S. and SPRINTHALL, N.A. (1980) 'Student teaching: A developmental approach', *Journal of Teacher Education*, **31**, 2, pp. 31–38.

HARVEY, O.Y., HUNT, D.E. and SCHRODER, H.M. (1961) *Conceptual Systems and Personality*, New York, Wiley.

HUBERMAN, M. (1989) 'On teachers' careers: Once over lightly, with a broad brush', *International Journal of Educational Research*, **13**, 4, pp. 347–361.

HUNT, D.E. (1987) *Beginning with Ourselves*, Toronto, OISE Press.

KELLY, G.A. (1985) *The Psychology of Personal Constructs*, New York, Norton.

LOEVINGER, J. and WESSLER, R. (1970) *Measuring Ego Development*, San Francisco, Jossey-Bass.

MARTON, F. (1981) 'Phenomenography — describing conceptions of the world around us', *Instructional Science*, **10**, pp. 177–200.

MOORE, S.J., LALIK, H. and POTTS, A.D. (1993, April) 'Intentions, Contradiction and Transformation: The Lived Experience of an Emergent Teacher Education', paper presented at the annual meeting of the American Educational Research Association, Atlanta.

MOSS, P. (1994) 'Can there be validity without reliability?' *Educational Researcher*, **23**, 2, pp. 5–12.

POWNEY, J. and WATTS. M. (1987) *Interviewing in Educational Research*, London, Routledge and Kegan Paul.

PIAGET, J. (1963) *Psychology of Intelligence*, Totowa, NJ, Littlefield Adams.

PINAR, W.F. (1975) 'Search for a method', in PINAR, W.F. (Ed) *Curriculum Theorizing: The Reconceptualization*, Berkeley, McCutcheon, pp. 415–426.

PERRY, W., JR. (1970) *Forms of Intellectual and Ethical Development in the College Years*, New York, Holt, Rinehart and Winston.

REIMAN, A.J. and THIES-SPRINTHALL, L. (1993) 'Promoting the development of mentor teachers: Theory and research programs using guided reflection', *Journal of Research and Development in Education*, **26**, 3, pp. 179–187.

SIKES, P. (1985) 'The life cycle of teachers', in BALL, S. and GOODSON, I. (Eds) *Teachers' Lives and Careers*, London, Falmer Press, pp. 27–60.

SPRINTHALL, N.A. and THIES-SPRINTHALL, L. (1983) 'The teacher as an adult learner: A cognitive-developmental view', in GRIFFIN, G.A. (Ed) *Staff Development* (82nd yearbook of the National Society for the Study of Education, part 2), Chicago, University of Chicago Press.

SUPER, D.E. (1957) *Psychology of Careers: An Introduction to Vocational Development*, New York, Harper and Row.

SUPER, D.E. (1981) 'A life span: Life space approach to career development', *Journal of Vocational Behavior*, **16**, pp. 282–298.

SUPER, D.E. (1985) 'Career development', in HUSEN, T. and POSTLETHWAITE, T.N. (Eds) *The International Encyclopedia of Education: Research and Studies, Vol. 2*, Oxford, Pergamon Press, pp. 639–641.

WATTS, H. (1982) 'Observations on stages in teacher development', *MATE Viewpoints*, **4**, 1, pp. 4–8.

WEATHERBY, R.P. (1981) 'Ego development', in CHICKERING, A.W. (Ed) *The Modern American College*, San Francisco, Jossey-Bass.

10 Towards Rigour with Relevance: How can Teachers and Teacher Educators Claim to Know?

Hugh Munby and Tom Russell

Introduction

The discourse in this chapter occurs on two quite different levels, both of which are very important to us in our work as teacher educators. On one level — a practical level — we address our version of Jack Whitehead's question: 'How can we improve the quality of our *student teachers'* learning?' We present data that came to our attention by using a construct — the authority of experience (Munby and Russell, 1994) — that encouraged us to try to improve the quality of our student teachers' learning by enabling them to recognize more fully how they have learned from experience. On another level — a theoretical level — we take very seriously that familiar academic question of rigour: 'How do you know?' We argue that we, as teacher educators, know that the construct of the authority of experience is a useful contribution to knowledge in teacher education, not on classical criteria but on the domain-specific criterion of its instrumental value in the conduct of teacher education. Thus we would have rigour with our relevance.

Teacher education demands a unique blend of theory and practice. As we teach new teachers by presenting claims about how to teach and improve one's teaching, we are expected by them to teach well and to improve our teaching as we teach. Every teacher educator faces a continuing challenge: 'Can you walk the walk, as you talk the talk?' We believe that teacher education as a profession is only beginning to discover the complexities of this challenge, and self-study within teacher education is one important strategy for the work that lies ahead. In this chapter we examine our own work with the authority of experience construct to illustrate the theoretical and practical challenges we experience as teacher educators.

We begin from the theoretical side, taking seriously the challenge recently posed by Fenstermacher (1944, p. 28): 'To claim that we have tacit knowledge does not relieve us of the obligation to show how it is objectively reasonable to believe what we are contending'. We adopt the view that, of the many stances available, the most practical and appropriate one is found within the experience of teacher education itself. When we move to the practical side, we present and discuss data obtained in 1994 from one of our classes of students in the Waterloo-Queen's

Concurrent Science Teacher Education Program, a program that has a two-to-one ratio of teaching experience to education coursework and that begins with a 16-week teaching placement. These data allow us to return to the theoretical questions with the conclusion that the discourse of theory may not be up to the task of establishing the validity of claims within the discourse of practice. This conclusion has important implications for teachers' and teacher educators' personal understanding of the basis on which they make claims to 'know' by virtue of experience.

How do teacher educators know?

Fenstermacher's (1994) extensive review and critique of research on teachers' knowledge is an overdue and welcome challenge to the field in which we have been working for the last decade. With few exceptions (e.g., Phillips, 1988), little attention has been given to what Fenstermacher calls 'the epistemic import' of the claims to know made within two strands of research that he identifies as seeking an understanding of the knowledge teachers (and teacher educators) bring to their work. 'The first strand encompasses the work of . . . Elbaz and Connelly and Clandinin. . . . The second strand is based on the reflective practice notions of Donald Schön . . .' (Fenstermacher, 1994, p. 9). Fenstermacher goes on to present a detailed analysis of performance knowledge and craft knowledge, of knowledge and belief, of the justification of knowledge claims, and of the concept of science for the study of teaching. He also distinguishes between two discourses — the discourse of practice and the discourse of theory. Fenstermacher concludes with a challenge that we take seriously:

> The work of Munby, Russell, Grimmett, Erickson, and MacKinnon (all within the Schön strand) is highly attentive to the fact that it is presenting knowledge of a particular kind, although it has yet to deal with the fragility of inferences by the researcher that the teacher knows this or that as a result of action or reflection on that action. Moreover, the Schön strand researchers have yet to come to grips with the difference between the justification of their own inferences of teacher knowledge and the justification of what the teacher knows (a problem of levels of discourse). (p. 49)

Formal validity is appropriate for theoretical work, just as predictive validity is expected of theories within the logical positivist paradigm. Our concern here is with what might be styled *'functional validity'*. In our view, if theoretical constructs are invoked for a purpose within a specific theatre of practice, then the optimal approach to establishing the validity of the constructs is to inspect the theatre of practice and see if the constructs have taken the practitioner where he or she wished to go. This approach to validity parallels parts of Simon's (1981) argument for attention to purpose (prescription) rather than just description when addressing issues of the validity of theories in the social sciences. For us, though, the theatre of practice is not precisely the same as the prescriptiveness that Simon finds in the social sciences, and a simple example shows why this is so. In athletic activity, coaches frequently use a language that seems to make no sense at all except within the theatre of practice. When Hugh Munby tells a novice fencer to make the hand 'follow the point' to the target, he is not expecting that anyone believes (or knows) that the hand really follows the point, because the point is controlled by the hand. Rather, the instruction is aimed at helping the fencer make the hand and arm stretch out straight when an attack is initiated. It turns out, then, that the construction is not making a claim about how points work; instead, it is designed for a function — to transform an inefficient and poorly defined action into an efficient and properly defined one.

The ground we select for addressing Fenstermacher's justification questions extends from our theoretical purposes in developing an epistemology of teacher education practice, to our practical purposes in working with teacher education students. Our approach is more like engineering than applied physics, in other words. Ultimately, the inquiry may help us and our teacher education colleagues to look differently at formal epistemological theory and verification.

The Schön strand's constructs and intent

Our involvement in 'the Schön strand' began ten years ago when we joined our separate work on teachers' constructions and learning to teach, and built upon the work of Schön (1983, 1987). This work had special appeal because it was founded on the view that professional knowledge (including that of teacher educators as well as that of teachers) was underrated in academic circles. Also, the work gave an internally consistent account of the nature of the knowledge of action using concepts that clearly distinguished it from the language of propositional forms of knowing. Our purpose in pursuing this research was to develop Schön's account into an epistemology of teaching knowledge that could be developed into a sound theoretical basis for teacher education. In our early case studies (e.g., Russell, 1988), we explored the suitability of such concepts as reflection-in-action in accounting for the experiences of those learning to teach. Later, we undertook similar explorations with the concept of reframing (e.g., Munby and Russell, 1992). As the research program was unfolding, Tom Russell was adapting his teaching of the physics curriculum and instruction course (Physics 351) in the B.Ed. program at Queen's to reflect what the research seemed to be suggesting. This dialogue between research and practice served to remind us of our purpose in undertaking the research in the first place. It also did more: it allowed continuous monitoring of the research in the theatre of action, and it prompted new insights.

Our 'invention' of the construct of the authority of experience exemplifies the interaction of the theatre of action with theory. Data collected from Tom's Physics 351 students during the 1992–1993 academic year revealed a variety of beliefs about learning to teach. Most students appeared dismayed at the lack of specific information about how to teach, while some expressed concern at their peers' high need for certainty. We examined these views in light of Pajares' (1992) review of beliefs, noting the strength of existing beliefs and the subsequent difficulty in changing these, and we were struck by the sentence, 'Belief change during adulthood is a relatively rare phenomenon, the most common cause being a conversion from one authority to another or a gestalt shift' (p. 326). Our initial discussions centred on the traditional distinction between the authority of reason and the authority of position, and we realized that the 351 students had seen these two basic types of authority at work during their many years of schooling. We speculated that these students had probably witnessed how their experience of schooling might have concealed the difference between the authority of reason and the authority of status (Barnes, 1976). Quite unexpectedly, as in Schön's reframing, we began to talk about a third form of authority, 'the authority of experience' (Munby and Russell, 1994). We knew that neither the authority of reason nor the authority of position captured the sense of authority that one has from experiencing something for oneself, and it suddenly seemed apt to speak of experience as *having* authority. There were two immediate consequences of invoking 'the authority of experience': explanatory and instructional.

> The explanatory potential of the authority of experience can be seen in the predicament of experienced teachers who are appointed to faculties and colleges of education. Their knowledge-in-action gives them the authority of experience. But the circumstances of telling their students about teaching unavoidably commits them to the authority of being in charge, and their students are automatically placed under authority. The authority of experi- ence gets transformed into the authority (of position) that says, *I know because I have been there and so you should listen.* The authority of experience simply does not transfer because it resides in having the experience. (Munby and Russell, 1994, pp. 92–93.)

More concisely, *experience cannot be taught; it must be had.* This recalls Schön's (1984) advice to beginning professionals: 'There is something you need to know, but your teachers cannot tell you what it is'. It also points to the character of our work: we are less interested in making claims about the knowledge that teachers possess and more interested in the relationship between their experiences and how they learn to teach. We return to this in the discussion when we review some of Fenstermacher's concerns.

The instructional consequence of the concept 'the authority of experience' lay, for us, in the recognition it gives to the significance of providing extensive teaching experience within pre-service programs and of establishing approaches within the 'in-college' portion of such programs that encourage students to make specific connections between their practice teaching and their experiences in a course such as Physics 351. This is not to say that our former work with Schön's concepts failed to direct Tom's teaching in this way. Rather, it is to note the power of linking our understanding of the forms of authority to elements of a teacher education program. An implicit claim here is that recognizing three very different forms of authority cautioned Tom to avoid in his teaching the conflation of the authority of experience with the authority of his position as a professor and former high-school physics teacher. As we have said, the authority of a teacher educator's previous classroom experience simply does not transfer.

The basis for believing our contentions

The challenge presented by Fenstermacher (1994) is that we must validate inferences we make about concepts such as 'the authority of experience'. This chapter is an initial response to this challenge, and so the range of our attempts to offer grounds for believing our contentions is restricted somewhat, yet we are able to use recent data to show that there are good reasons for introducing the concept of the authority of experience into an epistemology of professional knowledge. Before we present the context and data below, we need to consider the claims that we are making for this concept.

A significant feature of 'the authority of experience' is that it is primarily an instrumental concept whose ultimate force lies in its potential as a device for teaching about professional experience. We have secured the concept in the epistemology of professional practice developed by Schön, but our emphasis has been upon the importance of this epistemology to understanding how teaching is learned and can be taught. By invoking 'the authority of experience' to distinguish the personal knowledge of an experience from the knowledge of an experience related by someone else, we are clearly endowing it with some epistemological features, but these are plainly not propositional. The sense of knowledge conveyed by the concept is not unlike the sense captured by the notion of experience itself: it is *had*. Disputes about this form of knowledge are not resolved with evidence and argument, as are disputes about the epistemic status of propositional claims. Although this form of knowledge is tacit, its possession is not verified by witnessing later performance, as one might do to verify the claim that someone knows how to fence. A close approximation to verifying that someone has the authority of experience is gained from being present while that experience is had. Aside from the obvious practical difficulties that this poses for the social scientist, validating claims about the authority of experience presents further complications because the concept denotes a particular attentiveness to elements of the experience. As Hanson (1965) remarked of observation, there is a difference between having an experience and the way in which an experience is had. In like manner, the authority of experience suggests a particular awareness to what is experienced. Being there and observing is insufficient, and something more is needed.

The functional character of the authority of experience presents further problems for its own validation. It might appear that its validation as a teaching device could be approached with experimental research on instruction. But the character of experimental research is ill-suited to determining the overall impact of a methods course that builds upon the individual and uniquely varied experiences of its students, and that incorporates a wide variety of teaching approaches delivered over a

Table 10.1: *Routes to the Queen's B.Ed. degree, showing depth of experience before and after coursework*

	Queen's Consecutive Program	Queen's Concurrent Program	Queen's-Waterloo Concurrent Science Program
Prior to September	Bachelor's degree	Bachelor's degree. Two or three half-courses in education six weeks in schools (over three years)	Two years of university study. One week introduction to teaching
September–December	10 weeks in class 3 weeks teaching	10 weeks in class 3 weeks teaching	16 weeks teaching
January–April	10 weeks in class 6 weeks teaching	15 weeks teaching	10 weeks in class 3 weeks teaching
after April	collect B.Ed. degree	collect B.Ed. degree	Begin third year of undergraduate studies
during following fall or winter term			16 weeks teaching

period of a few months. The following data and their context are presented to demonstrate how claims about the epistemic status of concepts like 'the authority of experience' may be approached.

Background and context for the data

The data presented here are taken from students in the Waterloo-Queen's Concurrent Science Education Program. This program, which produced its first graduates in 1990, is operated jointly by the University of Waterloo and Queen's University in the province of Ontario. Its unique feature emerges from the co-operative work term structure of undergraduate education at Waterloo. Table 10.1 compares the structure of this program with the consecutive and concurrent programs at Queen's University. Students in the concurrent program are enrolled for two degrees at the same time; the consecutive has students who have completed their undergraduate studies when they begin their study of education.

Each person in the Queen's-Waterloo Concurrent Program completes two work terms in schools, with a term of education courses at Queen's following immediately after the first work term. Thus while Ontario requires a minimum of eight weeks of practice teaching experience for teacher certification, each graduate of this program has completed at least thirty-two weeks of practice teaching. Most B.Ed. candidates beginning the education year at Queen's have teaching experience ranging from none (most consecutive students) to five weeks (most concurrent students). In sharp contrast, the Queen's-Waterloo candidates arrive with sixteen weeks of very recent teaching experience. While the immediacy of their experience is important, it is the depth of their experience that is unique in pre-service teacher education. They enter their education courses knowing that they already know how to teach in some minimally successful ways. The need for education courses to attempt to 'teach them how to teach' is reduced significantly. Furthermore, they study issues in education knowing that they will return to the classroom for a further sixteen weeks of teaching before they assume full-time responsibilities for students. When Tom Russell began his work with a new cohort in January, 1994, as one of two science curriculum course instructors, he did so with considerable interest in the authority of the experience that the Queen's-Waterloo candidates had recently acquired. Tom's success in developing this attention to experience was enhanced considerably by the fact that the other science instructor for this group was Peter Chin, who is also familiar with the 'Schön strand' in both theory and action. The importance of listening to self and to students had emerged from analysis of teaching in the 1992–93 academic year (see Tom Russell's chapter in this collection), and this perspective had been accepted with interest and enthusiasm by the physics curriculum students with whom Tom began to work in September 1993. The most important step may have been that Tom 'took it for granted' that the Queen's-Waterloo students should be treated as having important experiences that needed to be interpreted and understood. At the end of the first week, Tom assigned written work that would draw on their recent teaching experience and do so in a particular way:

> This assignment is an attempt to capture some *detail* about one significant event in your teaching last term. On this page, describe as fully as possible the events of *two days' work with one class*. In particular, try to think of a day when you deliberately did something different on day two in response to what happened on day one. *Why* did you change, *what* did you do differently, *and what were the results*? What would you do next time?

Although the assignment makes no explicit reference to either the authority of personal experience or to Schön's 'reflection-in-action', it clearly requests their personal views of their own teaching experience and it clearly requests a comparison between one set of actions and those that immediately preceded it. It was seen by Tom as a request for events and perspectives that could help develop 'reflection-in-action', if the candidates revealed that they had already experienced a cycle of action-puzzle-reframing-new action.

With the written permission of the authors, we now present a few of the responses to this Day 1/Day 2 assignment. For Tom, the results were astonishing, in the sense that he had never seen such detailed and engaging writing by B.Ed. students so early in their studies at Queen's. We invite the reader to consider this perspective, but to also read for the instrumental value of the authority of experience concept. Put another way, do these data convey that experience is being recalled with a sense of personal authority?

Five responses to the Day 1/Day 2 Assignment

Italic typeface has been added to each account to call attention to the issue the teacher is concerned with and the learning that has resulted from the Day 1/Day 2 comparison.

Brigit: On Friday, Sept. 17th, I taught an OAC [Ontario Academic Credit, a university entrance course for 17–19 year olds] physics class about vector components, unit vectors and vector multiplication. I took a very theoretical approach, structuring my lesson from an algebra text (I don't like taking lesson plans from the students' text because I'd like them to use it as a different look at the same subject — a new angle, new examples, if they didn't understand what I taught). Well, the students were confused (and very vocal about it). Nothing I said made it any better and both they and I came away frustrated. I scrawled 'didn't work' on the top of the plan.

I decided to write a new lesson plan and try again because I felt it wasn't fair to the students to leave them so confused. I went to the school library that night and asked whether they had a copy of the physics text that I used and really liked in OAC, and was told they didn't but that they would order it (it was invaluable during the latter half of the term). Many students had been looking for other texts since the texts they had were difficult to read. Anyway, *I took five different texts home with me and combined the information into a more practical lesson which proceeded logically from step to step.* I made sure the students understood (or smiled and nodded) a step before moving on and providing more examples. This class went very well. By the end no one was yelling that they didn't understand. I believe it was a case of my needing to spend more time (which was difficult when there were two other plans to make that night) to make sure everything was clear and there was the fact that I hadn't known the class long enough to know 'how' they learn best. For the next classes *I tried to anticipate the questions students might have and I used many more resources to ensure that what I was teaching was as clear as it could be.* If the class didn't understand, I always tried another angle the next day.

Brad: I was teaching a chemistry review to my Grade 10 [15–16 year olds] science class when a significant event occurred. We had just covered material on the make-up of atoms, having discussed the number of protons, neutrons and electrons and how to find these numbers. I then started to teach them about the charges that the various elements could have. I showed them how to find the charges, the ions wanting to have a stable electronic configuration, which is to have complete electronic shells. Although most of the students were able to find the charges, many students asked what was the point of those ions. *Why would something which is stable without a charge want to strive for a stable electronic configuration, giving it a charge and thus making it unstable?* I tried explaining that when atoms and molecules received energy they could form ions. *It was too late.* Many students had concluded that this was a useless activity and could not understand why we were concerned with ions.

For the following day *I devised a couple of demonstrations to show why we were concerned about ions.* For the first, I took solid potassium iodide (KI) and mixed it with solid lead nitrate (Pb(NO$_3$)$_2$). I showed the students that no matter how hard I mixed these uncharged molecules together, nothing would occur. Then I made solutions of the two solids, explaining to them that the water contained enough energy to create charged ions. I then mixed the two solutions together, and the students observed a bright yellow precipitate (PbI$_3$). The colour change really impressed the students; colours seem to do that well. For the next demo, I had prepared a mixture of solid potassium chlorate (KClO$_4$) with sucrose. I layered the mixture in a large test tube. Each layer contains different metals in order to create a changing colour effect (strontium chloride, copper chlorate, sodium chloride, iron filings, etc.). I then explained that I was adding a few drops of a substance (sulphuric acid) that gave enough energy to form ions in the mixture, with the substance not actually participating in the reaction. When the sulphuric acid was added, the reaction produced a violent jet of flame with vibrant colours. This really wowed the students. *I think after those two demonstrations the class at least understood that ions = reactions.* We then continued with writing equations involving the combination of ions.

Frank: Relatively early in November, when the students began to get sick of school, a problem started to develop in my Grade 11 [16–17 year olds] Business Math class. A group of four girls sitting in the back corner started to get noisier than usual. On the first day of this problem, I simply dealt with it by pausing and waiting for quiet; this had worked on most occasions earlier in the term. *During this class, however, they did not stop talking for very long.* I expressed my displeasure by issuing a warning: '____, this is the last time I'm going to ask you to stop talking . . . all right?' The noise level did drop, but not for long. Soon after, the class ended.

The next day the same problem occurred, but this time I handled it differently. At that time that I gave them a warning, and I outlined the consequences of what would happen if they continued to talk. The next time the level of noise got to be intolerable, *I followed through with the consequences of separating them and moved one of the girls to another seat.* At that time, I explained that I would do it again if I had to. Ten seconds later, I moved another. This seemed to work and I decided that a permanent change to the seating plan was necessary. I changed the way I handled this situation because I did not want the problem to escalate and I also wanted them to respect the position they had put me in . . . after all I was only trying to do my job. I think the explanation of the consequences was not what changed them but *it was the following through* — something my associate had suggested. Next time I would not let the situation get as bad as it did by explaining the consequences earlier.

Steve: I had completed a unit on green plants with my grade 9 [14–15 year olds] science class two days before a test. The first day we worked on a review sheet and updated notebooks — basic pre-test stuff. *The problem was that they were bored of* *review and I had a day to go.* For the second day I came up with a fun review game. There were seven groups of three students. The students in each group were numbered 1 to 3. I made the groups by mixing stronger with weaker students. Then I would ask a question such as, 'Label eight parts in a cross-section of a leaf'. Each group then had two minutes to talk about the answer as a team so that all the members knew the answer. After the two minutes I would call a number (1, 2, or 3) and all the students of that number from each team would go to the front of the class. On my signal the students would begin writing the answer on the board, and as soon as one person was done, they would all stop and go back to their teams. We would then mark each person's answer with the entire class and give a mark out of 5. After three to six rounds we would tally up the scores to see who won. *The game worked very well because it was active, social, and the students were helping each other get answers.* If you weren't listening to the group answer and your number was called, you let your team down. The only problem was that I mistimed the game and we played right to the bell and some people didn't get prizes. Next time I will end the game sooner. The students seemed to like it.

Gina: This event happened in my 11G [16–17 year olds] chemistry class. I was teaching a lesson on ionic bonding. We had already covered how and why atoms form ions, and they seemed to be comfortable with that. The purpose of this lesson was for the students to be able to write the ionic formulas as a result of the formation of an ionic bond. In order to teach this, I started with an example and asked them what they thought would happen if we mixed sodium and chloride atoms together. Using this example, we went through the steps (ions are formed, positive attracts negative, etc.) By the end of the lesson they could follow the steps and get the correct formula, but *they all had questions about why they were doing it and what the crossover rule's purpose was.* They were attentive during the class, so I could tell they were really trying to understand. I discussed this with my associate teacher because I didn't want them to just go through the motions and not understand the how or why.

The next day I decided to basically re-teach the lesson with a whole new approach, hoping it would be clearer to them. I started the lesson with a short video clip of the reaction we discussed last day of sodium and chlorine. Then we discussed what happened, and the kids decided that the sodium and chlorine mixed together and formed a new substance. I then drew a picture on the board of a jar containing sodium and chlorine, e.g., NaCl. After questioning, they deduced that before the reaction of Cl with Na would occur, the sodium and chlorine must form ions. From previous NaCl lessons, they knew the ions were Na^+ and Cl^-. I added the signs to the diagram, and they then saw that they would be attracted like magnets, and one atom of Cl attracted one atom of Na. I then explained the formula would be $Na_{(1)}Cl_{(1)}$ and that the 'invisible' number ones meant one atom of each. We then worked through the formation of $BaCl_2$, using the same method. They understood that two atoms of Cl must join one atom of Ba. Then we did the example by the crossover rule, which I explained was just a short cut. They worked through more examples and the next day we followed up by doing a lab where everyone got to create an ionic compound. *The second day's lesson was much better because I used more visual teaching tools and a more concrete way of explaining things.* The first lesson, I made the mistake of concentrating too much on the theory and just getting the correct answer, instead of why we were doing it, how it is useful, and what the numbers and symbols actually meant. A lot of times I found it hard to remember that this wasn't university and that these kids weren't particularly interested in the theory, but that they need visual and tactile stimulation to understand things.

The experience of the classroom has two roles in these accounts of early professional learning. First, experience offers what Schön calls 'backtalk' — the unexpected consequences of our actions talking back to us. The students demonstrate their receptivity to backtalk, modify their approaches, and are then rewarded with further evidence of the appropriateness of their teaching. The Day 1/Day 2 accounts reveal this plainly, just as they reveal that the Queen's-Waterloo students have learned from experience. The second role of experience is as *an authority from which the student teachers learn.* No doubt we all recognize in the Day 1/Day 2 accounts, scenes and events that are familiar to us, especially to those who have taught science and mathematics in secondary schools. These accounts teach us all as we read them, *but the authority for our learning is the authority of those who have been there — it is the authority of position.* As readers, our learning is qualitatively different from the learning of the authors of these accounts; the authority for their learning was the authority of the experience itself.

We believe the preceding accounts of professional learning from experience have qualities that are evident *only* because their authors were in schools for a period as long as sixteen weeks. Even though they often refer to events early in their placements, the depth of their experiences appears to have been a major factor in their ability to write these accounts. Our understanding of our own teacher education practices has been advanced dramatically by the opportunity to work with student teachers following different program structures. We assume that a student teacher assigned for only three weeks could not write a similar account, and we will be testing that assumption with future student teachers. It is a familiar pattern to have individuals begin their education courses and then gradually add classroom teaching experience. It is much less common to have students gain extensive teaching experience *before* they attend education courses on the how and why of teaching. These student teachers had continuous extensive experience, knowing that they would proceed immediately to a term of education courses, even though they did not know the nature of those courses. Many of these accounts demonstrate that 'reframing' in response to 'puzzles or surprises' (terms used by Schön, 1983) occurred naturally to these students. Nevertheless, they do not always recognize these as moments in which they were learning from the authority of experience, and our work with them seeks to develop an initial understanding of that authority in ways that will be helpful to them in their learning from experience in their second sixteen week practicum. Here we see how our understanding of our work has moved from events of teacher education practice to developing the idea of the authority of experience, and how that idea now enriches our further practice.

Seeking rigour *and* relevance

Teacher education candidates quickly see the *relevance* of writing about their experiences, yet it is a long leap from that obvious relevance to anything they might associate with the *rigour* they know from their undergraduate studies of science. As future science teachers, rigour in any scientific sense will not be an important professional concern. We are now setting ourselves the personal professional challenge of developing ways to show how there can be rigour in the professional knowledge that teachers develop from experience.

Our arguments in this paper constitute an initial response to Fensternacher's (1994) concerns for the epistemic status of claims made in research on teacher knowledge that he has called 'the Schön strand'. We take issue with his use of *phronesis* as a model for determining the validity of claims to knowledge because of its clear dependence on propositional forms of knowledge. Our approach to the issue of validity has been to return to the purposes of our research and to argue that the constructs we invoke are *functional* — they are designed expressly to help us better prepare pre-service students for careers in teaching. Our recent work with the construct of the authority of experience illustrates this stance. The accounts from students in the Queen's-Waterloo program, we argue, represent learning that is qualitatively different from the learning that comes from being told. Thus the functional validity of the authority of experience lies in how we use the concept to point to this difference and how, in turn, it points to the significance of teaching practice. In using this concept, we are not claiming anything about the professional or practical knowledge of the Queen's-Waterloo students. But we are most certainly making a claim about our own professional knowledge as teacher educators — a claim about the conditions under which professional knowledge can be developed. The rich and varied experiences of teaching practice have an authoritative voice that can be heeded by pre-service candidates, but not automatically. Extensive teaching experience has obvious practical relevance. Our challenge now is to bridge the practice-theory divide by developing the less-obvious rigour of teachers' practical knowledge.

In our view, Schön is correct in insisting that the knowledge of action resides within the action. We take this further by arguing that the idea of learning from experience offers too limited an account of how experience can teach. A better account would incorporate the idea that learning is *in* the experience. The authority of experience reminds us of the immediacy of this learning, just as it also suggests that some of our students may not be ready to recognize and respond to that authority. Reports of data such as that presented here show that student teachers have met the conditions for significant professional learning. They have had experiences of sufficient depth and variety to begin to understand how they learn in and from experience — in short, to begin to recognize how experience has authority. Thus the data illustrate the instrumental value of the concept of authority of experience. We believe it is increasingly important for teacher educators to explore instrumental analyses of this type in order to better understand the basis for our claims to know in teaching and in teacher education.

Acknowledgments

We are grateful to members of the 1994 cohort of the Waterloo-Queen's Concurrent Science Education Program for permission to use their data here. An earlier version of this chapter was presented at the annual meeting of the Canadian Society for the Study of Education, Calgary, Alberta, June 1994. The analysis is part of the 1992–1995 research project, 'Case study research in teachers' professional knowledge' (Hugh Munby and Tom Russell, Principal Investigators), funded by the Social Sciences and Humanities Research Council of Canada.

References

BARNES, D. (1976) *From Communication to Curriculum*, Harmondsworth, Penguin.

FENSTERMACHER, G. (1994) 'The knower and the known: The nature of knowledge in research on teaching', in DARLING-HAMMOND, L. (Ed) *Review of Research in Education 20*, Washington, DC, American Educational Research Association, pp. 3–56.

HANSON, N. (1965) *Patterns of Discovery*, Cambridge, Cambridge University Press.

MUNBY, H., and RUSSELL, T. (1992) 'Transforming chemistry research into teaching: The complexities of adopting new frames for experience', in RUSSELL, T. and MUNBY, H. (Eds) *Teachers and Teaching: From Classroom to Reflection*, London, Falmer Press, pp. 90–108.

MUNBY, H., and RUSSELL, T. (1994) 'The authority of experience in learning to teach: Messages from a physics methods class', *Journal of Teacher Education*, **45**, 2, pp. 86–95.

PAJARES, M.F. (1992) 'Teachers' beliefs and educational research: Cleaning up a messy construct', *Review of Educational Research*, **62**, pp. 307–332.

PHILLIPS, D. (1988) 'On teacher knowledge: A skeptical dialogue', *Educational Researcher*, **38**, pp. 457–466.

PHILLIPS, D. (1993, April) 'Telling It Straight: Issues in Assessing Narrative Research', paper presented at the annual conference of the Philosophy of Education Society of Great Britain, Oxford.

RUSSELL, T. (1988) 'From pre-service teacher education to first year of teaching: A study of theory and practice', in CALDERHEAD, J. (Ed) *Teachers' Professional Learning*, London, Falmer Press, pp. 13–34.

SCHÖN, D.A. (1983) *The Reflective Practitioner: How Professionals Think in Action*, New York, Basic Books.

SCHÖN, D.A. (1984, October) *Reflection-in-action* (Videotaped lecture), Queen's University Faculty of Education, Kingston, Ontario.

SCHÖN, D.A. (1987) *Educating the Reflective Practitioner*, San Francisco, Jossey-Bass.

SIMON, H. (1981) *The Science of the Artificial*, 2nd ed., Cambridge, MIT Press.

Part 6

Epilogue

11 Teachers Who Teach Teachers: Some Final Considerations

Fred Korthagen and Tom Russell

The idea for this book grew out of amazement — our amazement at the type of research on teacher education that seemed to be acceptable to the research community at the beginning of the 1990s. There was a general trend to emphasize the importance of reflective teaching for teachers, and although the literature shows many studies discussing views of reflection and methods to promote its development during teacher education, teacher educators did not seem to apply these ideas to themselves. Articles published by teacher educators almost always showed a certain degree of 'distance' between the author and the topic described, a distance that could be very well accounted for by the author with the aid of the dominant research methodology. The result of this situation was that, as Zeichner (1981) noted, 'we know very little of what actually goes on inside teacher education programs'. We could add that we know even less about what goes on inside teacher educators as they pursue their profession. Our amazement was an incentive to look for the reasons for this gap between the rhetoric of teacher educators and their own practice. We now review briefly some historical issues in the development of teacher education that we found helpful in understanding a situation that appeared so perplexing to us. Then we reflect on the previous chapters in this book, which is the very tangible product of our initial surprise and concern about teacher education. Finally, we venture a look forward into the future of teacher education.

Some historical trends

A century ago, teaching was mastered mainly by gaining experience, without any formal theoretical professional training. Often a new teacher learned the tricks of the trade within an apprenticeship with an experienced teacher, after a study of the relevant subject matter, for example an academic study in a particular discipline. As more and more psychological and pedagogical knowledge developed and seemed to be relevant to the work of teachers, the professionalization of teacher education began. This development was influenced by a growing wish, worldwide, to educate not only the most gifted children, but to suit the educational needs of a broad group of students, if not all students. This democratization of education enhanced the need for developing teachers' professional knowledge.

At first, the general trend was to teach teachers courses in relevant knowledge domains, for example, the psychology of learning. This is an early sign of how slowly new ideas about teacher education were developing, because the existing paradigm was apparent in this approach. The idea was that acquiring a relevant knowledge base is sufficient for good teaching and that 'the rest' is learned on the job. Next came the view that there was 'poor application' of this knowledge base by teachers and that more was needed. This led to the introduction of 'competency-based teacher education' (CBTE) with the underlying idea that formulation of concrete and observable criteria for good teaching could serve as a basis for the training of teachers. For quite a long time, process–product studies were considered the type of research that could feed this approach to teacher education. Behind this line of thought one can still see what Jean Clandinin calls 'the sacred theory-practice story': teacher education conceived as the translation of theory on good teaching into practice. Even as late as 1986, Shulman (1986) noted that 'teacher education programs in general seem to be based on the view that teacher candidates will teach effectively once they have acquired subject matter knowledge, got acquainted with models of innovative curriculum and have practised using them'. The sacred theory-practice story persisted in spite of many studies showing the failure of this approach (for an overview, see Kagan, 1992), and in spite of many severe problems encountered by beginning teachers who felt so insufficiently prepared that the term 'transition shock' came into use (Veenman, 1984; Corcoran, 1981).

During the 1980s, a new approach to teacher education was proposed, based on an analysis of the failure of the old paradigm (see, for example, Zeichner and Tabachnick, 1981; Zeichner, 1981). It can be characterized by an emphasis on the importance of reflective teaching and by new methods to be used in teacher education, such as action research by (student) teachers and reflective journal writing. This approach implied a break with the traditional way of thinking about professional knowledge. No longer was the question how to implement academic knowledge (or 'formal' knowledge — Fenstermacher, 1994) in the practical setting. The question became how to make teachers aware of their *practical knowledge* — the conceptions, beliefs and personal theories embedded in their everyday teaching — and how to develop in teachers both a feeling of responsibility for the goals and effects of their teaching and the skills required to work towards those goals. This also meant a shift away from a general theory about good teaching towards more appreciation for the individuality of each teacher.

At the same time, at the research front, very little changed. This posed significant obstacles for teacher educators who wanted to publish material dealing with alternative models of teacher education or new views of professional knowledge, as in the story told by Gary Knowles and Ardra Cole. Research and practice in teacher education had become split personalities. In their practices, teacher educators often went through a paradigm shift by conquering the sacred theory-practice story and developing views in which knowledge was considered much more context-bound, personal and dynamic. In their research work, however, teacher educators had to show that they believed in traditional views of knowledge growth. A failure to live with this split-personality syndrome was, and still is, punished by expulsion from academia-tenure positions generally open only to staff members with a sufficiently long list of publications in the field's traditional journals, which generally support the old research paradigm. Moreover, the academic world has other means to safeguard its dominant paradigms; publications that are regarded as out of the mainstream are often just not cited by the veterans in teacher education.

A first sign of a breakthrough in this situation was visible at the 1993 Annual Meeting of the American Educational Research Association (AERA) in Atlanta. Suddenly, more than a few teacher educators were presenting reflective accounts and narratives about their own work in teacher education and their personal professional development. What made this development striking was that among these presenters were some well-known teacher educators. At the same meeting, an entire symposium was devoted to reflective analyses by teacher educators of their own practices. This was also the AERA meeting at which a new Special Interest Group was organized. The 'Self-Study of Teacher Education Practices' (S-STEP) group was in full operation at the 1994 Annual Meeting of AERA and saw a rapid growth to more than two hundred members from all over the world.

A book about the work of teacher educators

It was at the 1993 conference that we developed the idea for this book. Now that it is finished, we believe even more strongly that it fills a gap in our knowledge of teacher education. The chapters show many, often revealing, stories from within the reality of teacher education in a variety of countries, thanks to the willingness of the contributors to this book to be very open about their own practices, their concerns, their failures as well as their successes, their struggles and their continuous searching in unfamiliar areas.

First, it is notable that the professional development of experienced teacher educators is described by the teacher educators themselves. Often we assume that professional development is directed purely by the head, by cognitive or meta-cognitive factors. The contributions of experienced teacher educators in this book, however, show that their development is as much rooted in their hearts, in emotional life experiences, in something they feel is important to live for. Ken Zeichner, for example, makes very clear how his ongoing search for new directions in teacher education is based in his dramatic experiences as a teacher of students from economically poor backgrounds and in his commitment to a better society. When Jean Clandinin worked as a university teacher educator she took her own feeling of separation from the reality of the schools seriously and started to work for a teacher education program she could really believe in. The same motive stimulated Tom Russell to go back to the secondary school to be a physics teacher again and to make his experiences as useful as possible for his student teachers. What these teacher educators tried to establish contrasts sharply with common practices in their institutions, practices that made some feel both vulnerable and isolated. How could they have sustained their efforts without the power of their ideals, without their strong belief that an alternative should be possible? The reflective accounts of these teacher educators are fine illustrations of how valuable it can be, in one's professional development, to use as a compass Jack Whitehead's question, 'How do I live my values more fully in my practice?'

Ardra Cole and Gary Knowles discuss the influence of people's personal life histories on their professional development, offering a framework for a deeper understanding of how important personal experiences, and the associated beliefs and ideals, influence the developmental process of professionals. The analysis by Lya Kremer and Ruth Zuzovsky of the professional development of teacher educators adds the career stage or life phase perspective. Beginning teacher educators seem most concerned with survival in their new job, with sticking to what is expected of them, and with trying to 'sell' generally accepted theories to student teachers. Only in a later career stage do they develop an alternative view of knowledge and knowledge development, start to question the effectiveness of their work and begin to search for new methods.

Although this may be the general trend, it is important to raise the question of what we can learn from exceptional individuals such as Stefinee Pinnegar, Karen Guilfoyle, Mary Lynn Hamilton and Peggy Placier. All four show a remarkable resistance to rapid socialization into established practices within their institutions and a highly reflective attitude towards their own professional development. In the early stages of their careers, they maintain their sometimes unconventional ideals, even in a somewhat hostile environment. For example, Stefinee Pinnegar's belief in the intellectual capability of children to engage in processes of interpretation and re-interpretation and her commitment to trust as the basis for learning, helped her to go back to school as a teacher and really make a difference. She even succeeded in changing the attitude of an experienced teacher who at first had little reason to trust her views of teaching. Stefinee's narrative confirms that her ideals were strongly rooted in her life history, especially in her experiences on the Navajo Indian Reservation.

Apparently, it is possible that beginning teacher educators, like beginning teachers, find their personal styles, that they work in line with the ideals formed earlier in their lives. We consider this a very important contribution to the development of teacher education. This contribution was probably only possible through the support that these four beginning teacher educators (the 'Arizona group') gave each other. They shared their hopes and their problems with each other on a weekly and monthly, if not daily, basis. Although they lived and worked hours away from each other, electronic mail helped to fill in a gap left by the colleagues in their own institutions. At the same time, let us not be too negative about the support for these beginning teacher educators within their own universities. First, there were a few staff members who really tried to be helpful. Secondly, what are the possibilities for support in the traditional university environment anyway? There are the heavy teaching loads to be dealt with, the rules for promotion, the regulations for gaining tenure. And there is the total absence of formal training and a professional support system for beginning teacher educators. Almost all over the world, one becomes a teacher educator by being a good teacher in primary or secondary education (Ducharme, 1994; Korthagen, 1995). The general picture is that after an often informal recruitment procedure, one is given the responsibility for a group of student teachers and is left alone. The idea seems to be that one learns the profession by itself, through trial-and-error in practice. The ancient paradigm, over a century old, is still very strong. As Wilson (1990) notes, this situation is highly remarkable in an area where professional development is the operative word.

The professionalization of teacher education

Would it not be impressive if the seeds for professional growth within beginning teachers could be stimulated much earlier than at the middle or end of their careers? In this context we should acknowledge that the accounts in this collection may still be exceptions to the general rule — the stories of teacher educators who had such strong innovative attitudes that they survived in non-supportive contexts. One seldom hears the stories of those who dropped out through lack of support or loss of ideals.

We put forward here a strong plea for supportive systems of professional development for both beginning and experienced teacher educators. The formation of support groups in which teacher educators share their knowledge and mutually facilitate each other's development would be a start. Teacher education staff should be given time and other facilities for promotion of their professional growth, just as we usually require for teachers in schools. As studies showing the failure of teacher education are still very timely, the teacher education community has a responsibility to promote its own professionalism. Beginning teacher educators need not invent the wheel over and over again for themselves, now that there is a growing body of knowledge that we can begin to call a theory of teacher education. It is a mistake to consider the job of a teacher educator to be based on either formal theory and knowledge or practical experience alone. One essential characteristic for the profession of teacher educator is expertise on the relationship not just of theory to practice *but also of practice to theory*. And it is here that the reflective activities related in this volume are most relevant. Being an expert on the practice-theory relationship requires competencies quite different from those of teachers in schools or staff in other departments within the university. This is even more the case as the integration of theory and practice has to take place *within the person of the student*, which means that teacher educators require knowledge, skills and attitudes in the field of human development (adult development, social psychology, counselling, and the like). The low status of teacher education in many countries may be directly related to the inability of the teacher education community to take seriously the task of professional development for its members.

A professional program for teacher educators should not be confined to the presentation of theory on teacher education or the training of supervision skills, although these are indispensable elements. This book shows that teacher educators who are able to create real innovations in their field are highly reflective. They are able to analyze and challenge the basic assumptions in their work. They use their ideals as the compass that guides them on their route, and they reflect on this route over and over again and discuss it with colleagues. In short, what is advocated for teacher education — an emphasis on the development of reflection — deserves a similar place in the professionalization of teacher educators. It would be a major step forward if, through their professional training, teacher educators became accustomed to studying their own practices in a variety of ways, such as those described by Jack Whitehead and by Ardra Cole and Gary Knowles. We could not agree more with Ardra's statement: 'Knowing myself as person is very much part of knowing myself as professional'. A life history approach as described by Ardra and Gary could help teacher educators to become and remain aware of their personal strengths and thus to stick to their beliefs and ideals, to their hearts. This certainly does not mean that they will be successful and valued by their colleagues. The stories in this book also show that taking responsibility for one's ideals leads to a continuous process of search and struggle, in which one is over and over again confronted with the tensions within the 'I as a living contradiction', as Jack Whitehead describes it.

Is there another way? One day each teacher educator must confront Jack Whitehead's question: 'How do I help my teacher education students, and finally their students in the schools, to improve the quality of their learning?' In teacher education settings all over the world, this question has the potential to generate significant confrontations. We hope that such events will stimulate further sharing of reflections by teacher educators about their work, with their teacher education colleagues and with the teachers and students, whose time spent together in schools deserves the highest possible quality.

References

CORCORAN, C. (1981) 'Transition shock: The beginning teacher's paradox', *Journal of Teacher Education*, **32**, 3, pp. 19–23.

DUCHARME, E.R. (1993) *The Lives of Teacher Educators*, New York, Teachers College Press.

FENSTERMACHER, G.D. (1994) 'The knower and the known: The nature of knowledge in research on teaching', *Review of Research in Education*, **20**, pp. 3–56.

KAGAN, D.M. (1992) 'Professional growth among preservice and beginning teachers', *Review of Educational Research*, **62**, 2, pp. 129–169.

KORTHAGEN, F.A.J. (1995) 'A reflection on five reflective accounts', *Teacher Education Quarterly*, in press.

SHULMAN, L.S. (1986) 'Those who understand: Knowledge growth in teaching', *Educational Researcher*, **15**, 2, pp. 4–14.

VEENMAN, S. (1984) 'Perceived problems of beginning teachers', *Review of Educational Research*, **54**, 2, pp. 143–178.

WILSON, J.D. (1990) 'The selection and professional development of trainers for initial teacher training', *European Journal of Teacher Education*, **13**, 1/2, pp. 7–24.

ZEICHNER, K.M. (1981) 'Reflective teaching and field-based experience in teacher education', *Interchange*, **12**, 4, pp. 1–22.

ZEICHNER, K. and TABACHNICK, B. (1981) 'Are the effects of university teacher education "washed out by school experience"?', *Journal of Teacher Education*, **32**, 3, pp. 7–11.

Notes on Contributors

D. Jean Clandinin is a former teacher, counsellor and school psychologist. She is a Professor and Director of the Centre for Research for Teacher Education and Development at the University of Alberta. Jean is the co-author of several books on curriculum practice and teacher education. Her latest book (with Michael Connelly) is entitled *Teachers' Professional Knowledge Landscapes*.

Ardra L. Cole is Associate Professor at the Department of Applied Psychology, The Ontario Institute for Studies in Education, Toronto, Canada. Her research, writing, and teaching are in the areas of teacher education and development, and qualitative approaches to educational research. Ardra is particularly interested in autobiographical and life history methods. She is currently conducting a life history study of untenured teacher educators in Canadian universities.

Karen Guilfoyle is an Associate Professor in Teacher Education at the University of Idaho. Her field is literacy, language and culture, and her research focuses on learning and teaching using a critical social-constructivist framework.

Mary Lynn Hamilton is an Associate Professor in the Department of Curriculum and Instruction at the University of Kansas in Lawrence. Her research interests include the study of her own teaching practice and the dialogue that emerges from conversations with students and colleagues.

J. Gary Knowles is Visiting Scholar at the Ontario Institute for Studies in Education in 1995 and Assistant Professor at the School of Education, The University of Michigan, Ann Arbor, Michigan, USA. His teaching and researching are centred on issues of teacher education and development. In recent years he has helped develop an alternative, graduate, field-based pre-service teacher education program. His research includes an auto-ethnographic research project focused on beginning professors of teacher education.

Fred A.J. Korthagen is Senior Researcher and Head of the Teacher Education Program of IVLOS Institute of Education at Utrecht University in the Netherlands. He has published many research articles on the promotion of reflection in student teachers. His research interests include the role of non-rational, action-guiding images or Gestalts in teaching and the professional training of teacher educators.

Lya Kremer-Hayon is Professor of Education at the University of Haifa. She has been head of the Department of Education, and now heads the Center of Educational Administration and Evaluation. She is also editor of the *Journal of Educational Administration*. Her main interest is the professional development of teachers and educational administrators, an area in which she publishes regularly.

Hugh Munby is Professor of Education at Queen's University, Kingston, Ontario. He divides his time between teaching graduate courses on research and curriculum studies, collaborating with Tom Russell on their continuing research into how teachers learn to teach, and coaching sabre with the Queen's University Fencing Team.

Stefinee Pinnegar is an Assistant Professor of Secondary Education at Brigham Young University. She is involved in the school-university partnership, and her research interests include self-study, qualitative methodology and teacher thinking.

Margaret (Peggy) Placier is an Assistant Professor in the Foundations of Education at the University of Missouri-Columbia. She instructs pre-service teachers in the history and sociology of education with an emphasis on the dilemmas that cultural diversity introduces in a common public school system. Her research interests include educational policy, organizational culture and teacher education.

Anna Richert is an Associate Professor of Education at Mills College in Oakland, California where she is co-director of the teacher education program, 'Teachers for Tomorrow's Schools'. Her research on reflective practice and teacher learning at the pre-service level has led to her new work on school reform and teacher learning in school settings. She sees learning as the key activity of goods teaching, and her research is focused on understanding the conditions that make learning possible for all teachers.

Tom Russell is a Professor in the Faculty of Education at Queen's University, Kingston, Ontario, where his teaching responsibilities include pre-service methods courses in secondary science and a course in action research at the graduate level. He co-ordinates the Waterloo-Queen's Science Education Program, which provides extensive teaching experience both before and after pre-service education courses. His research with Hugh Munby on how teachers learn from experience has been supported by several grants from the Social Sciences and Humanities Research Council of Canada.

Jack Whitehead is a Lecturer in Education at the University of Bath, UK, where he has worked on teacher education programmes since 1973. He specializes in the design of educational action research programmes for continuing professional development. He convenes the Action Research in Educational Theory Research Group in the School of Education at Bath and supports action enquiries with teachers who are asking questions of the kind, 'How do I help my pupils to improve the quality of their learning?'

Kenneth Zeichner is Hoefs-Bascom Professor of Teacher Education, University of Wisconsin-Madison and Senior Researcher, National Center for Research on Teacher Learning, Michigan State University. His recent publications include *Beyond the Divide of Teacher Research and Academic Research* (in Teachers and Teaching), *Teacher Socialization for Cultural Diversity* (in the 'Handbook of Research on Teacher Education', 2nd. ed.) and (with Dan Liston) *Reflective Teaching*.

Ruth Zuzovsky is Senior Lecturer and Head of Pedagogical Studies at the State Teachers College, Seminar Hakibbutzim, Tel-Aviv. She presents papers regularly at international conferences, and she recently led a special program for cooperating teachers in the college where she teaches.

Author index

Subject index

academic freedom 46
action research 2, 3, 14, 17, 45, 97, 115, 188
  around world 114–17
  and authority of experience 107
  criteria, as teacher educator 117–19
  cycles of 38
  enquiry, development of 121, 126
  evidence 98
  and living educational theory 113–27
  participatory, in developing countries 113, 116, 119
  in physics teaching 97–9, 108
  projects 17
  questions 97
  /reflective cycle 118, 123, 124
  'second order' 19
alternative program: of teacher education 26–31 passim, 133
analysis: speculative 38
approximations: process of 51
assignments: design by university teachers 27
  and experience 178, 179–82
  negotiating 27, 29
  relevant 29
  student teacher centred 27
authority of experience 97, 113, 172, 174, 175, 182
  functional character of 176
  as instrumental concept 176
  in learning to teach 99–100, 105–6, 107
authority of position 100, 107, 175, 182
authority of reason 99, 101, 107, 175
autobiographical narrative 132–41

backtalk 182
  and problems 60, 61
  by students 99, 100, 108
beginners: teachers as 1, 6

behavioural objectives 63
beliefs: change in 175
  consciousness of 48
  teacher 67, 82
  in teacher education 47, 49
  student 4, 46, 53
biography 39–45
body knowledge 115
body language: role of 65
burnout, teacher 57

care: ethic of 26
categorizing: in analysis 38
classification: in analysis 38
classroom: as community 64
  content 59
  critical dimension of 18
  discipline 18, 59
  environments 16
  experience of 182
  as field site 81
  management 18, 58, 59, 65–7
  teachers 14
  world in 52
collaboration: in teacher education 26
  between teachers and students 28, 30
commitment: to students and/or society 15–19
  to teacher development 45
community: concept of 126
  educative 127
competence: personal 56
competency-based teacher education (CBTE) 188
concept formation 38
conceptual level (CL) 156
contextual analysis 142
conversation: role in professional work 72
critical analyses: of practice 131
critical awareness: student 17